Communications
in Computer and Information Science   380

Editorial Board

Simone Diniz Junqueira Barbosa
Pontifical Catholic University of Rio de Janeiro (PUC-Rio),
Rio de Janeiro, Brazil

Phoebe Chen
La Trobe University, Melbourne, Australia

Alfredo Cuzzocrea
ICAR-CNR and University of Calabria, Italy

Xiaoyong Du
Renmin University of China, Beijing, China

Joaquim Filipe
Polytechnic Institute of Setúbal, Portugal

Orhun Kara
TÜBİTAK BİLGEM and Middle East Technical University, Turkey

Igor Kotenko
St. Petersburg Institute for Informatics and Automation
of the Russian Academy of Sciences, Russia

Krishna M. Sivalingam
Indian Institute of Technology Madras, India

Dominik Ślęzak
University of Warsaw and Infobright, Poland

Takashi Washio
Osaka University, Japan

Xiaokang Yang
Shanghai Jiao Tong University, China

Cerstin Mahlow   Michael Piotrowski (Eds.)

Systems and Frameworks
for Computational Morphology

Third International Workshop, SFCM 2013
Berlin, Germany, September 6, 2013
Proceedings

 Springer

Volume Editors

Cerstin Mahlow
University of Konstanz
78457 Konstanz, Germany
E-mail: cerstin.mahlow@uni-konstanz.de

Michael Piotrowski
Leibniz Institute of European History
Alte Universitätsstr. 19
55116 Mainz, Germany
E-mail: piotrowski@ieg-mainz.de

ISSN 1865-0929   e-ISSN 1865-0937
ISBN 978-3-642-40485-6   e-ISBN 978-3-642-40486-3
DOI 10.1007/978-3-642-40486-3
Springer Heidelberg New York Dordrecht London

Library of Congress Control Number: 2013945728

CR Subject Classification (1998): I.2.7, J.5

© Springer-Verlag Berlin Heidelberg 2013
This work is subject to copyright. All rights are reserved by the Publisher, whether the whole or part of
the material is concerned, specifically the rights of translation, reprinting, reuse of illustrations, recitation,
broadcasting, reproduction on microfilms or in any other physical way, and transmission or information
storage and retrieval, electronic adaptation, computer software, or by similar or dissimilar methodology
now known or hereafter developed. Exempted from this legal reservation are brief excerpts in connection
with reviews or scholarly analysis or material supplied specifically for the purpose of being entered and
executed on a computer system, for exclusive use by the purchaser of the work. Duplication of this publication
or parts thereof is permitted only under the provisions of the Copyright Law of the Publisher's location,
in ist current version, and permission for use must always be obtained from Springer. Permissions for use
may be obtained through RightsLink at the Copyright Clearance Center. Violations are liable to prosecution
under the respective Copyright Law.
The use of general descriptive names, registered names, trademarks, service marks, etc. in this publication
does not imply, even in the absence of a specific statement, that such names are exempt from the relevant
protective laws and regulations and therefore free for general use.
While the advice and information in this book are believed to be true and accurate at the date of publication,
neither the authors nor the editors nor the publisher can accept any legal responsibility for any errors or
omissions that may be made. The publisher makes no warranty, express or implied, with respect to the
material contained herein.

Typesetting: Camera-ready by author, data conversion by Scientific Publishing Services, Chennai, India

Printed on acid-free paper

Springer is part of Springer Science+Business Media (www.springer.com)

Preface

This volume contains the papers presented at SFCM 2013: The Third International Workshop on Systems and Frameworks for Computational Morphology, held on September 6, 2013, at the Humboldt-Universität zu Berlin.

Morphological resources are the basis for all higher-level natural language processing applications. Morphology components should thus be capable of analyzing single word forms as well as whole corpora. For many practical applications, not only morphological analysis, but also generation is required, i.e., the production of surfaces corresponding to specific categories.

Apart from uses in computational linguistics, there are numerous practical applications that either require morphological analysis and generation, or that can greatly benefit from it, for example, in text processing, user interfaces, or information retrieval. These applications have specific requirements for morphological components, including requirements from software engineering, such as programming interfaces or robustness.

With the workshop on Systems and Frameworks for Computational Morphology (SFCM) we have established a place for presenting and discussing recent advances in the field of computational morphology. In 2013 the workshop took place for the third time. SFCM focuses on actual working systems and frameworks that are based on linguistic principles and that provide linguistically motivated analyses and/or generation on the basis of linguistic categories. The main theme for SFCM 2009 was systems for a specific language, namely, German; SFCM 2011 looked at phenomena at the interface between morphology and syntax in various languages. SFCM 2013 had three main goals:

– To discuss the role of morphological analysis and generation to improve the rather disappointing situation with respect to language technology for languages other than English, as described in the recently published White Paper Series by META-NET.
– To stimulate discussion among researchers and developers and to offer an up-to-date overview of available morphological systems for specific purposes.
– To stimulate discussion among developers of general frameworks that can be used to implement morphological components for several languages.

On the basis of the number of submissions and the number of participants at the workshop we can definitely state that the topic of the workshop was met with great interest from the community, both from academia and industry. We received 15 submissions, of which seven were accepted after a thorough review by the members of the Program Committee and additional reviewers. The peer review process was double-blind, and each paper received four reviews.

In addition to the regular papers, we had the pleasure of Georg Rehm giving an invited talk on the role of morphology systems in the META-NET Strategic Research Agenda.

The discussions after the talks and during the demo sessions, as well as the final plenum, showed the interest in and the need and the requirements for further efforts in the field of computational morphology. We will maintain the website for the workshop series at http://www.sfcm.eu.

This book starts with the invited paper by Georg Rehm ("The State of Computational Morphology for Europe's Languages and the META-NET Strategic Research Agenda"), emphasizing that computational morphology is all but a solved problem. Only for a few European languages appropriate resources and tools are available. He argues that a joint effort of the members of the European research community is needed to create "adequate, precise, robust, scalable and freely available morphology components" for all European languages.

The following paper "A Case Study in Tagging Case in German: An Assessment of Statistical Approaches" by Simon Clematide presents a study that assesses the performance of purely statistical approaches using supervised machine learning for predicting case in German nouns. The study evaluates different approaches—Hidden Markov Models, Decision Trees, and Conditional Random Fields—on two treebanks. The author shows that his CRF-based approach outperforms all other approaches and results in an improvement of 11% compared to an HMM trigram tagger.

In their paper "Jabalín: A Comprehensive Computational Model of Modern Standard Arabic Verbal Morphology Based on Traditional Arabic Prosody," Alicia González Martínez, Susana López Hervás, Doaa Samy, Carlos G. Arques, and Antonio Moreno Sandoval note that—despite its richness—the Arabic morphological system is in fact highly regular. By taking inspiration from the traditional description of Arabic prosody, the authors' Jabalín system implements a compact and simple morphological description for Modern Standard Arabic, which takes advantage of the regularities of Arabic morphology.

Both SFCM 2009 and SFCM 2011 featured papers on HFST, and we are happy to see this tradition continue: The paper "HFST—A System for Creating NLP Tools" by Krister Lindén, Erik Axelson, Senka Drobac, Sam Hardwick, Juha Kuokkala, Jyrki Niemi, Tommi Pirinen, and Miikka Silfverberg presents and evaluates various NLP tools that have been created using HFST. What makes this paper particularly interesting, however, is that the authors describe an implementation and application of pmatch finite-state pattern matching algorithm presented by Lauri Karttunen at SFCM 2011.

The next paper, "A System for Archivable Grammar Documentation" by Michael Maxwell, first describes a number of criteria for archivable documentation of grammars for natural languages and then presents a system for writing and testing morphological and phonological grammars, which aims to satisfy these criteria. The paper explains some of the decisions that went into the design of the formalism and describes experiences gained from its use with grammars for a variety of languages.

Fiammetta Namer's paper "A Rule-Based Morphosemantic Parser for French for a Fine-Grained Semantic Annotation of Texts" describes the DériF system. Unlike existing word segmentation tools, DériF annotates derived and compound words with semantic information, namely a definition, lexical-semantic features, and lexical relations.

Next, in their paper "Implementing a Formal Model of Inflectional Morphology," Benoît Sagot and Géraldine Walther describe the implementation of a formal model of inflectional morphology that aims to capture typological generalizations. The authors show that the availability of such a model—and an implementation thereof—is beneficial for studies in descriptive and formal morphology, as well as for the development of NLP tools and resources.

Finally, the paper "Verbal Morphosyntactic Disambiguation through Topological Field Recognition in German-Language Law Texts" by Kyoko Sugisaki and Stefan Höfler introduces an incremental system of verbal morphosyntactic disambiguation that exploits the concept of topological fields, and demonstrates that this approach is able to significantly reduce the error rate in POS tagging.

The contributions show that high-quality research is being conducted in the area of computational morphology: Mature systems are further developed and new systems and applications are emerging. Other languages than English are becoming more important. The papers in this book come from six countries and two continents, discuss a wide variety of languages from many different language families, and illustrate that, in fact, a rich morphology is better described as the norm rather than the exception—proving that for most languages, as we have stated above, morphological resources are indeed the basis for all higher-level natural language processing applications.

The trend toward open-source developments still goes on and evaluation is considered an important issue. Making high-quality morphological resources freely available will help to advance the state of the art and allow the development of high-quality real-world applications. Useful applications with carefully conducted evaluation will demonstrate to a broad audience that computational morphology is an actual science with tangible benefits for society.

We would like to thank the authors for their contributions to the workshop and to this book. We also thank the reviewers for their effort and for their constructive feedback, encouraging and helping the authors to improve their papers. The submission and reviewing process and the compilation of the proceedings was supported by the Easy-Chair system. We thank Aliaksandr Birukou, the editor of the series *Communications in Computer and Information Science* (CCIS), and the Springer staff for publishing the proceedings of SFCM 2013. We are grateful for the financial support given by the German Society for Computational Linguistics and Language Technology (GSCL). We thank Anke Lüdeling and Carolin Odebrecht and the staff from the Corpus Linguistics and Morphology Group at the Department of German Language and Linguistics at the Humboldt-Universität zu Berlin for the local organization.

June 2013   Cerstin Mahlow
                                                                  Michael Piotrowski

Organization

The Third International Workshop on Systems and Frameworks for Computational Morphology (SFCM 2013) was organized and chaired by Cerstin Mahlow and Michael Piotrowski. The workshop was held at Humboldt-Universität zu Berlin.

Program Chairs

Cerstin Mahlow	University of Konstanz, Germany
Michael Piotrowski	Leibniz Institute of European History, Germany

Program Committee

Bruno Cartoni	University of Geneva, Switzerland
Simon Clematide	University of Zurich, Switzerland
Piotr Fuglewicz	TiP Sp. z o. o., Katowice, Poland
Thomas Hanneforth	University of Potsdam, Germany
Kimmo Koskenniemi	University of Helsinki, Finland
Winfried Lenders	University of Bonn, Germany
Krister Lindén	University of Helsinki, Finland
Anke Lüdeling	Humboldt-Universität Berlin, Germany
Cerstin Mahlow	University of Konstanz, Germany
Günter Neumann	DFKI Saarbrücken, Germany
Michael Piotrowski	Leibniz Institute of European History, Germany
Benoît Sagot	INRIA/Université Paris 7, France
Helmut Schmid	University of Stuttgart, Germany
Angelika Storrer	University of Dortmund, Germany
Pius ten Hacken	Swansea University, UK
Andrea Zielinski	Fraunhofer IOSB, Germany

Additional Reviewers

Lenz Furrer	University of Zurich, Switzerland

Local Organization

Anke Lüdeling	Humboldt-Universität Berlin, Germany
Carolin Odebrecht	Humboldt-Universität Berlin, Germany

Sponsoring Institutions

German Society for Computational Linguistics and Language Technology (GSCL)
Humboldt-Universität Berlin, Germany

Table of Contents

The State of Computational Morphology
for Europe's Languages and the META-NET Strategic
Research Agenda

Georg Rehm

DFKI GmbH, Alt-Moabit 91c, 10559 Berlin, Germany
georg.rehm@dfki.de

Abstract. Recognising Europe's exceptional demand and opportunities for multilingual language technologies, 60 leading research centres in 34 European countries joined forces in META-NET, a European Network of Excellence. Working together with numerous additional organisations and experts from a variety of fields, META-NET has developed the *Strategic Research Agenda for Multilingual Europe 2020* (SRA) [42] – the complex planning and discussion process took more than two years to complete and involved ca. 200 experts. In this contribution we motivate the SRA, briefly describe the current state of Language Technology, especially Computational Morphology, in Europe and discuss the findings in the overall framework of the plans and strategies as specified in the META-NET Strategic Research Agenda.

Keywords: language technology, computational morphology, strategic research agenda, europe, digital agenda.

1 Introduction

The multilingual setup of our European society imposes grand societal challenges on political, economic and social integration and inclusion, especially in the creation of the single digital market and unified information space targeted by the European Commission's Digital Agenda [16]. As many as 21 European languages are at risk of digital extinction [41]. They could become victims of the digital age as they are under-represented online and under-resourced with respect to language technologies. Huge market opportunities remain untapped because of language barriers. If no action is taken, many European citizens will find that speaking their mother tongue leaves them at a social and economic disadvantage.

Language technology is the missing piece of the puzzle that will bring us closer to a single digital market. It is the key enabler and solution to boosting future growth in Europe and strengthening our competitiveness. The key question is: Will Europe wholeheartedly decide to participate in this fast growing market?

Although we use computers to write, phones to chat and the web to search for knowledge, IT does not yet have access to the meaning, purpose and sentiment behind our trillions of written and spoken words. Technology will bridge the rift separating IT and the human mind using sophisticated technologies for language understanding.

C. Mahlow and M. Piotrowski (Eds.): SFCM 2013, CCIS 380, pp. 1–21, 2013.
© Springer-Verlag Berlin Heidelberg 2013

Today's computers cannot understand texts and questions well enough to provide translations, summaries or reliable answers, but in less than ten years such services will be offered for many languages. Technological mastery of human language will enable a host of innovative IT products and services in commerce, administration, government, education, health care, entertainment and other sectors.

Recognising Europe's exceptional demand and opportunities, 60 leading research centres in 34 European countries joined forces in META-NET (http://www.meta-net.eu), a European Network of Excellence dedicated to the technological foundations of a multilingual, inclusive, innovative and reflective European society and partially supported through four EC-funded projects. META-NET assembled the Multilingual Europe Technology Alliance (META) with more than 700 organisations and experts representing multiple stakeholders. Working together with numerous additional organisations and experts from a variety of fields, META-NET has developed a Strategic Research Agenda (SRA) [42]. Our recommendations for Multilingual Europe 2020, as specified in the SRA, are based on a planning process involving more than one thousand experts.

We predict, in line with many other forecasts, that the next generation of IT will be able to handle human language, knowledge and emotion in competent and meaningful ways. These new competencies will enable an endless stream of novel services that will improve communication and understanding. Many services will help people learn about and understand things such as world history, technology, nature and the economy. Others will help us to better understand each other across language and knowledge boundaries. They will also drive many other services including programmes for commerce, localisation, and personal assistance.

Our ultimate goal is monolingual, crosslingual and multilingual technology support for all languages spoken by a significant population in Europe. We recommend focusing on three priority research topics connected to innovative application scenarios that will provide European R&D in this field with the ability to compete with other markets and subsequently achieve benefits for European society and citizens as well as an array of opportunities for our economy and future growth. We are confident that upcoming EU funding programmes, specifically Horizon 2020 [21] and Connecting Europe Facility [17], combined with national and regional funding, can provide the necessary resources for accomplishing our joint vision.

In the following, Section 2 provides some background and context for our overall initiative. Section 3 describes the results of the META-NET study "Europe's Languages in the Digital Age", taking a closer look at text analytics, especially computational morphology. Section 4 summarises the META-NET technology vision that we foresee for the year 2020, while Section 5 presents the core of the META-NET Strategic Research Agenda, i. e., five lines of action for large-scale research and innovation. The objective of these five themes is to turn our joint vision into reality and allow Europe to benefit from a technological revolution that will overcome barriers of understanding between people of different languages, people and technology, and people and the digitised knowledge of mankind.

2 Multilingual Europe: Facts and Opportunities for LT

During the last 60 years, Europe has become a distinct political and economic structure. Culturally and linguistically it is rich and diverse. However, everyday communication between Europe's citizens, enterprises and politicians is inevitably confronted with language barriers. They are an invisible and increasingly problematic threat to economic growth [12]. The EU's institutions spend about *one billion euros per year* on translation and interpretation to maintain their policy of multilingualism [22].

The only – unacceptable and rather un-European – alternative to a multilingual Europe would be to allow a single language to take a predominant position and replace all other languages. Another way to overcome language barriers is to learn foreign languages. However, given the 23 official EU languages plus 60 or more other languages spoken in Europe [20], language learning alone cannot solve the problem. Without technological support, our linguistic diversity will be an insurmountable obstacle for the entire continent. Only about half of the 500 million people who live in the EU speak English! There is no such thing as a lingua franca shared by the vast majority of the population.

Less than 10% of the EU's population are willing or able to use online services in English which is why multilingual technologies are badly needed to support and to move the EU online market from more than 20 language-specific sub-markets to one unified single digital market with more than 500 million users and consumers. The current situation with many fragmented markets is considered a critical obstacle [16].

In the late 1970s the EU realised the relevance of LT as a driver of European unity and began funding its first research projects, such as EUROTRA. After a longer period of sparse funding [27, 31], the EC set up a department dedicated to language technology and machine translation a few years ago. Selective funding efforts have led to a number of valuable results. For example, the EC's translation services now use Moses, which has been mainly developed in European research projects. However, these never led to a concerted European effort through which the EU and its member states systematically pursue the common goal of providing technology support for all European languages.

Through initiatives such as CLARIN and META-NET the research community is well connected and engaged in a long term agenda that aims gradually to strengthen language technology's role. What is missing in Europe is awareness, political determination and political will that would take us to a leading position in this technology area through a concerted funding effort. This major dedicated push needs to include the political determination to adopt a shared, EU-wide language policy that foresees an important role for language technologies.

Europe's more than 80 languages are one of its most important cultural assets and a vital part of its social model [13, 20]. While languages such as English and Spanish are likely to thrive in the emerging digital marketplace, many European languages could become marginal in a networked society. This would weaken Europe's global standing, and run counter to the goal of ensuring equal participation for every European citizen regardless of language [49, 50, 52, 54].

Only 57% of internet users in Europe purchase goods and services in languages that are not their native language. 55% of users read content in a foreign language while only 35% use another language to write e-mails or post comments on the web [19].

A few years ago, English might have been the lingua franca of the web but the situation has drastically changed. The amount of online content in other European as well as Asian and Middle Eastern languages has exploded [23]. Already today, more than 55% of web-based content is not in English.

The European market for translation, interpretation and localisation was estimated to be 5.7 billion euros in 2008. The subtitling and dubbing sector was at 633 million euros, language teaching at 1.6 billion euros. The overall value of the European language industry was estimated at 8.4 billion euros and expected to grow by 10% p. a., resulting in ca. 16.5 billion euros in 2015 [15, 18]. Yet, this existing capacity is not enough to satisfy current and future needs, e. g., with regard to translation [11]. Already today, Google Translate translates the same volume per *day* that all human translators on the planet translate in one *year* [38].

Despite recent improvements, the quality, usability and integration of machine translation into other online services is far from what is needed. If we rely on existing technologies, automated translation and the ability to process a variety of content in a variety of languages will be impossible. The same applies to information services, document services, media industries, digital archives and language teaching. The most compelling solution for ensuring the breadth and depth of language usage in tomorrow's Europe is to use appropriate technology. Still, the quality and usability of current technologies is far from what is needed. Especially the smaller European languages suffer severely from under-representation in the digital realm.

Drawing on the insights gained so far, today's hybrid language technology mixing deep processing with statistical methods could be able to bridge the gap between all European languages and beyond. In the end, high-quality language technology will be a must for all of Europe's languages for supporting the political and economic unity through cultural diversity. The three priority research themes are mainly aimed at Horizon 2020 [21]. The more infrastructural aspects, platform design and implementation and concrete language technology services are aimed at CEF [17]. An integral component of our strategic plans are the member states and associated countries: it is of utmost importance to set up, under the umbrella of the SRA, a coordinated initiative both on the national (member states, regions, associated countries) and international level (EC/EU).

We believe that *Language Technology made in Europe for Europe* will significantly contribute to future cross-border and cross-language communication, economic growth and social stability while establishing for Europe a worldwide, leading position in technology innovation, securing Europe's future as a world-wide trader and exporter of goods, services and information. There are many societal changes and challenges as well as economic and technological trends that confirm the urgent need to include sophisticated language technology in our European ICT infrastructure. Among these changes and challenges are language barriers [14], an ageing population, people with disabilities, immigration and integration, personal information services and customer care, operation and cooperation on a global scale, preservation of cultural heritage, linguistic diversity [51, 56], social media and e-participation as well as market awareness and customer acceptance.

3   LT and Computational Morphology: Current State

Answering the question on the current state of a whole R&D field is both difficult and complex, the same is true for a specific area such as computational morphology. For language technology at large, even though partial answers exist in terms of business figures, scientific challenges and results from educational studies, nobody has collected these indicators and provided comparable reports for a substantial number of European languages yet. In order to arrive at a comprehensive answer, META-NET prepared the White Paper Series *Europe's Languages in the Digital Age* [41] that describes the current state of language technology support for 30 European languages (including all 23 official EU languages). This immense undertaking has been in preparation since mid 2010 and was finally published in late 2012. More than 200 experts participated to the 30 volumes as co-authors and contributors.

The individual volumes of this series report on the specifics for a given language. In addition, we also prepared a comparison that goes across all languages and that takes a closer look at four important areas of language technology: *machine translation*; *interactive speech technologies*; *text analytics*; *language resources*. For each of these areas we ranked the level of support through language technology for each of the 30 languages on a five-point scale, from *excellent* to *weak/no support*. The *text analytics* area comprises, among others, the quality and coverage of existing text analysis technologies (morphology, syntax, semantics), coverage of linguistic phenomena and domains, amount and variety of available applications, quality and size of corpora, as well as quality and coverage of existing lexical resources and grammars. Figure 1 shows the results of the cross-language comparison for text analytics (the other three comparisons exhibit very similar tendencies). In addition to other processing components and technologies such as syntactic parsers, the results in Figure 1 also reflect computational morphology.

The differences in technology support between the various languages and areas are dramatic and alarming. In all four areas, English is ahead of the other languages but even support for English is far from being perfect. While there are good quality software and resources available for a few larger languages and application areas, others, usually smaller or very small languages, have substantial gaps. Many languages lack even basic technologies for text analytics and essential resources. Others have basic resources but the implementation of semantic methods is still far away. Currently no language, not even English, has the technological support it deserves. Also, the number of badly supported and under-resourced languages is unacceptable if we do not want to give up the principles of solidarity and subsidiarity in Europe.

For all four areas the positioning and ranking of all languages was carried out in a large meeting, held in Berlin, Germany, on October 21/22, 2011, in which representatives of all languages, i.e., members of all authoring teams of all white papers participated. This ranking exercise was informed by several statistics, discussions, comparisons, and examples. In addition to the positioning of a language, Figure 1 shows the average score of the category *grammatical analysis* which is part of a set of categories that are contained in each white paper and which provide more detailed information on a *language-specific* basis. The category *grammatical analysis* includes, among others, the area of computational morphology. The score shown in the Figure is an average

Table 1. Text analytics: state of language technology support for 30 European languages

Excellent support	Good support	Moderate support	Fragmentary support	Weak/no support
English (4.50)	Dutch (3.94)	Basque (3.36)	Croatian (2.43)	
	French (3.71)	Bulgarian (2.80)	Estonian (3.14)	
	German (3.36)	Catalan (3.21)	Icelandic (3.50)	
	Italian (3.50)	Czech (3.29)	Irish (3.71)	
	Spanish (3.77)	Danish (3.00)	Latvian (3.14)	
		Finnish (3.64)	Lithuanian (1.79)	
		Galician (3.43)	Maltese (0.80)	
		Greek (2.71)	Serbian (1.64)	
		Hungarian (3.79)		
		Norwegian (4.36)		
		Polish (4.07)		
		Portuguese (3.64)		
		Romanian (3.87)		
		Slovak (2.43)		
		Slovene (3.57)		
		Swedish (4.57)		

of the following seven dimensions: *quantity, quality, availability, coverage, maturity, sustainability, adaptability* (from 0, very low, to 6, very high). Neither the individual scores nor the average scores have been calibrated with regard to the scores assigned to the language technology support of other languages. This is why the scores cannot be used for a cross-language comparison alone; nevertheless, the average scores show how the respective authoring teams perceive the state of the *grammatical analysis* category for their respective language themselves (among the other categories are, for example, *speech recognition, speech synthesis, semantic analysis, text generation* and *machine translation*). To provide the complete picture, the individual scores assigned by the experts to the seven dimensions of the category *grammatical analysis* for their respective languages are shown in Table 2. This table represents a rating of the current state of existing tools in that category for the 30 languages examined by our study. Detailed explanations and interpretations are provided in the META-NET Language White Papers.

In the highly complex – and highly abstract – technology stack used in sophisticated language technology systems such as, for example, systems for machine translation, morphology tools and modules can almost be thought of as a well established, working technology, a solved problem. Instead of taking a bird's-eye view through our cross-language comparison that also takes into account many other technologies for text analytics we will now have a closer look at the individual languages and the level of support they have in terms of software for morphological analysis. While we delve into the concrete results of the META-NET White Paper Series concerning computational morphology in the order of the quality of support, we are unable to give a complete account of all aspects and issues discussed by the authors.

Table 2. Rating (from 0, very low, to 6, very high) of the current state of existing tools and technologies in the category *grammatical analysis* along seven different criteria; the scores were assigned by the members of the respective authoring teams who, in many cases, consulted with additional experts in order to arrive at scores that the whole regional/national community can agree upon; these scores for the seven dimensions were assigned individually and not calibrated among the 30 languages. In contrast, the information given in the column *Level of support* is the result of a cross-language comparison which was prepared at a large meeting with representatives of all authoring teams in Berlin on October 21/22, 2011.

Language	Quantity	Availability	Quality	Coverage	Maturity	Sustainability	Adaptability	Average	Level of support
Basque [26]	4	2.5	4	4	4	2.5	2.5	3.36	fragmentary
Bulgarian [2]	2.4	2	3.6	3.6	2.8	2.4	2.8	2.80	fragmentary
Catalan [37]	3	2.5	4	4	4	2.5	2.5	3.21	fragmentary
Croatian [47]	2	1.5	3.5	3	2	1	4	2.43	weak/no
Czech [3]	4	2	4	4	3	2	4	3.29	fragmentary
Danish [40]	3	2	4	4	3	2	3	3.00	fragmentary
Dutch [39]	3.6	5.4	4.8	3.6	4.8	3.6	1.8	3.94	moderate
English [1]	5	5	5.5	4.5	4.5	3	4	4.50	good
Estonian [32]	2.5	3.5	3.2	2.8	4	2.5	3.5	3.14	weak/no
Finnish [29]	3.5	3.5	3.5	4	4	3.5	3.5	3.64	fragmentary
French [33]	4	4	4	4	4	3	3	3.71	moderate
Galician [24]	3	5	4	4	3	2	3	3.43	fragmentary
German [6]	4	2.5	4	4	4	2.5	2.5	3.36	moderate
Greek [25]	2	1.5	3.5	3	3	3	3	2.71	fragmentary
Hungarian [45]	4.5	2	4	4.5	4	3	4.5	3.79	fragmentary
Icelandic [44]	2	5.5	4	3	3.5	3.5	3	3.50	weak/no
Irish [28]	4	4	3	3	4	4	4	3.71	weak/no
Italian [8]	3.5	3	4	5	4	3	2	3.50	moderate
Latvian [46]	2.5	2	3	3.5	4	3	4	3.14	weak/no
Lithuanian [43]	2	1.5	2.5	2	1.5	1	2	1.79	weak/no
Maltese [43]	0.8	0.8	0.8	0.8	0.8	0.8	0.8	0.80	weak/no
Norwegian [9, 10]	4	4.5	4	4	4.5	4.5	5	4.36	fragmentary
Polish [36]	4	4.5	4.5	4.5	4	4	3	4.07	fragmentary
Portuguese [5]	3	3	4	4	4.5	2.5	4.5	3.64	fragmentary
Romanian [48]	4	3.5	4	3.6	4.5	3.5	4	3.87	fragmentary
Serbian [55]	1	1	2.5	2	2	1.5	1.5	1.64	weak/no
Slovak [57]	2	2	3	2	2	3	3	2.43	fragmentary
Slovene [30]	2.5	4	4.5	3.5	3	3	4.5	3.57	fragmentary
Spanish [34]	3.5	3	5.4	4.5	3.5	3	3.5	3.77	moderate
Swedish [4]	4.5	3.5	5	4	5	5	5	4.57	fragmentary

Good Support. The only language that is considered to have "good support" in terms of text analytics is English. In comparison to certain other languages and language families, the morphology of English is usually considered as being rather simple and straight-forward. Many robust and precise off-the-shelf technologies exist which is most probably the main reason why the authors of the white paper on English [1] do not discuss morphology components at all, nor any related issues or challenges.

Moderate Support. The experts who wrote the white papers on the languages with "moderate support" concerning text analytics follow this trend. They mainly discuss other research and technology gaps, mentioning the existence of, for example, "medium- to high-quality software for basic text analysis, such as tools for morphological analysis and syntactic parsing" [6], mentioning morphology on a more superficial level [8, 34] or not at all [39]. The authors of the white paper on French [33] emphasise that large programmes were set up (1994–2000; 2003–2005) to build a more or less complete set of basic technologies for French, from spoken and written language resources to spoken and written language processing systems including evaluations.

Fragmentary Support. A total of 16 languages only have "fragmentary support" in the area of text analytics. Especially in this but also in the lowest category usually one or at most two different morphological components are mentioned by the authors [3, 26]. There is a clear tendency that these tools have limited functionality and a long history including an unclear copyright situation [45]; they are neither freely [40, 48] nor immediately available. However, these tools are usually employed in the large office application suites (MS Office, Open Office), localisation frameworks or national search engines [3, 9, 57].

Most experts discuss the complexity of the rich morphological systems of their languages, a high degree of inflection and maybe a complete lack of morphological distinction for certain nominal cases as a key contributing factor to the fact that only very few morphological modules exist for their languages; these linguistic features make morphological processing, as well as all approaches based primarily on statistics, a substantial challenge [2, 3, 25, 26, 29, 30, 36, 45, 48, 57]. Special characters and their encoding systems are also mentioned for languages with alphabets that go beyond plain ASCII; morphologically processing words when certain diacritics are actually missing (this often happens in web texts and emails) is a challenge as no cues for automatic processing exist. Such words are considered malformed which is why several experts demand more robust error detection algorithms, also to distinguish between genuine spelling errors and word forms which are correct but missing from the lexicon [3]. A simple but important observation, made for Basque [26] and for Greek [25], is related to the fact that algorithms and approaches developed for English cannot be directly transferred to other languages. An overarching reason for the lack of basic processing tools concerns the fact that languages spoken in smaller countries usually do not receive as much attention and research funding than larger languages in which typically also a larger base of researchers works on building actual technologies, maybe even breaking new ground

[25]. For Hungarian, the authors note that a lack of synchronisation between parallel efforts to build morphological processors lead to substantial friction loss [45]. This is why several morphological parsers for Hungarian exist but they use conflicting and incompatible formalisms. Some authors also discuss related technologies such as, for example, e-learning tools and systems for second language learners that employ complex morphological components [3].

Similar to the programmes set up to boost the technological support for French (1994–2000 and 2003–2005, see above) a project was set up in Portugal in 2005 to enable the development of a set of linguistic resources and software components to support the computational processing of Portuguese. The outcome of this project was a large annotated corpus and processing tools for tokenisation, morphosyntactic tagging, inflection analysis, and lemmatisation, among others [5]. A comparable project was set up in Slovakia to provide integrated computational processing of the Slovak language for linguistic research purposes within the framework of the national research and development programme *Current Issues in Society Development* [57]. Results of this project are tools and data sets that include processors and morphologically annotated corpora. In direct comparison, it can be seen that French had a clear head-start over Portuguese and Slovak, in addition to a longer, more established reasearch tradition in this area, which is why it was ranked higher. The authors of the white paper on Slovak [57] conclude that, while certain morphological tools do exist for their language, "those must be further developed and supported."

Weak/no Support. Eight languages were placed in this lowest category of language technology support. In general, the authors of the respective language white papers mention the same set of issues as the ones of the previous category. A small or very small number of morphological tools or components exist [28] and are widely used, even in well known applications, but they are not freely available or accessible for research purposes and also based on rather simple approaches that rely on extensive lists of correct word forms [32, 47, 53]. Several of these tools have been in development since the 1980ies and are under the control of companies. This is why researchers often use the open source software ispell or aspell as a technological fallback solution. Furthermore, the complex morphology of languages is mentioned in almost all cases along with the statement that morphology processing must be further developed [32, 43, 44, 47, 55].

Several authors of the white papers on the languages with only weak or no support explicitly demand intensified development for basic morphological tools in order to achieve better precision and performance for technologies supporting their languages. An important aspect is to design and model these approaches to the specific linguistic properties of the language in question without trying to adapt an approach developed and optimised for English to a completely different language [32, 55]. One such step is to set up specific language technology programmes, as has been done, among others, in France, Slovakia and Portugal. In 2000, the Icelandic government also set up a national programme with the aim of supporting institutions and companies in creating basic resources for Icelandic language technology. This initiative resulted in several projects which have had a profound influence on the field in Iceland. Among its main direct products are a full-form morphological database of Modern Icelandic inflections, a balanced morphosyntactically tagged corpus of 25 million words and a training model for data-driven part-of-speech taggers and an improved spell checker [44].

4   Language Technology 2020: The META-NET Technology Vision

Before we go into the details of the Strategic Research Agenda, we want to present, briefly, the overarching technology vision which drives the content and direction of the priority research themes and which is, in essence, the foundation of the SRA. The wide range of novel or improved applications in META-NET's shared vision represent only a fragment of the countless opportunities for LT to change our work and everyday life. Language-proficient technology will enable or enhance applications wherever language is present.

We believe that in the next IT revolution computers will master our languages. The operating systems of tomorrow will *know* human languages. They may not reach the linguistic performance of educated people and they will not yet know enough about the world to understand everything, but they will be much more useful than they are today and will further enhance our work and life.

The area of **communication among people** will see a dramatically increased use of sophisticated LT. By the year 2020, with sufficient research effort on high-quality automatic translation and robust accurate speech recognition, reliable dialogue translation for face-to-face conversation and telecommunication will be possible for at least hundreds of languages, across multiple subject fields and text types, both spoken and written. Authoring software will check for appropriate style according to genre and purpose, it will flag potential errors, suggest corrections, and use authoring memories to suggest completions of started sentences or even whole paragraphs. LT will be able to record, transcribe, and summarise tele-meetings. Brainstorming will be facilitated by semantic lookup and structured display of relevant data, proposals, pictures, and maps. Even before 2020, email communication will be semantically analysed, checked for sentiment indicators, and summarised in reports.

Human language will become the primary medium for **communication between people and technology**. Today's voice-control interfaces to smartphones and search engines are just the modest start of overcoming the communication barrier between humankind and the non-human part of the world. Only a few years ago the idea of talking to a car to access key functions would have seemed absurd, yet it is now commonplace. We will soon see much more sophisticated personal digital assistants with expressive voices, faces, and gestures. They will become an interface to any information provided online. Such assistants can be made sensitive to the user's preferences, habits, moods, and goals. By the year 2020 we could have a highly personalised, socially aware and interactive virtual assistant. Having been trained on the user's behaviour, it will offer advice and it will be able to speak in the language and dialect of the user but also digest information in other natural and artificial languages and formats. The assistant will translate or interpret without the user even needing to request it.

In the context of the Semantic Web, Linked Open Data and the general semantification of the web as well as knowledge acquisition and ontology population, LT can perform many tasks in the **processing of knowledge and information**. It can sort, categorise, catalogue, and filter content and it can deliver the data for data mining in texts. LT can connect web documents with meaningful hyperlinks and it can produce summaries of larger text collections. Opinion mining and sentiment analysis can find out what people think about products, personalities, or problems and analyse their feelings about such topics. In the next few years we will see considerable advances for all these techniques. For large parts of research and application development, language processing and knowledge processing will merge. Language and knowledge technologies for social intelligence applications will involve text and speech analytics, translation, summarisation, opinion mining, sentiment analysis, and several other technologies. In 2020, LT will enable forms of knowledge evolution, transmission and exploitation that speed up scientific, social, and cultural development.

5 Language Technology 2020: The META-NET Priority Research Themes

In ten years or less, basic language proficiency is going to be an integral component of any advanced IT. It will be available to any user interface, service and application. Additional language skills for semantic search, knowledge discovery, human-technology communication, text analytics, language checking, e-learning, translation and other applications will employ and extend the basic proficiency. The shared basic language competence will ensure consistency and interoperability among services. Many adaptations and extensions will be derived and improved through sample data and interaction with people through machine learning.

In the envisaged big push toward realising this vision by massive research and innovation, the technology community is faced with three enormous challenges:

1. *Richness and diversity.* A serious challenge is the sheer number of languages, some closely related, others distantly apart. Within a language, technology has to deal with dialects, sociolects, registers, jargons, genres and slangs.
2. *Depth and meaning.* Understanding language is a complex process. Human language is not only the key to knowledge and thought, it also cannot be interpreted without shared knowledge and active inference. Computational language proficiency needs semantic technologies.
3. *Multimodality and grounding.* Human language is embedded in our daily activities. It is combined with other modes and media of communication. It is affected by beliefs, desires, intentions and emotions and it affects all of these. Successful interactive LT requires models of embodied and adaptive human interaction with people, technology and other parts of the world.

It is fortunate for research and economy that the only way to effectively tackle the three challenges involves submitting the evolving technology continuously to the growing demands and practical stress tests of real world applications. Only a continuous stream of technological innovation can provide the economic pull forces and the evolutionary environments for the realisation of the grand vision. We propose five major action lines of research and innovation:

- **Three Priority Research Themes** along with application scenarios to drive research and innovation. These will demonstrate novel technologies in show-case solutions with high economic and societal impact. They will open up numerous new business opportunities for European language-technology and -service providers.
  1. **Translingual Cloud:** generic and specialised federated cloud services for instantaneous reliable spoken and written translation among all European and major non-European languages.
  2. **Social Intelligence and e-Participation:** understanding and dialogue within and across communities of citizens, customers, clients and consumers to enable e-participation and more effective processes for preparing, selecting and evaluating collective decisions.
  3. **Socially Aware Interactive Assistants** that learn and adapt and that provide proactive and interactive support tailored to specific situations, locations and goals of the user through verbal and non-verbal multimodal communication.
- Two additional themes focus upon base technologies and a service platform:
  4. **Core technologies and resources for Europe's languages:** a steadily evolving system of shared, collectively maintained interoperable core technologies and resources for the languages of Europe and selected other languages. These will ensure that our languages will be sufficiently supported and represented in the next generations of IT.
  5. A **European service platform for language technologies** for supporting research and innovation by testing and showcasing research results, integrating various services, even including professional human services, will allow SME providers to offer services, and share and utilise tools, components and data resources.

These priority themes have been designed with the aim of turning our vision into reality and to letting Europe benefit from a technological revolution that will overcome barriers of understanding between people of different languages, between people and technology and between people and the knowledge of mankind. The themes connect societal needs with LT applications. In the following we mainly focus upon the two additional themes as these are the most relevant ones for computational morphology. Detailed descriptions of the three priority research themes can be found in the SRA [42].

The three priority research themes overlap in technologies and challenges. The overlap reflects the coherence and maturation of the field. At the same time, the resulting division of labour and sharing of resources and results is a precondition for the realisation of this highly ambitious programme. The themes need to benefit from progress in core technologies of language analysis and production such as morphological, syntactic and semantic parsing and generation (see Figure 1).

5.1 Core Language Resources and Technologies

The three priority research themes share a large and heterogeneous group of core technologies for language analysis and production that provide development support

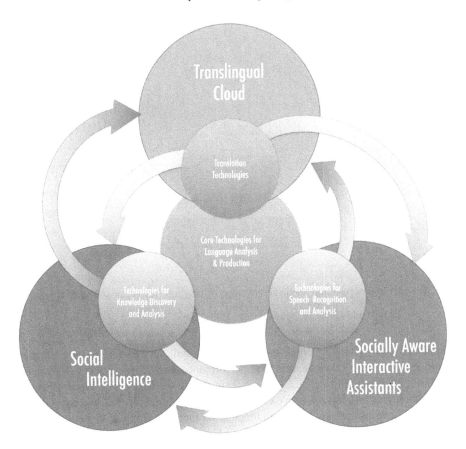

Fig. 1. Core language resources and technologies at the centre of the three priority research themes

through basic modules and datasets (see Figure 1). To this group belong tools and technologies such as, among others, tokenisers, part-of-speech taggers, morphology components, syntactic parsers, tools for building language models, information retrieval libraries, machine learning toolkits, speech recognition and speech synthesis engines, and integrated architectures. Many of these tools depend on specific datasets (i. e., language resources), for example, very large collections of linguistically annotated documents (morphologically annotated corpora, multilingual, aligned corpora, etc.), treebanks, grammars, lexicons, thesauri, terminologies, dictionaries, ontologies and language models. Both tools and resources can be rather general or highly task- or domain-specific, tools can be language-independent, datasets are, by definition, language-specific.

A key component of this research agenda is to collect, develop and make available core technologies and resources through a shared infrastructure so that the research and technology development carried out in all themes can make use of them. Over time, this approach will improve the core technologies including systems and frameworks for

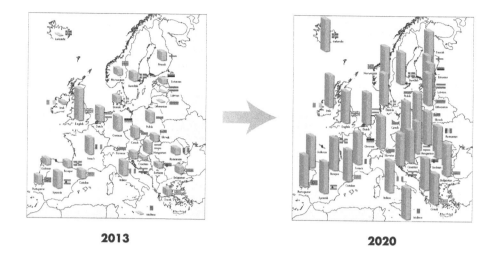

2013   **2020**

Fig. 2. Towards appropriate and adequate coverage of language resources and technologies for Europe

computational morphology, as the specific research will have certain requirements on the software, extending their feature sets, performance, accuracy, etc. through dynamic push-pull effects (see Figure 2). Conceptualising these technologies as a set of shared core technologies will have positive effects on their sustainability and interoperability. Also, as we have seen, many European languages other than English are heavily under-resourced [41].

The European academic and industrial technology community is fully aware of the need for sharing language resources and language technologies as a basis for the successful development and implementation of the priority themes. Initiatives such as FLaReNet [7] and CLARIN (http://www.clarin.eu) have prepared the ground for a culture of sharing, META-NET's open resource exchange infrastructure, META-SHARE, is providing the technological platform as well as legal and organisational schemes (http://www.meta-share.eu). All language resources and basic technologies including morphology tools and components will be created under this core technologies umbrella.

5.2   A European Service Platform for Language Technologies

We recommend the design and implementation of an ambitious large-scale platform as a central motor for research and innovation in the next phase of IT evolution and as a ubiquitous resource for the multilingual European society. The platform will be used for testing, show casing, proof-of-concept demonstration, avant-garde adoption, experimental and operational service composition, and fast and economical service delivery to enterprises and end-users (see Figure 3). The creation of a cloud platform for a wide

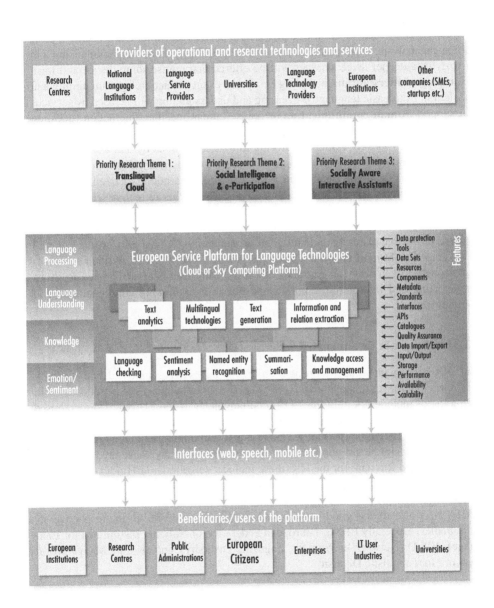

Fig. 3. European Service Platform for Language Technologies

range of services dealing with human language, knowledge and emotion will not only benefit the individual and corporate users of these technologies but also the providers. Large-scale ICT infrastructures and innovation clusters such as this one are foreseen in the Digital Agenda for Europe [16].

A top layer consists of **language processing** such as text filters, tokenisation, morphological analysis, spell, grammar and style checking, hyphenation, lemmatising and parsing. At a deeper level, services will be offered that realise some degree and form of **language understanding** including entity and event extraction, opinion mining and translation. Both basic language processing and understanding will be used by services that support **human communication** or realise human-machine interaction (question answering, dialogue systems, email response applications). Another component will bring in services for processing and storing **knowledge** gained by and used for understanding and communication (ontologies, linked data collections). These in turn permit a certain range of rational capabilities often attributed to a notion of intelligence. The goal is not to model the entire human intelligence but rather to realise selected forms of **inference** that are needed for utilising and extending knowledge, for understanding and for successful communication. These forms of inference permit better decision support, pro-active planning and autonomous adaptation. A final part of services will be dedicated to **human emotion**. Since people are largely guided by their emotions and strongly affected by the emotions of others, truly user-centred IT need facilities for detecting and interpreting emotion and even for expressing emotional states in communication.

5.3   Languages to Be Supported

The SRA has a much broader scope in terms of languages to be supported than our study "Europe's Languages in the Digital Age" [41]. The set of languages to be reflected with technologies include not only the 23 official languages of the EU but also recognised and unrecognised regional languages and the languages of associated countries or non-member states. Equally important are the minority and immigrant languages that are in active use by a significant population in Europe (for Germany, these are, among others, Turkish and Russian; for the UK, these include Bengali, Urdu/Hindi and Punjabi). An important set of languages outside our continent are those of important political and trade partners such as, for example, Chinese, Japanese, Korean, Russian, and Thai. META-NET already has good working relationships with several of the respective official bodies, especially EFNIL (European Federation of National Institutions for Language), NPLD (Network to Promote Linguistic Diversity), and also the Maaya World Network for Linguistic Diversity.

6   Conclusions: Computational Morphology for Europe

In the Strategic Research Agenda, META-NET recommends setting up a large, multi-year programme on language technologies to build the technological foundations for a truly multilingual Europe. The research strands and associated sets of applications we suggest to build in the next ten years are of utmost importance for Europe. Through these technologies we will be able to overcome language barriers in spoken and written communication, we will be able to carry out both regional and national and language-border-crossing debates and we will enable new forms and means of communication. We are confident that the impact of our technologies will be so immense that they will be able to help establishing a sense of a European identity in the majority of European citizens. The research plan described in the SRA will generate a countless number of opportunities, it will significantly contribute to Europe's future growth and will secure its position in many global markets.

Due to the scope and duration of the suggested action, our preferred option is to set up a shared programme between the European Commission and the Member States as well as Associated Countries. First steps along those lines have been taken at our META-FORUM 2012 conference in Brussels, Belgium, on June 21, 2012, when representatives of several European funding agencies (Bulgaria, Czech Republic, France, Hungary, The Netherlands, Slovenia) who participated in a panel discussion on this topic, unanimously expressed the urgent need for setting up such a shared programme [35].

The overview of the results of our study "Europe's Languages in the Digital Age" with regard to the area of text analytics, specifically computational morphology, clearly shows that this sub-area cannot and must not be considered a "solved problem". Quite the contrary: while, overall, several good technologies exist for a small number of languages, many languages lack adequate support in this technology area. This is why the whole European research community needs to team up in order to discuss potential synergies and to boost technology transfer so that adequate, precise, robust, scalable and freely available morphology components will be available for all European languages sooner rather than later. Among the many new challenges and opportunities in this area are real-time processing, web-scale processing of and training on documents using big data technologies such as Hadoop, interoperability and standardisation of data formats, morphology as a service and "multilingual" processing of closely related languages. The sophisticated applications foreseen in our language technology vision and the priority research themes are criticially dependent on reliable and precise basic processing components including computational morphology.

Acknowledgements. The work presented in this article would not have been possible without the dedication and commitment of our colleagues Aljoscha Burchardt, Kathrin Eichler, Tina Klüwer, Arle Lommel, Felix Sasaki and Hans Uszkoreit (all DFKI), the 60 member organisations of the META-NET network of excellence, the ca. 70 members of the Vision Groups, the ca. 30 members of the META Technology Council, the more than 200 authors of and contributors to the META-NET Language White Paper Series [41] and the ca. 200 representatives from industry and research who contributed to the META-NET SRA [42].

META-NET is co-funded by the 7th Framework Programme of the European Commission through the following grant agreements: T4ME Net (no. 249 119), CESAR (no. 271 022), METANET4U (no. 270 893) and META-NORD (no. 270 899). More information: http://www.meta-net.eu, office@meta-net.eu.

References

[1] Ananiadou, S., McNaught, J., Thompson, P.: The English Language in the Digital Age. META-NET White Paper Series: Europe's Languages in the Digital Age. Springer, Heidelberg (2012), http://www.meta-net.eu/whitepapers/volumes/english

[2] Blagoeva, D., Koeva, S., Murdarov, V.: Българският език в дигиталната епоха – The Bulgarian Language in the Digital Age. META-NET White Paper Series: Europe's Languages in the Digital Age. Springer, Heidelberg (2012), http://www.meta-net.eu/whitepapers/volumes/bulgarian

[3] Bojar, O., Cinková, S., Hajič, J., Hladká, B., Kuboň, V., Mírovský, J., Panevová, J., Peterek, N., Spoustová, J., Žabokrtský, Z.: Čeština v digitálním věku – The Czech Language in the Digital Age. META-NET White Paper Series: Europe's Languages in the Digital Age. Springer, Heidelberg (2012), http://www.meta-net.eu/whitepapers/volumes/czech

[4] Borin, L., Brandt, M.D., Edlund, J., Lindh, J., Parkvall, M.: Svenska språket i den digitala tidsåldern – The Swedish Language in the Digital Age. META-NET White Paper Series: Europe's Languages in the Digital Age. Springer, Heidelberg (2012), http://www.meta-net.eu/whitepapers/volumes/swedish

[5] Branco, A., Mendes, A., Pereira, S., Henriques, P., Pellegrini, T., Meinedo, H., Trancoso, I., Quaresma, P., de Lima, V.L.S., Bacelar, F.: A língua portuguesa na era digital – The Portuguese Language in the Digital Age. META-NET White Paper Series: Europe's Languages in the Digital Age. Springer, Heidelberg (2012), http://www.meta-net.eu/whitepapers/volumes/portuguese

[6] Burchardt, A., Egg, M., Eichler, K., Krenn, B., Kreutel, J., Leßmöllmann, A., Rehm, G., Stede, M., Uszkoreit, H., Volk, M.: Die Deutsche Sprache im digitalen Zeitalter – German in the Digital Age. META-NET White Paper Series: Europe's Languages in the Digital Age. Springer, Heidelberg (2012), http://www.meta-net.eu/whitepapers/volumes/german

[7] Calzolari, N., Bel, N., Choukri, K., Mariani, J., Monachini, M., Odijk, J., Piperidis, S., Quochi, V., Soria, C.: Language Resources for the Future – The Future of Language Resources (September 2011), http://www.flarenet.eu/sites/default/files/FLaReNet_Book.pdf

[8] Calzolari, N., Magnini, B., Soria, C., Speranza, M.: La Lingua Italiana nell'Era Digitale – The Italian Language in the Digital Age. META-NET White Paper Series: Europe's Languages in the Digital Age. Springer, Heidelberg (2012), http://www.meta-net.eu/whitepapers/volumes/italian

[9] De Smedt, K., Lyse, G.I., Gjesdal, A.M., Losnegaard, G.S.: Norsk i den digitale tidsalderen (bokmålsversjon) – The Norwegian Language in the Digital Age (Bokmål Version). META-NET White Paper Series: Europe's Languages in the Digital Age. Springer, Heidelberg (2012), http://www.meta-net.eu/whitepapers/volumes/norwegian-bokmaal

[10] De Smedt, K., Lyse, G.I., Gjesdal, A.M., Losnegaard, G.S.: Norsk i den digitale tidsalderen (nynorskversjon) – The Norwegian Language in the Digital Age (Nynorsk Version). META-NET White Paper Series: Europe's Languages in the Digital Age. Springer, Heidelberg (2012), http://www.meta-net.eu/whitepapers/volumes/norwegian-nynorsk

[11] DePalma, D.A., Kelly, N.: The Business Case for Machine Translation. How Organizations Justify and Adopt Automated Translation (August 2009), http://www.commonsenseadvisory.com

[12] Economist, E.I.U.T.: Competing across borders. How Cultural and Communication Barriers Affect Business (2012),
http://www.managementthinking.eiu.com/competing-across-borders.html

[13] European Commission: Multilingualism: an Asset for Europe and a Shared Commitment (2008), http://ec.europa.eu/languages/pdf/comm2008_en.pdf

[14] European Commission: Report on cross-border e-commerce in the EU (2009),
http://ec.europa.eu/consumers/strategy/docs/com_staff_wp2009_en.pdf

[15] European Commission: Size of the Language Industry in the EU (2009),
http://ec.europa.eu/dgs/translation/publications/studies

[16] European Commission: A Digital Agenda for Europe (2010),
http://ec.europa.eu/information_society/digital-agenda/publications/

[17] European Commission: Connecting Europe Facility: Commission adopts plan for €50 billion boost to European networks (2011),
http://europa.eu/rapid/pressReleasesAction.do?reference=IP/11/1200

[18] European Commission: Languages mean business (2011),
http://ec.europa.eu/languages/languages-mean-business/

[19] European Commission: User Language Preferences Online (2011),
http://ec.europa.eu/public_opinion/flash/fl_313_en.pdf

[20] European Commission: Europeans and their Languages european Commission. Special Eurobarometer 386/77.1 (June 2012), http://ec.europa.eu/languages/languages-of-europe/eurobarometer-survey_en.htm

[21] European Commission: Horizon 2020: The Framework Programme for Research and Innovation (2012), http://ec.europa.eu/research/horizon2020/

[22] European Commission: Languages (2012), http://ec.europa.eu/languages/

[23] Ford, D., Batson, J.: Languages of the World (Wide Web) (July 2011),
http://googleresearch.blogspot.com/2011/07/languages-of-world-wide-web.html

[24] García-Mateo, C., Arza, M.: O idioma galego na era dixital – The Galician Language in the Digital Age. META-NET White Paper Series: Europe's Languages in the Digital Age. Springer, Heidelberg (2012),
http://www.meta-net.eu/whitepapers/volumes/galician

[25] Gavrilidou, M., Koutsombogera, M., Patrikakos, A., Piperidis, S.: – The Greek Language in the Digital Age. META-NET White Paper Series: Europe's Languages in the Digital Age. Springer, Heidelberg (2012),
http://www.meta-net.eu/whitepapers/volumes/greek

[26] Hernáez, I., Navas, E., Odriozola, I., Sarasola, K., de Ilarraza, A.D., Leturia, I., de Lezana, A.D., Oihartzabal, B., Salaberria, J.: Euskara Aro Digitalean – Basque in the Digital Age. META-NET White Paper Series: Europe's Languages in the Digital Age. Springer, Heidelberg (2012), http://www.meta-net.eu/whitepapers/volumes/basque

[27] Joscelyne, A., Lockwood, R.: The EUROMAP Study. Benchmarking HLT progress in Europe (2003), http://cst.dk/dandokcenter/FINAL_Euromap_rapport.pdf

[28] Judge, J., Chasaide, A.N., Dhubhda, R.N., Scannell, K.P., Dhonnchadha, E.U.: An Ghaeilge sa Ré Dhigiteach – The Irish Language in the Digital Age. META-NET White Paper Series: Europe's Languages in the Digital Age. Springer, Heidelberg (2012), http://www.meta-net.eu/whitepapers/volumes/irish

[29] Koskenniemi, K., Lindén, K., Carlson, L., Vainio, M., Arppe, A., Lennes, M., Westerlund, H., Hyvärinen, M., Bartis, I., Nuolijärvi, P., Piehl, A.: Suomen kieli digitaalisella aikakaudella – The Finnish Language in the Digital Age. META-NET White Paper Series: Europe's Languages in the Digital Age. Springer, Heidelberg (2012),
http://www.meta-net.eu/whitepapers/volumes/finnish

[30] Krek, S.: Slovenski jezik v digitalni dobi – The Slovene Language in the Digital Age. META-NET White Paper Series: Europe's Languages in the Digital Age. Springer, Heidelberg (2012), http://www.meta-net.eu/whitepapers/volumes/slovene

[31] Lazzari, G.: Human Language Technologies for Europe (2006), http://cordis.europa.eu/documents/documentlibrary/90834371EN6.pdf

[32] Liin, K., Muischnek, K., Müürisep, K., Vider, K.: Eesti keel digiajastul – The Estonian Language in the Digital Age. META-NET White Paper Series: Europe's Languages in the Digital Age. Springer, Heidelberg (2012), http://www.meta-net.eu/whitepapers/volumes/estonian

[33] Mariani, J., Paroubek, P., Francopoulo, G., Max, A., Yvon, F., Zweigenbaum, P.: La langue française à l' Ère du numérique – The French Language in the Digital Age. META-NET White Paper Series: Europe's Languages in the Digital Age. Springer, Heidelberg (2012), http://www.meta-net.eu/whitepapers/volumes/french

[34] Melero, M., Badia, T., Moreno, A.: La lengua española en la era digital – The Spanish Language in the Digital Age. META-NET White Paper Series: Europe's Languages in the Digital Age. Springer, Heidelberg (2012), http://www.meta-net.eu/whitepapers/volumes/spanish

[35] META-NET: META-FORUM 2012: A Strategy for Multilingual Europe. Panel discussion "Plans for LT Research and Innovation in Member States and Regions" (June 2012), videos available at http://www.meta-net.eu/events/meta-forum-2012/programme

[36] Miłkowski, M.: Język polski w erze cyfrowej – The Polish Language in the Digital Age. META-NET White Paper Series: Europe's Languages in the Digital Age. Springer, Heidelberg (2012), http://www.meta-net.eu/whitepapers/volumes/polish

[37] Moreno, A., Bel, N., Revilla, E., Garcia, E., Vallverdú, S.: La llengua catalana a l'era digital – The Catalan Language in the Digital Age. META-NET White Paper Series: Europe's Languages in the Digital Age. Springer, Heidelberg (2012), http://www.meta-net.eu/whitepapers/volumes/catalan

[38] Och, F.: Breaking down the language barrier – six years in (April 2012), http://googleblog.blogspot.de/2012/04/breaking-down-language-barriersix-years.html

[39] Odijk, J.: Het Nederlands in het Digitale Tijdperk – The Dutch Language in the Digital Age. META-NET White Paper Series: Europe's Languages in the Digital Age. Springer, Heidelberg (2012), http://www.meta-net.eu/whitepapers/volumes/dutch

[40] Pedersen, B.S., Wedekind, J., Bøhm-Andersen, S., Henrichsen, P.J., Hoffensetz-Andresen, S., Kirchmeier-Andersen, S., Kjærum, J.O., Larsen, L.B., Maegaard, B., Nimb, S., Rasmussen, J.E., Revsbech, P., Thomsen, H.E.: Det danske sprog i den digitale tidsalder – The Danish Language in the Digital Age. META-NET White Paper Series: Europe's Languages in the Digital Age. Springer, Heidelberg (2012), http://www.meta-net.eu/whitepapers/volumes/danish

[41] Rehm, G., Uszkoreit, H. (eds.): META-NET White Paper Series: Europe's Languages in the Digital Age. Springer, Heidelberg (2012), http://www.meta-net.eu/whitepapers, 31 volumes on 30 European languages

[42] Rehm, G., Uszkoreit, H. (eds.): The META-NET Strategic Research Agenda for Multilingual Europe. Springer, Heidelberg (2013), http://www.meta-net.eu/sra

[43] Rosner, M., Joachimsen, J.: Il-Lingwa Maltija Fl-Era Diġitali – The Maltese Language in the Digital Age. META-NET White Paper Series: Europe's Languages in the Digital Age. Springer, Heidelberg (2012), http://www.meta-net.eu/whitepapers/volumes/maltese

[44] Rögnvaldsson, E., Jóhannsdóttir, K.M., Helgadóttir, S., Steingrímsson, S.: Íslensk tunga á stafrænni öld – The Icelandic Language in the Digital Age. META-NET White Paper Series: Europe's Languages in the Digital Age. Springer, Heidelberg (2012), http://www.meta-net.eu/whitepapers/volumes/icelandic

[45] Simon, E., Lendvai, P., Németh, G., Olaszy, G., Vicsi, K.: A magyar nyelv a digitális korban – The Hungarian Language in the Digital Age. META-NET White Paper Series: Europe's Languages in the Digital Age. Springer, Heidelberg (2012), http://www.meta-net.eu/whitepapers/volumes/hungarian

[46] Skadiņa, I., Veisbergs, A., Vasiļjevs, A., Gornostaja, T., Keiša, I., Rudzīte, A.: Latviešu valoda digitālajā laikmetā – The Latvian Language in the Digital Age. META-NET White Paper Series: Europe's Languages in the Digital Age. Springer, Heidelberg (2012), http://www.meta-net.eu/whitepapers/volumes/latvian

[47] Tadić, M., Brozović-Rončević, D., Kapetanović, A.: Hrvatski Jezik u Digitalnom Dobu – The Croatian Language in the Digital Age. META-NET White Paper Series: Europe's Languages in the Digital Age. Springer, Heidelberg (2012), http://www.meta-net.eu/whitepapers/volumes/croatian

[48] Trandabăt, D., Irimia, E., Mititelu, V.B., Cristea, D., Tufis, D.: Limba română în era digitală – The Romanian Language in the Digital Age. META-NET White Paper Series: Europe's Languages in the Digital Age. Springer, Heidelberg (2012), http://www.meta-net.eu/whitepapers/volumes/romanian

[49] UNESCO: Intersectoral Mid-term Strategy on Languages and Multilingualism (2007), http://unesdoc.unesco.org/images/0015/001503/150335e.pdf

[50] UNESCO: UNESCO Information for All Programme: International Conference Linguistic and Cultural Diversity in Cyberspace: Final Document. Lena Resolution (July 2008)

[51] UNESCO: UNESCO Information for All Programme, AFP (2011), http://www.unesco.org/new/en/communication-and-information/intergovernmental-programmes/information-for-all-programme-ifap/

[52] UNESCO: UNESCO Information for All Programme: Second International Conference Linguistic and Cultural Diversity in Cyberspace: Final Document. Yakutsk Call for Action (July 2011), http://www.maayajo.org/IMG/pdf/Call_for_action_Yakutsk_EN-2.pdf

[53] Vaišnien, D., Zabarskaitė, J.: Lietuvių kalba skaitmeniniame amžiuje – The Lithuanian Language in the Digital Age. META-NET White Paper Series: Europe's Languages in the Digital Age. Springer, Heidelberg (2012), http://www.meta-net.eu/whitepapers/volumes/lithuanian

[54] Vannini, L., Crosnier, H.L. (eds.): Net.Lang – Towards the Multilingual Cyberspace. C&F éditions, Paris (March 2012), http://net-lang.net

[55] Vitas, D., Popović, L., Krstev, C., Obradović, I., Pavlović-Lažetić, G., Stanojević, M.: Српски језик у дигиталном добу – The Serbian Language in the Digital Age. META-NET White Paper Series: Europe's Languages in the Digital Age. Springer, Heidelberg (2012), http://www.meta-net.eu/whitepapers/volumes/serbian

[56] WSIS: World Summit on the Information Society: Declaration of Principles – Building the Information Society: a global challenge in the new Millennium (December 2003), http://www.itu.int/wsis/docs/geneva/official/dop.html

[57] Šimková, M., Garabík, R., Gajdošová, K., Laclavík, M., Ondrejović, S., Juhár, J., Genči, J., Furdík, K., Ivoríková, H., Ivanecký, J.: Slovenský jazyk v digitálnom veku – The Slovak Language in the Digital Age. META-NET White Paper Series: Europe's Languages in the Digital Age. Springer, Heidelberg (2012), http://www.meta-net.eu/whitepapers/volumes/slovak

A Case Study in Tagging Case in German: An Assessment of Statistical Approaches

Simon Clematide

University of Zurich, Institute of Computational Linguistics
Binzmühlestrasse 14, 8050 Zürich, Switzerland
simon.clematide@uzh.ch
http://www.cl.uzh.ch/siclemat

Abstract. In this study, we assess the performance of purely statistical approaches using supervised machine learning for predicting case in German (nominative, accusative, dative, genitive, n/a). We experiment with two different treebanks containing morphological annotations: TIGER and TUEBA. An evaluation with 10-fold cross-validation serves as the basis for systematic comparisons of the optimal parametrizations of different approaches. We test taggers based on Hidden Markov Models (HMM), Decision Trees, and Conditional Random Fields (CRF). The CRF approach based on our hand-crafted feature model achieves an accuracy of about 94%. This outperforms all other approaches and results in an improvement of 11% compared to a baseline HMM trigram tagger and an improvement of 2% compared to a state-of-the-art tagger for rich morphological tagsets. Moreover, we investigate the effect of additional (morphological) categories (gender, number, person, part of speech) in the internal tagset used for the training. Rich internal tagsets improve results for all tested approaches.

Keywords: German, Case, Tagging, Supervised Learning, Decision Trees, Conditional Random Fields, Hidden Markov Models, Morphologically annotated treebanks, Evaluation.

1 Introduction

Within linguistic analysis of the German language, determining the case of a token is a basic and important step. Usually, the case of a token is not determined in isolation but in connection with other morphological features. The objective of this study is to gain insight into the difficulties of case tagging independently from other morphological categories. The current availability of large, morphologically annotated corpora allows for a comprehensive and systematic evaluation.

It is a general assumption about the morphological analysis of inflecting languages like German, that good results cannot be achieved without applying richly resourced morphological systems, such as the commercial tool GERTWOL [1] or the freely available Morphisto [2]. In the current study, we answer the question how viable an approach can be that requires only a certain amount of morphologically annotated sentences available from current treebanks. With the help of supervised machine learning algorithms for probabilistic tagging of token sequences, such training material can be used to build systems which are able to predict comparable classifications given a similar raw text as

C. Mahlow and M. Piotrowski (Eds.): SFCM 2013, CCIS 380, pp. 22–34, 2013.
© Springer-Verlag Berlin Heidelberg 2013

input. An advantage of the statistical sequence taggers used in this study is their robustness and their ability to degrade gracefully on unseen input. On the other hand, such tools typically derive their decisions from a restricted local context. This leads to the disadvantage that they become easily confused when linguistic evidence from non-local places has to be combined in order to determine case correctly.

Broad coverage systems which disambiguate morphological categories (among these also case) have been available with MORPHY [3] and, more recently, with the state-of-the-art RFTagger for German [4]. An HMM-based case tagger for German forms part of the Durm Lemmatizer [5].

As a baseline system for our assessment, we use the trigram tagger tnt [6], which is based on HMMs. Secondly, we test the statistical part of the RFTagger (henceforth abbreviated as rft) [4], a specialized tagger for fine-grained POS tags that uses decision trees to estimate the transition probabilities of the subunits of complex tags. This tagger has proven excellent performance on the task of tagging the full morphological STTS[1] tagset for German [7]. Thirdly, we apply the state-of-the-art technique for sequence tagging, i.e., sequential Conditional Random Fields (CRFs) [8]. In particular, we developed our own feature model for case tagging based on the general purpose CRF tool wapiti [9].

It has been known since [10] that statistical approaches for PoS tagging can profit from enriched and fine-grained internal tagsets. In our experiment, we also try to assess the effect of training on internal tagsets that are enriched by additional morphological features such as PoS, gender, number, and person.

The main advantage of the tested approaches lies in the fact that only tokenized input is needed after training. One more advantage arises if tools like wapiti are used, which are able to calculate class probabilities for the assigned tags. Such confidence scores can be combined with the results of morphological analyzer tools as GERTWOL, which simply list all linguistically admissible analyses for a given token without contextual disambiguation.

When working with supervised learning methods, it is relatively easy to set up comparative evaluations. Typically, a system is built from a training corpus and afterwards evaluated on a test set, which has not been used for training. However, the obtained results are only precise for the specific training and testing corpus. A different splitting of training and testing set can lead to substantially different results. In order to properly estimate the performance of an approach, it is necessary to vary training and test sets. In this study, we use the prevalent method of 10-fold cross validation, which provides a mean measure of performance, its standard deviation, and a confidence interval. Furthermore, a t-test can decide on the statistical significance of performance improvements.

The paper is organized as follows: In the next section, we describe the resources and tools used in our experiments. In section 3, we compare the results that the different tools achieve. Moreover, we assess in detail the effect of rich internal tagsets, varying context sizes in HMM-based solutions, and the performance on known and unknown words.

---

[1] For a comprehensive overview of the different instances of the Stuttgart-Tübingen-Tagset (STTS), see http://www.ims.uni-stuttgart.de/forschung/ressourcen/lexika/GermanTagsets.html

2   Methods

2.1   Treebanks and Tagsets

We experiment with two different German treebanks. The TIGER corpus version 2.1 [11] contains 50474 sentences or segments.[2] The TüBa-D/Z corpus version 7.0 (henceforth TUEBA) [12] contains 65524 sentences.[3] Both corpora consist entirely of newspaper articles and include syntactic and detailed morphological annotations. For training and evaluation of the statistical tools, the treebanks were split as follows: 10% for testing, 90% for training. Contiguous slices were selected from the corpora. We did not randomly sample individual sentences from the treebank because the percentage of unknown words has a significant impact on the overall performance of a system. Sampling on individual sentences would decrease this percentage and therefore lead to over-optimistic results. In order to train the CRF tool `wapiti`, a development set is required. For this purpose, the training set for `wapiti` was further split into 4 parts for training (72% in total) and 1 part (18% in total) for development.

Table 1. Empirical sizes of the rich internal tagsets

Tagset	Size		Example
	TUEBA	TIGER	
case	5	5	Frage/Dat
case, number	15	15	Frage/Dat.Sg
case, gender	20	20	Frage/Dat.Fem
case, gender, number	50	56	Frage/Fem.Acc.Sg
case, PoS	113	127	Frage/NN.Acc
case, PoS, number	197	236	Frage/NN.Dat.Sg
case, PoS, gender	277	318	Frage/NN.Dat.Fem
case, PoS, number, person	296	349	ihn/PPER.Acc.Sg.3
case, PoS, gender, number	460	588	ihn/PPER.Masc.Acc.Sg
case, PoS, gender, number, person	492	638	ihn/PPER.Masc.Acc.Sg.3

Tagsets. An enriched tagset used for training is commonly referred to as an *internal* tagset. Prior to any evaluation, this internal and more fine-grained tagset is mapped to a smaller *external* tagset, in our case the tags "Nom" (nominative), "Acc" (accusative), "Dat" (dative), "Gen" (genitive), and "-" (unspecified). Already very early experiments of Brants [10] on PoS tagging with the `tnt` tagger have shown that fine-grained internal tagsets yield more than 1% performance improvement when measured on the so called *external* tagset. Within our experiments, we systematically refined our external tagset of 5 cases by morphological categories such as gender, number, person, and PoS. Table 1 shows the sizes of the refined tagsets for TIGER and TUEBA. Although TIGER and TUEBA's tagset for PoS has the same size, they are slightly different. TIGER enhances the German standard tagset STTS by the tag NNE (combination of a proper name and a

---

[2] http://www.ims.uni-stuttgart.de/forschung/ressourcen/korpora/tiger.html
[3] http://www.sfs.uni-tuebingen.de/ascl/ressourcen/corpora/tueba-dz.html

common noun) and doesn't differentiate between indefinite pronouns with determiners (PIDAT) or without determiners (PIAT) as done in TUEBA.

An important difference between TIGER and TUEBA consists in the fact that prepositions and postpositions in TIGER do not bear case tags as originally required by the full morphological STTS specification. This can be seen as an unfortunate choice since some common prepositions in German vary their required case according to their semantic function, for instance, the most frequent preposition "in" (*in*) has a local meaning in dative and a directional meaning in accusative case. Schmid and Laws [4] automatically insert case tags for unambiguous prepositions or create lexicalized tags for ambiguous prepositions. Given the fact that approx. 10% of all tokens are prepositions (e.g., 75897 of total 768971 tokens in TIGER), this may have an impact on tagging accuracy. According to Schmid and Laws [4], such language-specific optimizations yield an additional improvement of almost 1% for the full morphological tagset of TIGER. Since TIGER is a syntactically annotated treebank, we can in principle derive the case tag of a preposition if the dependent noun phrase is explicitly marked for case. However, simple and error-prone heuristics for case guessing could easily distort the gold standard. In German, head words can have complex prenominal modifiers which are marked with a case different from the head's case, e.g., prepositional phrases depending on attributive adjectives, or prenominal genitive attributes.

2.2   Statistical Tagging Tools

We deliberately refrain from a complete technical description of the statistical models of the four tools used in our experiments and refer to the corresponding literature instead. A description of our baseline system, the standard trigram tagger tnt, can be found in Brants [6]. Our second HMM-based tagger hunpos [13] is an open-source reimplementation of tnt. This tool allows for flexible parametrization of the order of tag transition and tag emission. The current study assesses the performance increase we can gain by tuning these parameters. Tnt uses a default context of 2 preceding tags for tag transition probabilities: $P(t_n|t_{n-1},t_{n-2})$. In Section 3, we encode the varying context sizes of hunpos as follows: c2 means a context of 2 preceding tags, c3 means a context of 3 preceding tags. See Figure 1 for an illustration of the corresponding feature spaces. The same convention applies for rft. The default emission order of 1 (encoded as e1 in Section 3) specifies the lexical probability as follows: $P(w_n|t_n)$. An emission order of 2, i.e., $P(w_n|t_{n-1},t_n)$, is encoded as e2 in the evaluation.

Our third tagger rft [4] proved state-of-the-art performance on the large fine-grained STTS tagset for German. Only the context width for tag order is varied in our experiments. The rft tagger needs a simple finite-state word class guesser. For the experiments we used the one provided by the rft software distribution for German.

CRFs, or more precisely, sequential Conditional Random Fields are well known for their state-of-the-art performance in sequence tagging problems. In our experiments, we use the freely available tool wapiti that supports parallel training on multiprocessor systems [9]. Unlike the HMM-based tools presented above, wapiti needs a handcrafted feature model. As illustrated in Figure 2, the whole sequence of input elements can be used to specify features. These features can be automatically conditioned on bigrams (B) or unigrams (U) of the output tags, or both (*). Bigram features are similar

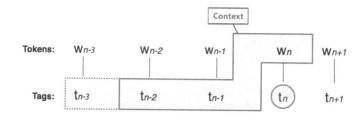

Fig. 1. Feature space of quadrigram and trigram HMM taggers

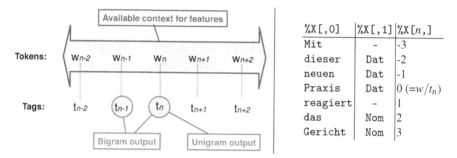

Fig. 2. Feature space in sequential CRFs (left part) and the matrix notation of the feature template expressions (right part)

to emission probabilities in HMM taggers and can quickly lead to feature explosion and slow training. Therefore, we use only one carefully selected bigram features in our model. Below is the complete listing of the features templates for our case tagger:

```
U:word LL=%X[-2,0]
U:word  L=%X[-1,0]
U:word  O=%X[ 0,0]
U:word  R=%X[ 1,0]
U:word RR=%X[ 2,0]
U:suf-1 O=%m[ 0,0,".?$"]
U:suf-2 O=%m[ 0,0,".?.?$"]
U:suf-3 O=%m[ 0,0,".?.?.?$"]
U:pre-1 O=%m[ 0,0,"^.?"]
U:pre-2 O=%m[ 0,0,"^.?.?"]
U:pre-3 O=%m[ 0,0,"^.?.?.?"]
U:word R/O=%X[ 1,0]/%X[0,0]
U:word L/O=%X[-1,0]/%X[0,0]
U:word R/L=%X[1,0]/%X[-1,0]
*:is-upper X=%t[ 0,0,"^\u"]
U:suf-2 L/O/R=%m[-1,0,".?.?$"]/%m[ 0,0,".?.?$"]/%m[1,0,".?.?$"]
U:presuf-1 O=%m[ 0,0,"^."]/%m[ 0,0,".$"]
```

As other CRF tools, `wapiti` supports the automatic extraction of features using feature templates, for instance, string features (%X), regular expression matches (%m), and regular expression tests (%t). A matrix-like notation with relative addressing as shown in the right part of Figure 2 can be used to access and combine different parts of the input sequence. For instance, the unigram feature template U:word L=%X[-1,0] at the position of the token "Praxis" results in a filled feature U:word L=neuen. The more complex unigram feature template U:word R/0=%X[1,0]/%X[0,0] is instantiated to U:word R/0=neuen/Praxis at the same position. In principle, feature templates can combine an arbitrary amount of information into a single feature.

wapiti offers different optimization algorithms for adjusting the weights of the features in the resulting model. In our experiments we used the option rprop- which selects a less memory demanding algorithm that can deal with all tagsets used in the experiments.

3   Results and Discussion

In this section, we present selected comparative evaluations of tested configurations for the problem of case tagging. The evaluation tables given here, present the results in the same consistent way, showing:

– Mean and standard deviation (SD) of tagging accuracy from the 10 runs produced by the cross-validation. In the tables, all rows are sorted in increasing order by the mean accuracy.
– The absolute (Δabs) and relative (Δrel) amount of performance improvement. Additionally, the cumulative relative amount (Δrel$_{bs}$) in comparison to the baseline performance is shown.
– The statistical significance of the improvement given as the P value of an exact pairwise t-test computed on the difference between two adjacent rows. Statistically not significant P values > 0.05 are shown in italics.
– The minimal improvement expected in 95% of all cases, i.e., the lower limit of the 95% confidence interval (ΔCI$_l$) as produced by the t test statistics.

Performance Increase of Rich Feature Sets. Table 2 shows in how far the additional morphological features have a positive or negative impact on the tnt baseline system. It is interesting to note that for a standard trigram tagger as tnt the biggest internal tagset is not the best solution. Especially the features person and gender do not contribute to the best overall performance. This is probably due to the fact that fine-grained tagsets increase data sparseness and therefore the model has less reliable estimates. The most important additional feature is PoS, which, compared to the baseline, yields an optimization of more than 6.5%. To sum up, additional morphological categories PoS and number give also best results for hunpos and wapiti. Only rft with its structured representation of fine-grained tags and its decision tree based transition probabilities can achieve better results with even richer feature sets (see Table 4).

Influence of Tag Order and Emission Order. The hunpos tool allows for flexible testing how tag order and emission order influence the tagging accuracy. Table 3 shows that a quadrigram tagger delivers the best results. On the other hand, raising the emission order to 2 does not yield (significant) improvements on the best internal tagset.

Table 2. Performance improvement for `tnt` using enriched internal tagsets

TIGER							
System	Mean	SD	Δabs	Δrel	Δrel$_{bs}$	P value	ΔCI$_l$
tnt:case	84.36	0.44					
tnt:case,numb	85.90	0.50	+1.54	+1.83	+1.83	0.0000	+1.43
tnt:case,gend	86.02	0.51	+0.12	+0.14	+1.97	0.0144	+0.04
tnt:case,gend,numb	87.28	0.52	+1.26	+1.47	+3.47	0.0000	+1.21
tnt:case,pos	89.90	0.42	+2.62	+3.00	+6.57	0.0000	+2.46
tnt:case,numb,pers,pos	90.03	0.40	+0.13	+0.14	+6.72	0.0004	+0.08
tnt:case,gend,pos	90.04	0.40	+0.01	+0.01	+6.74	0.0004	+0.01
tnt:case,gend,numb,pers,pos	90.29	0.45	+0.24	+0.27	+7.03	0.0000	+0.20
tnt:case,gend,numb,pos	90.31	0.44	+0.02	+0.02	+7.05	0.0001	+0.02
tnt:case,numb,pos	90.47	0.41	+0.16	+0.18	+7.25	0.0000	+0.12
TUEBA							
System	Mean	SD	Δabs	Δrel	Δrel$_{bs}$	P value	ΔCI$_l$
tnt:case	84.68	0.36					
tnt:case,gend	87.40	0.31	+2.71	+3.20	+3.20	0.0000	+2.65
tnt:case,numb	87.51	0.31	+0.11	+0.13	+3.33	0.0013	+0.06
tnt:case,gend,numb	88.53	0.27	+1.02	+1.17	+4.54	0.0000	+0.98
tnt:case,numb,pers,pos	90.38	0.28	+1.85	+2.09	+6.72	0.0000	+1.79
tnt:case,gend,pos	90.38	0.27	+0.01	+0.01	+6.73	0.0399	+0.00
tnt:case,pos	90.40	0.29	+0.02	+0.03	+6.75	*0.2101*	−0.03
tnt:case,gend,numb,pers,pos	90.55	0.27	+0.14	+0.16	+6.92	0.0007	+0.09
tnt:case,gend,numb,pos	90.56	0.28	+0.01	+0.01	+6.93	0.0256	+0.00
tnt:case,numb,pos	90.82	0.27	+0.26	+0.29	+7.24	0.0000	+0.21

Table 3. Influence of tag order and emission order in `hunpos`

TIGER							
System	Mean	SD	Δabs	Δrel	Δrel$_{bs}$	P value	ΔCI$_l$
hp-c2-e2:case,numb,pos	90.74	0.40					
hp-c2-e1:case,numb,pos	90.87	0.39	+0.13	+0.14	+0.14	0.0003	+0.08
hp-c3-e2:case,numb,pos	90.95	0.41	+0.09	+0.10	+0.24	0.0014	+0.05
hp-c4-e2:case,numb,pos	90.97	0.44	+0.02	+0.02	+0.26	*0.2145*	−0.02
hp-c4-e1:case,numb,pos	90.97	0.43	+0.00	+0.00	+0.26	*0.4478*	−0.03
hp-c3-e1:case,numb,pos	91.01	0.39	+0.04	+0.04	+0.30	*0.1080*	−0.01
TUEBA							
hp-c2-e2:case,numb,pos	91.04	0.26					
hp-c2-e1:case,numb,pos	91.15	0.28	+0.11	+0.12	+0.12	0.0009	+0.06
hp-c3-e2:case,numb,pos	91.30	0.26	+0.15	+0.17	+0.29	0.0023	+0.08
hp-c4-e1:case,numb,pos	91.33	0.27	+0.02	+0.02	+0.31	*0.2142*	−0.03
hp-c4-e2:case,numb,pos	91.35	0.27	+0.02	+0.02	+0.33	*0.1004*	−0.01
hp-c3-e1:case,numb,pos	91.35	0.29	+0.01	+0.01	+0.34	*0.3892*	−0.03

Altogether, only small improvements can be noticed when varying the tag order and emission order. The setting hp-c2-e1 corresponds to the setting of tnt. It should be noted that hunpos reaches slightly better values with the same settings: for TIGER 90.87% (tnt 90.47%), for TUEBA 91.15% (tnt 90.82%).

Accuracy on Unknown and Known Words. Table 4 shows the performance for the best settings of the examined tools. Tnt deals worst with unknown words. Remarkably better results are reached by the unknown words guesser of hunpos and by including a context window of 3 preceding tags. For TUEBA, the best mean accuracy is reached by rft, however, the advantage towards wapiti can not be considered statistically significant with a P value > 0.1. wapiti performs substantially better than rft on known words. This is probably due to the richer contextual model of the CRF approach which also includes evidence from the righthand side of the current token.

Confusion Matrix of Errors. In order to quantify and characterize the problems of case tagging that cannot be solved by the best system, we collected all errors from the test data of our wapiti system. Table 6 sums these numbers up into confusion matrices for both corpora. Given that our system has more or less the same performance on both corpora one might have expected a slightly more similar error distribution. The error differences therefore probably reflect genuine differences in the morphological annotation in both corpora. The most important difference concerning missing case tags in TIGER has already been mentioned above. In TUEBA, most prepositions bear dative case (56,651), followed by accusative (24,120) and genitive (1,823). Of course, there is no nominative case marked by prepositions. The differences in the confusion matrices seem to match this distribution.

The main source of errors is the confusion of nominative and accusative case. This is due to the fact that in German many inflected word forms are morphologically ambiguous regarding these cases. Additionally, German has a relatively free word order which renders positional information in a sentence unreliable for case disambiguation.

Qualitative Error Analysis. In order to spot the main sources of remaining errors in our best system, we randomly sampled 50 errors from TIGER and TUEBA. These errors were manually classified into 3 categories by the author.

Category S stands for case ambiguity where syntactic knowledge beyond NPs and PPs is needed for proper resolution, typically, whole phrases are tagged with the wrong case. For instance, *Der/Nom Polizist/Nom greift/- ihre/Acc Arme/Acc und/- biegt/- sie/Acc/Nom* nach/- hinten/- ,...* ("The police man takes her arms and bends them back, ..."). The erroneous tag is printed in bold and marked by a star.

Category N stands for difficult and complex constructions in nominal phrases, including coordinated phrases and appositions, where some parts were tagged correctly and other parts of the same phrase were not. For instance, *Besonders/- neue/Nom Unternehmensfelder/Nom wie/- die/Nom Informations-/- und/- Kommunikationsbranche/Nom/Acc** ("Especially new business as the information and communications industry").

Category O collects all other cases. Some of them are due to domain-specific textual segments, e.g., introductory mentions of the place and date of a news article as

Table 4. Accuracy of best performing systems on known and unknown words

System	Mean	SD	Δabs	Δrel	Δrel$_{bs}$	P value	ΔCI$_l$
Unknown words							
TIGER							
tnt:case,numb,pos	76.57	1.16					
hp-c3-e1:case,numb,pos	80.90	1.09	+4.33	+5.66	+5.66	0.0000	+4.11
rft-c5:case,numb,pos	82.16	0.93	+1.26	+1.56	+7.30	0.0000	+0.98
wap:case,numb,pos	83.71	1.24	+1.56	+1.90	+9.34	0.0000	+1.23
TUEBA							
tnt:case,numb,pos	78.29	0.28					
hp-c3-e1:case,pos	82.74	0.55	+4.45	+5.68	+5.68	0.0000	+4.15
wap:case,numb,pos	84.08	0.51	+1.33	+1.61	+7.39	0.0000	+0.98
rft-c7:case,numb,pos	84.32	0.43	+0.24	+0.29	+7.69	*0.1157*	*−0.10*
Known words							
TIGER							
tnt:case,numb,pos	91.65	0.30					
hp-c3-e1:case,numb,pos	91.87	0.29	+0.22	+0.24	+0.24	0.0000	+0.19
rft-c8:case,gend,numb,pers,pos	92.31	0.33	+0.44	+0.48	+0.72	0.0000	+0.39
wap:case,numb,pos	94.71	0.23	+2.40	+2.60	+3.34	0.0000	+2.26
TUEBA							
tnt:case,numb,pos	91.87	0.25					
hp-c4-e2:case,numb,pos	92.12	0.25	+0.25	+0.27	+0.27	0.0000	+0.19
rft-c4:case,gend,numb,pers,pos	92.54	0.21	+0.42	+0.46	+0.73	0.0000	+0.36
wap:case,numb,pos	94.75	0.15	+2.21	+2.39	+3.13	0.0000	+2.13
All words							
TIGER							
tnt:case,numb,pos	90.47	0.41					
hp-c3-e1:case,numb,pos	91.01	0.39	+0.54	+0.59	+0.59	0.0000	+0.51
rft-c5:case,gend,numb,pers,pos	91.50	0.40	+0.49	+0.54	+1.14	0.0000	+0.44
wap:case,numb,pos	93.77	0.29	+2.27	+2.48	+3.65	0.0000	+2.14
TUEBA							
tnt:case,numb,pos	90.82	0.27					
hp-c3-e1:case,numb,pos	91.35	0.29	+0.54	+0.59	+0.59	0.0000	+0.49
rft-c4:case,gend,numb,pers,pos	91.87	0.24	+0.52	+0.56	+1.16	0.0000	+0.47
wap:case,numb,pos	93.84	0.16	+1.97	+2.14	+3.33	0.0000	+1.88

Table 5. Overall improvement over the baseline system

System	Mean	SD	Δabs	Δrel	Δrel$_{bs}$	P value	ΔCI$_l$
TIGER							
tnt:case	84.36	0.44					
wap:case,numb,pos	93.77	0.29	+9.41	+11.16	+11.16	0.0000	+9.29
TUEBA							
tnt:case	84.68	0.36					
wap:case,numb,pos	93.84	0.16	+9.15	+10.81	+10.81	0.0000	+9.02

Table 6. Confusion matrix of the best system

TIGER												
	System Output wapiti											
	-		Acc		Dat		Gen		Nom		Total	
Gold	#	%	#	%	#	%	#	%	#	%	#	%
-			557	1.0	587	1.1	324	0.6	1051	1.9	2519	4.5
Acc	509	0.9			3183	5.7	529	1.0	13308	24.0	17529	31.7
Dat	1122	2.0	2921	5.3			2474	4.5	2748	5.0	9265	16.7
Gen	442	0.8	243	0.4	1453	2.6			680	1.2	2818	5.1
Nom	2617	4.7	15252	27.5	3860	7.0	1507	2.7			23236	42.0
Total	4690	8.5	18973	34.3	9083	16.4	4834	8.7	17787	32.1	55367	100.0

TUEBA												
	System Output wapiti											
	-		Acc		Dat		Gen		Nom		Total	
Gold	#	%	#	%	#	%	#	%	#	%	#	%
-		0.0	875	1.3	815	1.2	568	0.8	1360	1.9	3618	5.2
Acc	775	1.1		0.0	5111	7.3	693	1.0	15805	22.7	22384	32.1
Dat	966	1.4	4412	6.3		0.0	2999	4.3	3098	4.4	11475	16.4
Gen	286	0.4	400	0.6	1756	2.5		0.0	961	1.4	3403	4.9
Nom	2105	3.0	19657	28.2	4816	6.9	2311	3.3		0.0	28889	41.4
Total	4132	5.9	25344	36.3	12498	17.9	6571	9.4	21224	30.4	69769	100.0

Table 7. Error classification of the best system

Error => Key	=>Acc	=>Nom	Acc=>-	Acc=>Dat	Acc=>Nom	Dat=>-	Dat=>Acc	Dat=>Gen	Dat=>Nom	Gen=>Acc	Gen=>Dat	Nom=>-	Nom=>Acc	Nom=>Dat	Nom=>Gen	Grand Total
S				7	20			1		1	1		18			48
O	1		3	1	3	1	1		3			4				17
N	1	1		3	9			2	2	1	2		7	4	3	35
Grand Total	2	1	3	11	32	1	1	3	5	2	3	4	25	4	3	100

in *LAGOS/Nom ,/- 5./Nom/Dat* Juli/Nom/Dat** ("LAGOS, July 5 (AP)"). There are also latent PoS tagging errors that are covered by this category. For instance, *Um/-/Acc* seine/Acc Jugendwelle/Acc ausstrahlen/- zu/- können/-* ... ("In order to be able to broadcast the program called 'Jugendwelle'...").

Table 7 shows the distribution of errors according to their category. Morpho-syntactic ambiguity between nominative and accusative case is very common, which is expected. Complex nominal phrases containing intermitting prepositional phrases and/or coordinated elements follow as the second largest source of errors.

Tagging the TIGER Corpus by TUEBA, and Vice Versa. We took the best system (i.e., wapiti with case, PoS, and number) and tagged each corpus with the model from round 1 of the cross validation (trained on the last 72% of TIGER resp. TUEBA).

The mentioned differences in annotating case tags for prepositions in the two corpora were resolved by deleting case tags from prepositions where needed. For the TIGER corpus we achieve an accuracy of 92.13% using the TUEBA model, and the TIGER model results in 92.29% accuracy for the TUEBA corpus. For known tokens, accuracy is 93.40% (TIGER) and 93.68% (TUEBA), for unknown tokens 82.05% (TIGER) and 81.28% (TUEBA). As expected, these results are slightly lower than the cross-validation results in Table 4.

It is difficult to decide in how far the additional error is caused by normal lexical differences between these newspaper corpora, or by the differences of the underlying annotation guidelines.

Speed and Memory Analysis. The tools compared in this evaluation have different requirements concerning memory consumption and processing time. In Table 8 we present the mean values for the best system configurations for training and tagging. All experiments were performed on a Linux machine with 2 Intel Xeon E5-2660 processors @ 2.2 GHz providing 32 cores and 320GB of RAM. For `wapiti` we made heavily use of parallel threads. The numbers in the columns labelled with "training" report the resources used for building the models from the training part in the 10-fold cross-validation. The columns labelled with "testing" report the average numbers for applying the models to the test data. Memory consumption was measured as maximum resident size of memory allocation. Processing time was measured in seconds as user time spent by the processors. The overview in Table 8 shows clearly that performance improvements have to be paid in terms of speed and memory. Training the CRF model is especially expensive, but our main goal here was high accuracy and not a cost-benefit optimization. Note that once a CRF model has been built less resources are needed and the speed is also acceptable.

Table 8. Mean of memory consumption (maximum resident size) and user processing time in seconds for training (90% of the corpora) and testing (10% of the corpora)

System	User time in secs.		Max. RAM in MB		User time in secs.		Max. RAM in MB	
	Training	Testing	Training	Testing	Training	Testing	Training	Testing
	TIGER				TUEBA			
tnt	1.8	1.3	43	84	2.8	1.7	52	103
hunpos	14.4	3.8	780	558	23.2	6.4	967	696
rft	288.2	26.6	1,291	167	356.1	27.2	1,630	176
wapiti	56,780.2	110.1	49,468	11,809	71,779.0	137.3	51,366	12,644

4   Conclusions

Tagging case in German newspaper corpora has a baseline accuracy of 84.5% using a standard trigram tagger. Applying our own feature model and an enriched internal tagset with the CRF tool `wapiti` improves these results by 11%. Our model also clearly outperforms the existing state-of-the-art approach of the `rft` for tagging morphologically rich tagsets by about 2%. However, this performance increase requires a substantial amount of additional computing power.

Even though the focus of this study is on case tagging, we want to emphasize the finding that assigning case works best if one classifies case, PoS, gender, and number jointly. Therefore, it's straightforward to use our CRF model for assigning the tags of the more fine-grained internal tagset.

The results of [4] show that the tagging accuracy on the fine-grained German STTS tagset increases from 86% to 91% if broad-coverage morphological analyses are provided as an external lexicon. In a future study, we will test whether case tagging performance improves similarly if we add the output of a morphological analyzer such as GERTWOL. Tools as `hunpos` or `rft` support the addition of external lexicons as a standard option when applying an existing model to new text. For `wapiti`, the lexical information has to be provided as part of the evidence in the training phase of a model as well as in the application phase of a model. Different approaches for making use of external lexical resources in combination with CRFs are discussed in [14].

Acknowledgements. I wish to thank Tilia Ellendorff for her support concerning content and proof-reading.

References

1. Koskeniemmi, K., Haapalainen, M.: GERTWOL – Lingsoft Oy. In: Hausser, R. (ed.) Linguistische Verifikation: Dokumentation zur Ersten Morpholympics 1994, Niemeyer, Tübingen. Sprache und Information, vol. 34, pp. 121–140 (1996)
2. Zielinski, A., Simon, C.: Morphisto: An open-source morphological analyzer for German. In: Seventh International Workshop on Finite-State Methods and Natural Language Processing, pp. 177–184 (2008)
3. Lezius, W., Rapp, R., Wettler, M.: A freely available morphological analyzer, disambiguator and context sensitive lemmatizer for German. In: Proceedings of COLING-ACL 1998: 36th Annual Meeting of the Association for Computational Linguistics and 17th International Conference on Computational Linguistics, Montreal, vol. 2, pp. 743–748 (1998)
4. Schmid, H., Laws, F.: Estimation of conditional probabilities with decision trees and an application to fine-grained POS tagging. In: Proceedings of the 22nd International Conference on Computational Linguistics (Coling 2008), Manchester, UK, pp. 777–784 (August 2008)
5. Perera, P., Witte, R.: A self-learning context-aware lemmatizer for German. In: Proceedings of Human Language Technology Conference and Conference on Empirical Methods in Natural Language Processing (HLT/EMNLP 2005), October 6-8, pp. 636–643. Association for Computational Linguistics, ACL, Vancouver (2005)
6. Brants, T.: TnT – a statistical part-of-speech tagger. In: Proceedings of the Sixth Applied Natural Language Processing Conference ANLP 2000, pp. 224–231 (2000)
7. Schiller, A., Teufel, S., Stöckert, C.: Guidelines für das Tagging deutscher Textcorpora mit STTS (Kleines und großes Tagset) (1999)
8. Sutton, C.A., McCallum, A.: An introduction to conditional random fields. Foundations and Trends in Machine Learning 4(4), 267–373 (2012)
9. Lavergne, T., Cappé, O., Yvon, F.: Practical very large scale CRFs. In: Proceedings of the 48th Annual Meeting of the Association for Computational Linguistics (ACL), pp. 504–513. Association for Computational Linguistics (July 2010)

In the field of Arabic language processing, the existing models have exploited the regularities encountered in the language to a variable extent, yet we believe there is still some scope for improvement. We intend to fill this gap developing a robust and compact system that covers all Arabic verbal morphology by means of simple and general procedures.

Modern Standard Arabic (MSA) is the formal language most widely used nowadays in the whole Arab world. It is spoken across more than 20 countries by over 300 million speakers [1]. MSA stands out for being the language of the media, and in general it is used in all formal situations within society. It is also the language of higher education, and it is used in most written texts. MSA is not a natural language, since it does not have real native speakers [2, 3, 4]. The native languages of Arab people are what we call the Arabic spoken varieties—they learn MSA through the educational system, thus in a non-natural way.

As it is not a natural language, MSA morphology has been described as an extremely regular system [5], susceptible of being represented by means of precise formal devices. As Kaye describes it, MSA presents an "almost (too perfect) algebraic-looking grammar" [2:665]. Broadly speaking, stems—word-forms without the affixal material [6]—are generally built by the organized combination of two types of morphemes—what we call the *root* and the *pattern*. The MSA lexicon contains between 4000 to 5000 different roots [7,8], and verbal morphology exhibits 24 different patterns, of which 16 are really common. Semantically related words tend to share the same root morpheme. Thus, the root turned out to be the basic component of Arabic lexicography, to the extent that dictionaries are organized by roots [9]. At a more superficial level, the inflectional system applies several operations to turn stems into specific verbal word forms. This stage is considerably complicated by the interaction of phonological and orthographic alterations. All these phenomena hinder the process of formalizing the system, thus making it an extremely interesting and challenging task.

1.1   MSA Morphotactics

MSA presents two morphological strategies: *concatenative* and *non-concatenative*—also known as *templatic morphology*. Concatenative morphemes are discrete segments which are simply attached to the stem regardless of the position, i.e., they have the form of an uninterrupted string. Non-concatenative morphemes are interleaved elements inserted within a word—they do not form a compact unit, but a discontinuous string whose 'internal blanks' are filled out with other morphemes. In MSA, derivational morphology is mainly marked by non-concatenative schemes, whereas inflectional morphology tends to be concatenative.

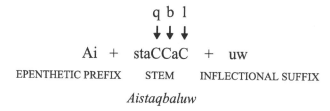

Fig. 1. Example of concatenative and non-concatenative processes in the formation of the verbal word form اِسۡتَقۡبَلُوا *Aistaqbaluw* 'they received'

Templatic morphology is known in the field of Arabic linguistics as *root-and-pattern morphology*. It takes its name from the Arabic morphemes which have a non-concatenative shape: the root and the pattern. This theoretical description attempts to describe how Arabic stems are built—root-and-pattern morphology states that stems are composed by these two elements. A *root* is a decomposable morpheme that provides the basic meaning of a word, and generally consists of 3 or 4 ordered consonants in non-linear position within the word [10,11,12,13,1]. The *pattern* is a syllabic structure which contains vowels, and sometimes consonants, in which the consonants of the root are inserted and occupy specified places [14,15]. Thus, by the interdigitation of a root and a pattern stems are created [16,17,18,10,15]. Some authors have proposed to separate the vowels from the template and to consider it a separate morpheme. This morpheme is commonly known as *vocalism* [19,20,21,22].

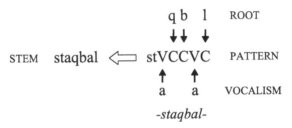

Fig. 2. Decomposition of the stem *-staqbal-* from the verbal word form اِسْتَقْبَلُوا *Aistaqbaluw* 'they received' into root, vocalism and pattern

1.2 MSA Verbal System

MSA exhibits 24 different verbal patterns. Some of them belong in fact to Classical Arabic and are rarely used. Traditionally they are classified in patterns from 3-consonant roots and patterns from 4-consonant roots. The different patterns add extensions to the basic meaning expressed by the root, i.e., they are of derivational nature. Below, we include the list of patterns using the root فعل *fçl* 'doing'. This root is traditionally used in Arabic to refer to grammatical forms. Patterns are shown using the lemma of the verb, which corresponds to the third person masculine singular of the perfective active inflection [4,10,18,23,24].

Following the Arabic western linguistic tradition, we use Roman numerals to refer to the different patterns. Patterns I include two vowels in their specification: one corresponds to the thematic vowel of the perfective and the other one to the thematic vowel of the imperfective—both correspond to the second vowel position of the stem. Some verbs share the same lemma form, but they are considered different since they present different forms in their conjugation. 4-consonant roots are distinguished from 3-consonant roots by the addition of a 'Q' to the Roman numeral.

Table 1. List of all verbal patterns in Arabic. Information on the transliteration system used throughout the whole paper can be found at http://elvira.lllf.uam.es/ING/transJab.html.

Pattern	Lemma from root فعل *fçl*	Example
Iau	فَعَل *façala*	كَتَبَ *kataba* 'to write'
Iai	فَعَل *façala*	رَمَى *ramaY* 'to throw'
Iaa	فَعَل *façala*	ضَرَبَ *Daraba* 'to hit'
Iuu	فَعُل *façula*	كَبُرَ *kabura* 'to grow'
Iia	فَعِل *façila*	رَضِيَ *raDiya* 'to agree'
Iii	فَعِل *façila*	وَرِثَ *wariþa* 'inherit'
II	فَعَّل *faç~ala*	عَلَّمَ *çal~ama* 'to teach'
III	فاعَل *faAçala*	شَاهَدَ *XaAhada* 'to watch'
IV	أَفْعَل *Áafçala*	أَحَبَّ *ÁHab~a* 'to love'
V	تَفَعَّل *tafaç~ala*	تَعَلَّمَ *taçal~ama* 'to learn'
VI	تَفاعَل *tafaAçala*	تَآمَرَ *taĀmara* 'to plot'
VII	إِنْفَعَل *Ain·façala*	إِنْقَضَى *Ain·qaDaY* 'to pass'
VIII	إِفْتَعَل *Aif·taçala*	إِتَّفَقَ *Ait~afaqa* 'to agree'
IX	إِفْعَلَّ *Aif·çalla*	إِحْمَرَّ *AiH·mar~a* 'to turn red'
X	إِسْتَفْعَل *Aistaf·çala*	إِسْتَمَرَّ *Ais·tamar~a* 'to continue'
XI	إِفْعالَّ *Aif·çaAlla*	إِحْمَارَّ *AiH·maAr~a* 'to turn red'
XII	إِفْعَوْعَل *Aif·çaw·çala*	إِحْضَوْضَرَ *AiHDawDara* 'to become green'
XIII	إِفْعَوَّل *Aif·çaw~ala*	إِجْلَوَّذَ *Aijlaw~aða* 'to last long'
XIV	إِفْعَنْلَل *Aif·çan·lala*	إِسْحَنْكَكَ *Ais·Han·kaka* 'to be dark'
XV	إِفْعَنْلَى *Aif·çan·laA*	إِعْلَنْدَى *Aiç·lan·daY* 'to be stout'
QI	فَعْلَل *façlala*	تَرْجَمَ *tar·jama* 'to translate'
QII	تَفَعْلَل *tafaç·lala*	تَدَحْرَجَ *tadaH·raja* 'to roll'
QIII	إِفْعَنْلَل *Aif·çanlala*	إِسْلَنْطَحَ *Ai·slan·TaHa* 'to lie on one's face'
QIV	إِفْعَلَلَّ *Aif·çalal~a*	إِقْشَعَرَّ *Aiq·Xaçar~a* 'to shudder with horror'

Regardless of the pattern, each verb may present a full conjugational paradigm. The paradigm exhibits a tense/aspect marking, opposing perfective and imperfective. Imperfective, in turn, includes three possible moods: indicative, subjunctive and jussive. There is an imperative conjugation, derived from the imperfective form. At the same time verbs exhibit voice opposition in active and passive, which consists only in a different vocalization. Each conjugational paradigm shows the features of person, number and gender [4,10,18,23,24]. Obviously, verbs do not cover all the possible inflectional alternatives. In the following table, we can see the full conjugational paradigm of the active verb فَعَل *façala* 'to do'.

Table 2. Complete conjugational paradigm of the Arabic active verb فَعَلَ *façala* 'to do'. The information of the inflectional tag is as follows. First position: 1=first person; 2=second person; 3=third person. Second position: S=singular; D=dual; P=plural. Third position: M=masculine; F=feminine; N=non-marked for gender.

Inflect Tag	Perfective	Imperfective			Imperative
		Nominative	Subjunctive	Jussive	
3SM	فَعَلَ façala	يَفْعُلُ yaf·çulu	يَفْعُلَ yaf·çula	يَفْعُلْ yaf·çul·	
3SF	فَعَلَتْ façalat·	تَفْعُلُ taf·çulu	تَفْعُلَ taf·çula	تَفْعُلْ taf·çul·	
3DM	فَعَلَا façalaA	يَفْعُلَانِ yaf·çulaAni	يَفْعُلَا yaf·çulaA	يَفْعُلَا yaf·çulaA	
3DF	فَعَلَتَا façalataA	تَفْعُلَانِ taf·çulaAni	تَفْعُلَا taf·çulaA	تَفْعُلَا taf·çulaA	
3PM	فَعَلُوا façaluwA	يَفْعُلُونَ yaf·çuluwna	يَفْعُلُوا yaf·çuluwA	يَفْعُلُوا yaf·çuluwA	
3PF	فَعَلْنَ façal·na	يَفْعُلْنَ yaf·çul·na	يَفْعُلْنَ yaf·çul·na	يَفْعُلْنَ yaf·çul·na	
2SM	فَعَلْتَ façal·ta	تَفْعُلُ taf·çulu	تَفْعُلَ taf·çula	تَفْعُلْ taf·çul·	اُفْعُلْ Auf·çul·
2SF	فَعَلْتِ façal·ti	تَفْعُلِينَ taf·çuliyna	تَفْعُلِي taf·çuliy	تَفْعُلِي taf·çuliy	اُفْعُلِي Auf·çuliy
2DN	فَعَلْتُمَا façal·tumaA	تَفْعُلَانِ taf·çulaAni	تَفْعُلَا taf·çulaA	تَفْعُلَا taf·çulaA	اُفْعُلَا Auf·çulaA
2PM	فَعَلْتُم façal·tum	تَفْعُلُونَ taf·çuluwna	تَفْعُلُوا taf·çuluwA	تَفْعُلُوا taf·çuluwA	اُفْعُلُوا Auf·çuluwA
2PF	فَعَلْتُنَّ façaltun~a	تَفْعُلْنَ tafçul·na	تَفْعُلْنَ tafçulna	تَفْعُلْنَ tafçulna	فْعُلْنَ fçul·na
1SN	فَعَلْتُ façal·tu	أَفْعُلُ Áaf·çulu	أَفْعُلَ Áaf·çula	أَفْعُلْ Áaf·çul·	
1PN	فَعَلْنَا façal·naA	نَفْعُلُ naf·çulu	نَفْعُلَ naf·çula	نَفْعُلْ naf·çul·	

At a superficial level, the whole verbal system is highly affected by allomorphism. Allomorphism is the situation in which the same morpheme exhibits different phonological shapes depending on the context [6]. This determines that a set of surface representations can be related to a single underlying representation [6]. Allomorphism is one of the most complicated aspects of Arabic morphological analysis.

The main causes of allomorphism in MSA are phonological constraints on the semiconsonants *w* and *y*. Verbs with roots containing at least one semiconsonant phoneme typically present phonological alterations. Another cause of allomorphism is the presence of two identical consonants in the second and third place of the root, which is known as *geminated or doubled roots* [4,10,23]. In spite of the uniform nature of these phonological alterations, which are susceptible to systematization, verbs suffering these phenomena are considered irregular in traditional Arabic grammar.

Orthographic idiosyncrasies are closely related with these phonological alterations. Thus, we can refer to them as *orthographic allomorphism*. Although not having linguistic nature, they are relevant computationally.

1.3 Traditional Arabic Prosody

Medieval Arab scholars developed an interesting analysis of Arabic morphological structure. With the development of Arabic poetry, scholars noticed that Arabic prosodic units were subjected to a marked rhythmic uniformity. This may be partially due to the fact that Arabic phonotactics restricts many types of syllables. Essentially, MSA accepts three types: CV, CVC and CVV. Exceptionally CVVC and CVCC are permitted [24].

The most important contribution in this field was made by Al Khalil, an acclaimed Arab scholar considered the father of Arabic lexicography. He described and systematized the metrical system of Arabic poetry, based directly on orthography. One of the interesting things of the Arabic writing system is that only consonants are considered letters. Vowels are diacritic symbols written on or below the consonant they accompany. In order to define the different metrical patterns, Al Khalil classified letters in two types [25]:

1. *sakin* letter حرف ساكن 'static letter', i.e. an unvocalized letter. A consonant without a vowel, or a semiconsonant. It is important to note that semiconsonants are used to represent long vowels when preceded by a short vowel.
2. *mutaharrik* letter حرف متحرك 'moving letter', i.e. a vocalized letter. A *mutaharrik* letter is a consonant followed by a diacritic vowel.

The fundamental principle of the analysis of al-Khalil is that a *mutaharrik* letter is heavier than a *sakin*. To represent this, they are marked with different weight symbols. A mutaharrik letter is going to be assigned the value 1, and a sakin letter the value of 0^1. Thus, an orthographic word can be represented as 1-0 combinations. These combinations are subsequently classified in wider groups of weight, which in fact unravel the different syllabic structures. First, 1-0 combinations compute the value 2; then 1-2 combinations compute the value 3; at last, 2-2 combinations compute the value 4. Finally, we can sum the resulting numbers and get the total weight for a word. Below, this computation of lexical weight is shown.

Word	يُعَلِّمُ *yuçal~imu* 'he teaches'				
Letters segmentation	yu	ça	l	li	mu
Weights	1	1	0	1	1
Cumulative weights	1		2	1	1
		3		1	1
Total weight of lexical item		5			

The fact that a small number of syllabic structures is allowed by Arabic phonotactics has interesting implications: as the formation of words belonging to the same morphological class is the product of a *quasi* mathematical combination of similar morphemic material, the resulting syllabic structure will tend to follow the same patterns. Thus, it seems possible to propose a precise formalism which predicts the syllabic structures for Arabic lexical items.

---

[1] In Arabic, the letter hamza ء is used to represent the *sakin* letter and the numeral ١ for the *mutaharrik* [25].

1.4   Current Computational Systems of MSA Morphology

The aim of Natural Language Processing (NLP) is to find the most efficient way to describe formally a language for a specific application. The core task in this field is to build a morphological analyzer and generator. Morphological analyzers are composed of two basic parts [21]:

1. Lexical units, i.e., a lexicon responsible for the coverage of the system. Ideally, the lexicon should include all the morphemes of a given language.
2. Morphosyntactic knowledge, i.e., a set of linguistic rules responsible for the robustness of the system. There are mainly two types of rules:
   (a) rewrite rules, which handle the phonological and orthographic variations of the lexical items;
   (b) morphotactic rules, which determine how morphemes are combined.

In fact both the lexicon and the rule components are closely related: linguistic rules can be codified in the lexicon, and consequently the size of both parts is directly related.

An early implementation of a computational model of Arabic morphology was carried out by Kenneth Beesley [8,15,16]. He created the Xerox Arabic morphological Analyzer, which uses finite-state technology to model MSA morphology. Beesley created a separate lexicon for each morpheme type: prefixes, suffixes, roots (4,930 entries) and patterns (about 400 entries). Information on root and pattern combinations is stored in the lexicon of roots, so he included full phonotactic coding in the entries. The system extracts the information stored in the lexicons and compiled it into a finite state transducer (FST). Phonotactics and orthographic variation rules are also compiled into FSTs. The combination of prefixes, stems and suffixes yields over 72 million hypothetical forms—with the disadvantage that it overgenerates. The phonotactic treatment includes 66 finite-state variation rules.

Beesley's system presents a fairly elegant description of MSA morphology. On the negative side, he uses an extensive list of patterns, as it is common in the traditional descriptions of Arabic morphology.

The most famous analyzer for the Arabic language is the Standard Arabic Morphological Analyzer (SAMA), formerly known as Buckwalter Arabic Morphological Analyzer (BAMA)—up to version 3—which was created by Tim Buckwalter in 2002 [1,26]. It has become the standard tool in the field of Arabic NLP [27]. SAMA is strongly lexicon-based—Buckwalter sacrifices the possibility of using a linguistic model in favor of a very practical solution: he codifies all linguistic processes in the lexicon and uses the stem as the basic lexical entry. He then specifies various sets of rules based on concatenative procedures to establish the permitted combinations of the different lexical items. The lexicon of stems includes 79,318 entries, representing 40,654 lemmas. Stems are turned into underlying forms by the addition of affixes, compiled in a lexicon of prefixes (1,328 entries) and a lexicon of suffixes (945 entries) These lexicons include both affixes and clitics.

This system presents two important disadvantages: first, it has a lot of obsolete words, reducing considerably its efficiency [27, 28]. Attia estimates that about 25% of the lexical items included in SAMA are outdated [27]. Second, it does not follow a linguistic analysis of MSA morphology. The design of morphology implies that phonological, morphological and orthographic alterations are simply codified in the lexicon: the same word may have more than one entry in the lexicon according to the number of lexemes its inflectional set of forms presents.

A very recent analyzer is the AraComLex, a large-scale finite-state morphological analyzer toolkit for MSA developed principally by Mohammed Attia[14,27]. Its lexical database uses a corpus of contemporary MSA to reject outdated words. It also makes use of pre-annotation tools and machine learning techniques, as well as knowledge-based pattern matching, to automatically acquire lexical knowledge. As a result, AraComLex is the only Arabic morphological analyzer which includes strictly contemporary vocabulary and is highly enhanced with additional linguistic features. Attia chooses the lemma as the basic lexical entry. The lexicon of lemmas has 5,925 nominals, 1,529 verbs; the lexicon of patterns 456 nominal patterns and 34 verbal. There are 130 alteration rules to handle all alterations encountered in the lexicon. Attia notes that a stem-based system, like that of the SAMA, is more costly for it has to list all the stem variants of a form, whereas a lexeme-based system simply includes one entry for each lexical form and a set of generalized rules for handling the variations. He also rejects a root-based approach, as it is more complex and tends to cause overgeneration problems.

The AraComLex is possibly the most consistent morphological analyzer for MSA, not only for its accuracy and efficient implementation, but also for its ease of use—and gladly it is available under a GNU GPL license. However, it did not intend to present a comprehensive model of Arabic internal morphology.

2   Methodology

The computational system has been implemented in Python programming language (version 3.2). In recent years it has come to be one of the best options for developing applications in the field of NLP. Further, version 3 of Python fully supports Unicode, so it can directly handle Arabic script. In relation to orthography, we handle fully diacritized forms. Arabic uses diacritics to disambiguate words [29], and thus we keep them to create a lexicon as unambiguous as possible. The rules of phonotactic and orthotactic nature, which cause a gap between the underlying—regularized—form and the surface form, were formalized using regular expressions.

We have manually created a lexicon of Arabic verb lemmas which consists of 15,453 entries with unambiguous information of each verbal item. The lexicon will be used as an input for the system of verbal generation. It was taken from a list of verbs included in the book *A dictionary of Arabic verb conjugation* by Antoine El-Dahdah [30]. The lexicographical sources used by El-Dahdah to compose his lexicon are widely known classical dictionaries. Thus, the lexicon includes many outdated vocabulary. Although this is a drawback for the development of a practical and accurate resource, this is going to allow us to have a complete overview of the MSA verbal system.

3   Results

Based on the ideas of Arabic traditional prosody, we have designed and built a computational model that describes the MSA verbal system. The computational model is based on generation. The output of the system is a large-scale lexicon of fully diacritized inflected forms. The lexicon has been subsequently used to develop an online interface of a morphological analyzer for verbs.

3.1   The Design of MSA Verbal Morphology

Our first aim was to clearly separate morphological phenomena from phonological and orthographic operations. We noticed that all verbs, regardless their nature, can be generated as regular, and then subjected to the constraints of phonology and orthography. By doing so, we can describe a completely regular morphology, applicable to all verbs. On a superficial level, phonological and orthographic alterations can be applied to these regular forms so they get their real surface form. This allows us to focus on morphological traits independently.

At a deep level, we decompose the stem into four elements: a root, derivational processes—consisting mainly of the insertion of consonantal material—a vocalism and a template.

The root is specific for each verb. As we have already said, it consists of three or four consonants interdigitated throughout the verbal stem. For instance, the root of the verb أرسل *Ársala* 'to send' is رسل *rsl*. There are cases, however, in which the root is not transparent, as in the verb استجاب *AistajaAba* 'to respond', whose root is جوب *jwb*.

The derivational processes—which correspond to parts of the traditional patterns—tend to add semantic connotations to the basic sense of the verb's root. The processes consist of three types of operations:

1. Insertion of one or more consonants, as the affix 'st' in the verb استجاب *AistajaAba* 'to respond'.
2. Insertion of a vowel lengthening mark, as the element *A* in the verb شاهد *XaAhada* 'to watch' which, is used to lengthen the vowel *a*.
3. Duplication of a consonant, as in the verb علّم *çal~ama* 'to teach', which doubles the *l*. The symbol ~ is used in the transliteration to represent the Arabic character ّ, whose function is to double the sound of a consonant.

In MSA there are only three short syllables *a*, *i* and *u*. The vocalism morpheme, which consists of two vowels—a first vowel and a second vowel within the stem—just presents different combinations of vowels in the vocalic slots of the template. For instance, in the inflected form يرسل *y-ursil-u* 'he sends', the stem shows two vowels, *u* and *i*. In this case, the vowels depend on the form of the stem, i.e., they have a default content, but in other cases they must be marked lexically.

The template is the most interesting element in the formation of the stem, for it has to deal with the combination of all the previous elements. This leads us to the challenging task of devising an algorithm that specifies how the lexical items are combined and merged into a well defined template.

We stated that we believe that the syllabic skeleton of Arabic verbal stems can be formalized in a reduced set of basic structural units. We base this hypothesis on al-Khalil's works on quantitative prosodic theory, for it computes syllabic shape by means of a systematic and simple mathematical device based on orthography. Al-Khalil's counting procedure hints at the existence of an extremely regular system of syllabic structure in Arabic. The interesting thing here is that verbs belonging to the same morphological class, overwhelmingly show the same weight, regardless being classified as regular or irregular.

Following this idea, we established that templates are formed by two basic units: first, consonants and vowel lengthening elements, and second, vowels themselves. We refer to the former as F, and to the latter as V or W (for first and second vowel respectively). A detailed analysis led us to propose that there are only two types of templates which cover all the traditional verbal patterns in the Arabic system. The basic difference between these two types is the length of the penultimate syllable: on one type this syllable is heavy, and on the other it is light. Hence, we are going to name the first type H, for *heavy,* and the second L, for *light*. Both types distinguish a perfective stem (*p-stem*), an imperfective stem (*i-stem*), and an imperative stem (*m-stem*), as each verb presents these three stems along its conjugation[2].

Table 3. Classification of verbal templates

Template type	p-stem	i-stem	m-stem
L	FFVFWF	VFFFWF	FFFWF
H	FFVFFWF	VFFFFWF	FFFFWF

The algorithm for combining the lexical items and the template is quite simple. First, the root and the derivational material are merged to form a string. This string is inserted into the template by a simple procedure. Each character from the root plus derivation string replaces an F of the template, starting from the end. If there are some F slots left after the replacement process, they are removed from the resulting string. Then, the specific vowels of the stem replace the V and W symbols. This straightforward algorithm is shown in figure 3. Strikingly, this algorithm implies that verbs of 3-consonant and 4-consonant roots are treated the same, so we do not need to have different conjugational categories for them, as is the general custom.

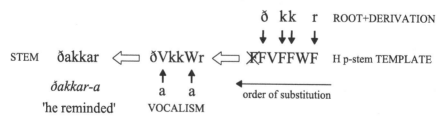

Fig. 3. Algorithm for template adjustment. Example of word form ذكّر *ðakkara* 'he reminded', root ذكر *ðkr.*

---

[2] m-stem is actually the same as i-stem but without the first vowel. For the sake of simplicity, we preferred to keep it as an autonomous template.

Table 4. Inflectional Chart. Symbol 'E' represents vowel lengthening.

TAG	p-stem	i-stem all	indicative	subjunctive	jussive	m-stem
1SN	ـُت	ـأ	ـÓ	ـÓ	-	None
1PN	Eـ'ن	ـن	ـÓ	ـÓ	-	None
2SM	ـُت	ت-	ـÓ	ـÓ	-	-
2SF	ـِت	ت-EQ	ـَن	-	-	EQ-
2DN	Eـِت	ت-EÓ	ـَن	-	-	EÓ-
2PM	ـُم	ت-EÓ	ـَن	ا	ا	اEÓ-
2PF	ـُّت	ت-ـَن	-	-	-	ـَن
3SM	ـÓ	ي-	ـÓ	ـÓ	-	None
3SF	ـَتÓ	ت-	ـÓ	ـÓ	-	None
3DM	EÓ-	ي-EÓ	ـَن	-	-	None
3DF	EـَتÓ	ت-EÓ	ـَن	-	-	None
3PM	EÓ-	ي-EÓ	ـَن	ا	ا	None
3PF	ـَن	ي-ـَن	-	-	-	None

As for the conjugational paradigm, we simply defined the inflectional morphemes that must be added to a base stem so that it turns into an inflected word form. The whole inflectional paradigm can be seen in Table 4.

In a superficial layer, phonological and orthographic operations modify the underlying form to yield the superficial form of the inflected verb. Even though these phenomena are considered irregular in traditional Arabic grammar, it is essential to note that these alterations are by no means arbitrary, but they entail systematizable subregularities. These operations are formalized as rewrite rules and implemented as regular expressions. The rewrite rules are represented as follows:

a → b / _c

> *If you find* a *in the word-form, and if* a *is followed by* c, *then change* a *to* b; *where* a *is the pattern we are looking for,* b *is the replacement for the pattern, and* c *is the surrounding context; and the underscore indicates the position of* a *in relation to* c.

For instance, one of the phonological rules is defined as [uwi -> iy / _Ca]. This rule deals with the sound *wi*, which is a segment discouraged by the Arabic phonological system [31]. Hence, the rule handles the transformation of this sound into a more harmonic sound *iy*. The context specified by the rule indicates that the *pattern* must be followed by a consonant plus a vowel *a*, so that the rule is applied. We can see the behavior of this rule in the perfective passive formation of the common verb قال *qaAla* 'to say', whose root is *qwl*. By applying this rule, the regularly generated passive **quwila* is substituted for the more melodious sound—and correct—*qiyla*.

In a nutshell, our model is essentially based on the division of stems in a root plus derivational affixation amalgam, a vocalization and a template. These three lexical items are merged by means of a formal device to build verbal stems. The keystone of this procedure are the 2 types of templates and their insertion algorithm, which abstract the syllabic structure of the underlying representation of verbal stems based on predefined basic units.

3.2   The Generation Model

The generation system relies on a lexicon of verb lemmas manually compiled for the present project. The sources of this lexicon were described in section 2. Based on our description of verbal morphology, each verb would need two pieces of information: the root, which must be lexically associated to each verb, and a code that codifies the morphemes of the verb stem and its template, i.e., the code shows if the verb presents derivational processes, the vowels it uses for its conjugation and if it adjusts to an L template or to a H template.

The code is formed by six digits and one letter. The latter is placed in position 3 of the code. The meaning of each position is as follows: positions 1, 2 and 4 indicate if the verb has derivational material; position 3 indicates the template the verb follows; and position 5, 6 and 7 indicate the conjugational vowels of the verb. For example, the verb اِسْتَمَرَّ *Aistamar~a* 'to continue' has a root مرر and a code 04H0000. The 4 in the code indicates that a prefix 'st' must be added to the root, and the H specifies that this verb adjusts to an H template. The zeros indicate that this verb does not have other derivational processes and that the vowels of its conjugation do not have to be lexically marked, i.e., this verbal class has default vowels in its conjugation.

The generation process is as follows. The system generates the conjugation of a verb starting from the verb's root. The code associated to that root is used to keep track of the generation path the verb must follow through the formation of the stem. The system is divided in 7 modules, which follow a hierarchical structure.

Module 1: Root and derivational material merging: in the first stage, the derivational processes are applied to the root. There are 7 processes of consonant insertion, 3 processes of vowel lengthening insertion and 2 process of duplication of a consonant.

Module 2: Insertion into template: the root and derivation amalgam is inserted into the template following the algorithm described in the previous section.

Module 3: Insertion of derivational affix ta- (patterns II and V). We left this single derivational affix to be inserted after the template adjustment for it has a completely different nature, compared to the others. This affix is the only affix constituted by a syllable, contrary to the other affixes, which are single consonants.

Module 4: Insertion of vocalization: vowels are inserted into the template.

Module 5: Phonotactic preprocessing: prohibited syllables are resyllabized and, at this point, deep phonological alterations are carried out—which consist of assimilation processes suffered by forms belonging to the VIII pattern. At the end of this stage the stem if completely formed.

Module 6: Generation of inflectional paradigm: the created stem is passed through the inflectional chart to yield all conjugated forms.

Module 7: Phonotactic constraints and orthographic normalization: all inflected forms are passed through a series of rewrite rules in the form of regular expressions. The rules are hierarchically organized, so if the same form suffers various phonological processes, all are applied in a cascade process. The system has 30 orthographic rules and 33 phonological, making a total of 63 rules to handle verbal allomorphism.

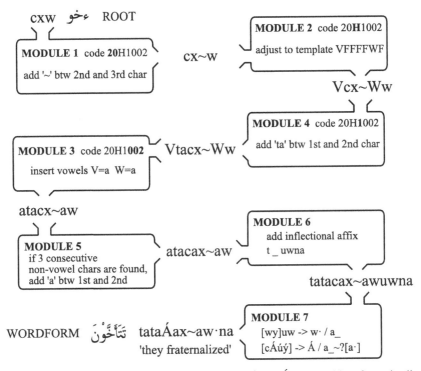

Fig. 4. Example of generation of the word worm تَتَأَخُّوْنَ tataÁx~aw·na 'they fraternized'

3.3   Evaluation of the Model

To evaluate the accuracy of the morphological model, we needed to compare the lexicon generated by our system with a reference lexicon. We carried out the evaluation against the list of inflected verbs extracted from the morphological analyzer ElixirFM [32]. We assumed that the lexicon extracted from the ElixirFM software is a validated database of Arabic conjugation, so we consider it our gold standard. We based this assumption on the fact that ElixirFM is an improvement on the BAMA analyzer,

Table 5. Data on number of lemmas and forms in ElixirFM and Jabalín

	No. Lemmas	No. Forms	Forms per lemma
ElixirFM	9,009	1,752,848	192
Jabalín	15,452	1,684,268	109
Common	6,878	749,702 (44%)	109

which has reportedly achieved 99.25% precision [33]. Starting from this assumption we normalized the ElixirFM lexicon, so that it shares a common format with our lexicon. In the table below we find the data of both lexicons.

The ElixirFM tagset is redundant, thus the higher number of forms per lemma. Another peculiarity of the ElixirFM tagset is that there may be more than one form corresponding to the same tag. This explains that the total number of forms does not equal the number of lemmas plus the number of forms per lemma.

There are 2,131 lemmas only present in ElixirFM and 8,581 only present in Jabalín. This means that we have a low recall rate with respect to the ElixirFM database. Even though both gaps may seem substantial, we believe that it is an inherent problem of working with Classical Arabic lexicon and, ultimately, both ElixirFM and Jabalín include a high percentage of obsolete lexical entries. There are a total of 749,702 common forms. From these, 651 forms were not evaluable because some discrepancies were found in grammar books. This means that the total number of evaluated forms was reduced to 749,051, which represents 44% of our lexicon.

For the evaluation task, we compared the reference lexicon with our generated lexicon and searched for each of our verbal entries in the reference lexicon, obtaining a number of successes and failures. From the evaluable forms, we achieved a precision of 99.52% of correct analyses. We believe that this high accuracy validates our model.

Table 6. Results from the evaluation

	No. forms	% from total	% from eval.
Correct	745,436	44,26%	99.52%
Incorrect	3,615	0.21%	0.48%
No data	935,217	55.53%	–
Total	1,684,268	–	–

3.4   The Jabalín Online Interface

The Jabalín Online Interface is a web application for analyzing and generating Arabic verbs. It uses the lexicon of inflected verbs provided by the generation system described in the previous section. The online interface is hosted at the LLI-UAM laboratory web page, under the address http://elvira.lllf.uam.es/jabalin/.

JABALÍN Online Interface of the Arabic Analyzer

Home | Quantitative Data | Explore Database | Inflect verb | Derive root | Analyze form

Jabalín is an application for analyzing and generating verbs in Modern Standard Arabic. It uses a large-scale lexicon of inflected forms which has been generated following a root-and-pattern approach. The system provides three functionalities: **inflect verb**, **derive root** and **analyze form**. In addition, the application offers the possibility to **explore the database** containing the lexicon of verbs and additional information. It also provides **quantitative data** extracted from the lexicons that can be used to perform statistical analysis on Arabic morphology.

Explore Database

This options allows you to look into the lexicon of Jabalín.

Quantitative Data

This options provides quantitative data extracted from the Jabalín lexicons, the lexicon of verbal lemmas and the lexicon of inflected forms.

Inflect verb

This functionality provides the conjugation paradigm of a given verb lemma. If the verb has shadda, it must be written.

Derive root

This functionality lists all the verb lemmas generated from a given root.

Analyze form

This functionality provides all the possible analyses of a given verb form. It accepts fully vocalized, partially vocalized or unvocalized forms.

© Alicia Gónzalez 2012, Susana L. Hervás 2012, Antonio Moreno Sandoval 2012, Otakar Smrž 2012, Viktor Bielický 2012, Tim Buckwalter 2002. GNU General Public License GNU GPL 3.

Jabalín is an open source online project developed by Alicia González Martínez, computational linguist, and Susana López Hervás, computer scientist, and directed by Prof. Antonio Moreno Sandoval, principal investigator of the LLI-UAM, The Laboratorio de Lingüística Informática, Universidad Autónoma de Madrid.

The evaluation has been carried out thanks to the ElixirFM morphological analyzer, Otakar Smrž 2012.

The interface provides five functionalities: explore database, quantitative data, inflect verb, derive root and analyze form. *Explore database* allows one to look into the lexicon of Jabalín. It includes information about all the inflected forms from the lexicon and indicates if the form has been evaluated. *Quantitative data* shows various types of frequency data extracted from both the lexicon of lemmas and the lexicon of inflected forms. *Inflect verb* provides the conjugation paradigm of a given verb lemma, including the root and the pattern of the verb. *Derive root* lists all the verb lemmas generated from a given root and its corresponding patterns. *Analyze form* provides all the possible analyses of a given verbal form. It accepts fully vocalized, partially vocalized or unvocalized forms.

4   Conclusions and Future Work

Our model intends to present a compact and efficient implementation of MSA verbal morphology. Our design of morphology is based on a linguistically motivated analysis which takes full advantage of the inner regularities encountered in Arabic morphology.

As a first goal, our descriptive model aims to clearly separate morphological, phonological and orthographic phenomena, avoiding treating different types of linguistic layers by means of the same operations. One of the keystones of the model is that we present a robust and simple algorithm for dealing with the non-concatenative nature of Arabic morphology, which gave us strikingly good results. As a consequence, we achieved to reduce the traditional classification of Arabic patterns from 24 classes to only 2 conjugational classes. Another remarkable conclusion drawn by the model is that there is no need to morphologically distinguish between verbs of 3-consonant and 4-consonant roots.

We created a total of 63 rules to handle both phonological and orthographic alterations. As a way of testing the robustness of the model, we automatically evaluated 44% of the output lexicon of the system against a gold standard. The results achieved by the evaluation show 99.52% correct forms.

Perhaps, the most remarkable conclusion we take from the template categorization and the ordering algorithm is that Arabic syllabic structure is overwhelmingly regular. The highly restrictive phonotactic system of Arabic makes the syllabic structure of stems predictable. In a nutshell, we have demonstrated that it is possible to develop a precise formalism which predicts the syllabic structures for Arabic lexical items.

As for future works, we strongly believe that in the long run a morphological system based on a precise description of the Arabic morphological system would benefit from high efficiency and better adaptability to numerous applications. Therefore, our forthcoming endeavors will be focused on extending the proposed model to nominal morphology, so that we can develop a complete system to handle Arabic morphology. The nominal system has the disadvantage of being more complex than verbal morphology, yet we believe that the basic principles of our analysis would be maintained in a nominal model.

Furthermore, the efficiency obtained from this system strongly suggests that this description model must have linguistic implications, so one of our most interesting future endeavors is to place this description framework inside current linguistic theory.

Acknowledgements. The present work benefited form the input of Jiři Hana and Theophile Ambadiang, who provided valuable comments to the research summarized here. We would like to thank Otakar Smrž too, for his invaluable help regarding the ElixirFM analyzer. This research was supported and funded by an FPU-UAM scholarship from the Universidad Autónoma de Madrid and by a grant from the Spanish Government (R&D National Plan Program TIN2010-20644-C02-03).

References

1. Habash, N.Y.: Introduction to Arabic Natural Language Processing. Morgan & Claypool, San Rafael (2010)
2. Kaye, A.S.: Formal vs. Informal Arabic: Diglossia, Triglossia, Tetraglossia, etc., Polyglossia viewed as a continuum. In: Comrie, B. (ed.) The World's Major Languages, pp. 664–685. Oxford University Press, Oxford (1990)
3. Ferrando Frutos, I.: El plural fracto en semítico: nuevas perspectivas. Estudios de Dialectología Norteafricana y Andalusí 4, 7–24 (1999)
4. Holes, C.: Modern Arabic: Structures, Functions, and Varieties. Georgetown University Press, Washington, D.C (2004)

5. Danks, W.: The Arabic Verb: Form and Meaning in the Vowel-Lengthening Patterns. John Benjamins, Amsterdam (2011)
6. Lieber, R.: Introducing Morphology. Cambridge University Press, Cambridge (2009)
7. Robin, C.: L'Arabie antique de Karib'il à Mahomet: nouvelles données sur l'histoire des Arabes grâce aux inscriptions. Édisud, Aix-en-Provence (1992)
8. Beesley, K.R.: Arabic Finite-State Morphological Analysis and Generation. In: Proceedings of COLING 1996 (1996)
9. Ratcliffe, R.R.: The "Broken" Plural Problem in Arabic and Comparative Semitic: Allomorphy and Analogy in Non-Concatenative Morphology. John Benjamins, Amsterdam (1998)
10. Cowan, D.: An Introduction to Modern Literary Arabic. Cambridge University Press, Cambridge (1958)
11. Versteegh, K.: The Arabic language. Edinburgh University Press, Edinburgh (2001)
12. Shimron, J.: Language Processing and Acquisition in Languages of Semitic, Root-Based, Morphology. John Benjamins, Amsterdam (2003)
13. Pierrehumbert, J.: Dissimilarity in the Arabic Verbal Roots. In: Proceedings of the 23rd Meeting of the Northeastern Linguistic Society, pp. 367–381. Graduate Student Association, U. Mass. Amherst (1993),
http://faculty.wcas.northwestern.edu/~jbp/publications/arabic_roots.pdf
14. Attia, M., Pecina, P., Toral, A., Tounsi, L., van Genabith, J.: An Open-Source Finite State Morphological Transducer for Modern Standard Arabic. In: Proceedings of the International Workshop on Finite State Methods and Natural Language Processing (FSNLP), pp. 125–136 (2011)
15. Beesley, K.R.: Finite-state Morphological Analysis and Generation of Arabic at Xerox Research: Status and plans in 2001. In: ACL Workshop on Arabic Language Processing: Status and Perspective, pp. 1–8 (2001)
16. Beesley, K.R.: Arabic Morphology Using only Finite-State Operations. In: Proceedings of the Workshop on Computational Approaches to Semitic Languages, pp. 50–57 (1998)
17. McCarthy, J.J.: A Prosodic Theory of Nonconcatenative Morphology. Linguistic Inquiry 12, 373–418 (1981)
18. Abu-Chacra, F.: Arabic: An Essential Grammar. Taylor & Francis, New York (2007)
19. Kiraz, G.A.: Computational Analyses of Arabic Morphology (1994)
20. Soudi, A., Eisele, A.: Generating an Arabic Full-Form Lexicon for Bidirectional Morphology Lookup. In: Proceedings of LREC 2004 (2004)
21. Kiraz, G.A.: Computational Nonlinear Morphology: With Emphasis on Semitic Languages. Cambridge University Press, Cambridge (2001)
22. Kiraz, G.A.: Computing Prosodic Morphology. In: Proceedings of the 16th Conference on Computational Linguistics, vol. 2, pp. 664–669 (1996)
23. Wright, W., Smith, W.R., de Goeje, M.J.: A Grammar of the Arabic Language. Cambridge University Press, Cambridge (1896)
24. Ryding, K.C.: A Reference Grammar of Modern Standard Arabic. Cambridge University Press, Cambridge (2005)
25. Khashan, K.M.: Al-Khalil Ibn Ahmad and Numerical Prosody I. Journal of Arabic Linguistic Tradition 1, 25–34 (2003)
26. Habash, N.: Large-Scale Lexeme-Based Arabic Morphological Generation. In: Proceedings of Traitement Automatique du Langage Naturel, TALN 2004 (2004)

27. Attia, M., Pecina, P., Toral, A., Tounsi, L., van Genabith, J.: A Lexical Database for Modern Standard Arabic Interoperable with a Finite State Morphological Transducer. In: Mahlow, C., Piotrowski, M. (eds.) SFCM 2011. CCIS, vol. 100, pp. 98–118. Springer, Heidelberg (2011)
28. Sawalha, M., Atwell, E.S.: Comparative Evaluation of Arabic Language Morphological Analysers and Stemmers. In: Proceedings of COLING 2008 (Poster Volume), pp. 107–110 (2008), http://eprints.whiterose.ac.uk/42635/
29. Al Shamsi, F., Guessoum, A.: A Hidden Markov Model-Based POS Tagger for Arabic. In: Proceedings of the 8th International Conference on the Statistical Analysis of Textual Data, pp. 31–42 (2006)
30. El-Dahdah, A.: A Dictionary of Arabic Verb Conjugation. Librairie du Liban, Beirut (1991)
31. Owens, J.: A Linguistic History of Arabic. Oxford University Press, Oxford (2006)
32. Smrž, O.: Functional Arabic Morphology. Formal System and Implementation (2007)
33. Rodrigues, P., Cavar, D.: Learning Arabic Morphology Using Statistical Constraint-Satisfaction Models. In: Benmamoun, E. (ed.) Papers from the 19th Annual Symposium on Arabic Linguistics, Urbana, Illinois, pp. 63–76. John Benjamins, Amsterdam (2007)

HFST — A System for Creating NLP Tools

Krister Lindén, Erik Axelson, Senka Drobac, Sam Hardwick,
Juha Kuokkala, Jyrki Niemi, Tommi A. Pirinen, and Miikka Silfverberg

University of Helsinki
Department of Modern Languages
Unioninkatu 40 A
FI-00014 University of Helsinki, Finland
{krister.linden,erik.axelson,senka.drobac,sam.hardwick,
juha.kuokkala,jyrki.niemi,tommi.pirinen,miikka.silfverberg}@helsinki.fi

Abstract. The paper presents and evaluates various NLP tools that have been created using the open source library HFST – Helsinki Finite-State Technology and outlines the minimal extensions that this has required to a pure finite-state system. In particular, the paper describes an implementation and application of Pmatch presented by Karttunen at SFCM 2011.

Keywords: finite-state technology, language identification, morphological guessers, spell-checking, named-entity recognition, language generation, parsing, HFST, XFST, Pmatch.

1 Introduction

In natural language processing, finite-state string transducer methods have been found useful for solving a number of practical problems ranging from language identification via morphological processing and generation to part-of-speech tagging and named-entity recognition, as long as the problems lend themselves to a formulation based on matching and transforming local context.

In this paper, we present and evaluate various tools that have been created using HFST – Helsinki Finite-State Technology[1] and outline the minimal extensions that this has required to a pure FST system. In particular, we describe an implementation of Pmatch presented by Karttunen at SFCM 2011 [7] and its application to a large-scale named-entity recognizer for Swedish.

The paper is structured as follows: Section 2 is on applications and their evaluation. In Section 3, we present examples of user environments supported by HFST. In Section 4, we present some of the solutions and extensions needed to implement the applications. This is followed by the Sections 5 and 6 with an outline of some future work and the discussion, respectively.

2 Applications and Tests

In this section, we describe and evaluate some applications implemented with HFST. When processing text corpora, it is useful to first identify the language of the text

---

[1] http://hfst.sf.net

C. Mahlow and M. Piotrowski (Eds.): SFCM 2013, CCIS 380, pp. 53–71, 2013.
© Springer-Verlag Berlin Heidelberg 2013

before analyzing its words morphologically. Words unknown to the morphological lexicon need a guesser derived from the lexicon. The reverse operation of morphological analysis is morphological generation. Generating inflections of words unknown to the morphological lexicon can be used for eliciting information from native speakers before adding the words to the lexicon. For information extraction, it is important to be able to identify multi-word expressions such as named entities, for which purpose HFST has a pattern matching tool. Finally, we also describe a traditional application area of finite-state morphology, i.e., spell-checking and spelling correction, which is now served by a uniform implementation using weighted finite-state technology.

2.1 Language Identification

Language identification is the task of recognizing the language of a text or text fragment. It is useful in applications that need to process documents written in various languages where the language might not be explicitly marked in the document. For example, a translation application might need to identify the language of a document in order to apply the correct translation model. Another example is a speller for Finnish, which might need to identify paragraphs written in English, in order not to spell-check those paragraphs.

In this section we outline how to use HFST tagger tools and language identification tools for creating language identifiers. We also present an experiment on language identification for documents written in Dutch, English, Estonian, Finnish, German or Swedish. The experiment shows that HFST language identifiers are highly accurate (99.5% of the input sentences were correctly classified).

There are several methods for performing language identification. Highly accurate language identification can be accomplished by treating data as a letter sequence and training a Markov chain from training documents whose language is known [3]. One Markov chain is trained for each language that the system recognizes. Language identification consists of applying each Markov chain on input and choosing the language whose model gives the highest likelihood for the text.

HFST language identifiers adopt a Markov chain framework, which can be implemented with weighted finite-state technology. Using HFST tagger tools [19], we train Markov models for all languages. A program, hfst-guess-language, reads the models and input text and labels each sentence with the language whose model gave the highest likelihood for the sentence.

We present an experiment on applying HFST language identifiers for guessing the language of sentences written in six languages. For all languages except Swedish, we used training data from corpora containing newspaper text. For Swedish, we used more general text.

For Dutch we used the Alpino treebank [1], for English we used the Penn Treebank [12], for Estonian we used the Estonian National Corpus[2], for Finnish we used text from the largest Finnish newspaper Helsingin Sanomat year 1995[3], for German we used the TIGER Corpus [2] and for Swedish we used Talbanken [5].

---

[2] http://www.cl.ut.ee/korpused/segakorpus/
[3] http://www.csc.fi/kielipankki/

Table 1. For each language, we used 2000 sentences for training and 200 sentences for testing. We give the sizes of the data sets in UTF-8 characters.

Language	Training data (UTF-8 chars)	Test data (UTF-8 chars)
Dutch	245,000	24,000
English	265,000	26,000
Estonian	238,000	23,000
Finnish	155,000	14,000
German	280,000	28,000
Swedish	164,000	16,000

Table 2. Accuracy of the language guesser per language and for all languages

Language	Accuracy
Dutch	99.0%
English	99.5%
Estonian	99.5%
Finnish	99.5%
German	100.0%
Swedish	99.5%
ALL	99.5%

For each language, we chose 2200 sentences for training and testing. Of the sentences, every eleventh sentence was used for testing and the rest for training. This totals 2000 sentences for training and 200 sentences for testing for each language. The sizes of the data sets in UTF-8 characters are described in Table 1. The average length of a sentence in characters was shorter for Finnish and Swedish than for the other languages.

We ran the language identifier for test sentences from all six languages (1200 sentences in total) and computed the accuracy of the language identification system as $corr/all$, where $corr$ is the number of sentences whose language was correctly guessed and all is the number of all sentences. In Table 2, we show results for each individual language and all the languages combined.

Of all sentences, 99.5% were correctly classified, which demonstrates that the language identification system is accurate. This is encouraging because Finnish and Estonian have similar orthographies. This applies to German, Swedish and Dutch as well.

Currently identification is limited to identifying the closest language corresponding to a sentence. There is no option to label a sentence as belonging to an unknown language.

2.2 Morphologies and Guessers

Language technology applications for agglutinating languages such as Finnish and Hungarian benefit greatly from high-coverage morphological analyzers, which supply word forms with their morphological analyses. This makes applications dependent on the coverage of the morphological analyzer. Building a high-coverage morphological analyzer (with recall over 95%) is a substantial task, and even with a high-coverage analyzer, domain-specific vocabulary presents a challenge. Therefore, accurate methods for dealing with out-of-vocabulary words are needed.

With HFST tools it is possible to use an existing morphological analyzer to construct a morphological guesser based on word suffixes. Suffix-based guessing is sufficient for many agglutinating languages such as Finnish [10], where most inflection and derivation is marked using suffixes. Even if a word is not recognized by the morphological analyzer, the analyzer is likely to recognize some words which inflect similarly to the unknown word. These can be used for guessing the inflection of the unknown word.

The guessing of an unknown word like "twiitin" (the genitive form of "twiitti", tweet in Finnish) is based on finding recognized word forms like "sviitin" (genitive form of "sviitti", hotel suite in Finnish) that have long suffixes, such as "-iitin", which match the suffixes of the unrecognized word. The longer the common suffix, the more likely it is that the unrecognized word has the same inflection as the known word. The guesser will output morphological analyses for "twiitin" in order of likelihood.

Besides the length of the matching suffix, guesses can also be ordered based on the probability that a suffix matches a given analysis. This can be estimated using a labeled training corpus. In addition, any existing weighting scheme in the original morphological analyzer can be utilized.

If the morphological analyzer marks declension class, the guesser can also be used for guessing the declension class. If the declension class is marked, the guesser can be used for the generation of word forms as well as analysis. This is described in Section 2.3.

Constructing a morphological guesser from OMorFi[4] – The open-source Finnish morphology [15], the three top guesses for "twiitin" are (the markup is slightly simplified):

```
twiit   [POS=NOUN]  [GUESS_CATEGORY=5]   [NUM=SG] [CASE=GEN]
twiiti  [POS=NOUN]  [GUESS_CATEGORY=33]  [NUM=SG] [CASE=NOM]
twiit   [POS=VERB]  [GUESS_CATEGORY=53]  [VOICE=ACT] [MOOD=INDV]  ...
```

The first field corresponds to the stem of the word, the second field to its main part of speech and the third to its declension class. The fourth field shows the inflectional and derivational information of the guess. In this case, the first guess is correct. It is modeled after declension class number 5, which is a class of nouns containing among others the noun "sviitti".

2.3   Language Generation for Out-of-Vocabulary Words

Natural-language user interfaces, such as dialogue systems, need a language generation component for generating messages for the user. The aim is to supply the user with information about the internal state of some database containing information such as airline connections or weather phenomena.

---

[4] http://code.google.com/p/omorfi/

Language generation systems for agglutinating languages will benefit from morphological analyzers, because generating syntactically correct sentences requires inflecting words according to syntactic context. Depending on the domain and coverage of the morphological analyzer, it might also be necessary to inflect words that are not recognized by the morphological analyzer.

HFST morphological guessers presented in Section 2.2 can be used for generation as well as morphological analysis. For example, using the OMorFi morphology for Finnish, the best morphological guess for the unknown word "twiitin" is

```
twiit   [POS=NOUN] [GUESS_CATEGORY=5]   [NUM=SG] [CASE=GEN]
```

Replacing the inflectional information [NUM=SG] [CASE=GEN] (singular genitive case) by [NUM=PL] [CASE=PAR] (plural partitive case) gives the analysis

```
twiit   [POS=NOUN] [GUESS_CATEGORY=5]   [NUM=PL] [CASE=PAR]
```

which can be fed back to the guesser to generate the surface forms "twiitteja" and "twiittejä". The latter one is correct, though the first one would also be possible in theory, since the variation between "-ja" and "-jä" is governed by Finnish vowel harmony and the stem "twiit" is neutral with respect to vowel harmony.

2.4   Extending a Lexicon with the Help of a Guesser

The morphological guesser has proven to be a useful tool when adding large bulks of new vocabulary to a lexicon. We tested this on the Finnish Open Source lexicon OMorFi. According to our experience with handling ca. 260.000 proper nouns, the guesser achieved roughly 90% accuracy in assigning the correct inflection class to new lexicon entries on the first guess, so the manual work needed was reduced to only checking the guesser's results and correcting ca. 10% of the suggested entries.

The names to be added to the lexicon were given in their base form, so we could benefit from accepting only suggestions by the guesser in the nominative case [CASE=NOM]. The data was presented to native speakers with key word forms generated for each entry, which could be used to distinguish between different inflection classes, so that it was not necessary to understand the linguistic encoding scheme:

```
Aura     9 Aura : Auraa : Aurat : Aurain, Aurojen : Auroja : Auroihin
Oura    10 Oura : Ouraa : Ourat : Ourain, Ourien : Ouria : Ouriin
Pura    10 Pura : Puraa : Purat : Purain, Purien : Puria : Puriin
Saura    9 Saura : Sauraa : Saurat : Saurain, Saurojen : Sauroja :
           Sauroihin
Peura    9 Peura : Peuraa :  Peurat : Peurain, Peurojen : Peuroja :
           Peuroihin
Tiura   10 Tiura : Tiuraa : Tiurat : Tiurain, Tiurien : Tiuria : Tiuriin
Heikura 13 Heikura : Heikuraa : Heikurat : Heikurojen, Heikuroiden,
           Heikuroitten : Heikuroja, Heikuroita : Heikuroihin
```

We did a preliminary test to assess the accuracy of the guesser when only some basic proper nouns were included in OMorFi's lexicon. A sample of 100 words from each proper noun list to be added (place names, companies, organizations, given names, family names) showed that the guesser's success rate for finding the correct inflection class within first five guesses ranged from 68% (companies) to 93% (place names). The differences between the groups are readily explained by the facts that the place names most often have endings corresponding to regular nouns, whereas the organization and company names often contain foreign and acronym components not recognized by the guesser.

When doing bulk additions of large numbers of lexical entries based on their suffixes, it is practical to sort the entries alphabetically according to the end of the word. As the first guess was very often correct, only one guess was provided. If the first guess is marked as incorrect by a native speaker, several words needing the same correction are likely to follow, so it is quick to apply the same correction.

After two lists of person names (ca. 12,000 family names and ca. 4,000 given names) had been manually corrected, they were included in OMorFi's lexicon in order to improve the guesser's performance when handling further proper noun data.

The guesser indeed performed well with the Finnish geographical names (ca. 230,000): 91% of the first inflection class codes generated were correct without any editing. A smaller collection of foreign geographical names – states, provinces and cities (ca. 12,000) – also yielded quite good results, considering the tiny amount of foreign lexical data previously known by OMorFi: 73% of the guesses were correct as such, and 6% with some added information.

The last batch of our proper names consisted of ca. 6,600 organization names. These included mostly Finnish but to some extent also international companies, societies and other organizations. Before handling the organizations, the geographical names were incorporated into OMorFi and the guesser was rebuilt. With this guesser, we got 86% of the organization names correctly assigned and 3% correctly with some additions. This was a significant improvement over the initial guesser.

2.5   Named-Entity Recognition

Named entities are among the most important elements of interest in information retrieval. In addition, names indicate agents and objects which are important in information extraction. Often named entities are denoted by multi-word expressions. In HFST, a pattern-matching tool, hfst-pmatch, has been implemented for identifying multi-word expressions and recognizing named entities.

Background. In his keynote speech at SFCM 2011, Karttunen presented toy examples of named-entity recognition (NER) with his FST pattern matching tool (pmatch) [7]. The HFST Pmatch tool has been modeled after Karttunen's, but it is an independent implementation with some differences in features. We have converted a full-scale named-entity recognizer for Swedish to use HFST Pmatch, and we are in the process of developing one for Finnish.

A named-entity recognizer marks names in a text, typically with information on the type (class) of the name [14]. Major types of names include persons, locations, organizations, events and works of art. NER tools often also recognize temporal and numeric expressions. Names and their types can be recognized based on internal evidence, i.e., the structure of the name itself (e.g., *ACME Inc.* probably denotes a company), or based on external evidence, i.e., the context of the name (e.g., *she works for ACME*; *ACME hired a new CEO*) [13]. In addition, NER tools typically use gazetteers, lists of known names, to ensure that high-frequency names are recognized with the correct type.

Named-Entity Recognition with Pmatch. A key feature of Pmatch that makes it well-suited for NER is the ability to efficiently add XML-style tags around substrings matching a regular expression, as in [7]. Such regular expressions are specified by suffixing the expression with EndTag(*TagName*). For example, the following expressions mark company names ending in a company designator:

```
Define NSTag [? - [Whitespace|"<"|">"]] ;
Define CorpSuffix [UppercaseAlpha NSTag+ " "]+ ["Corp" | "Inc"]
    EndTag(EnamexOrgCrp) ;
Define TOP CorpSuffix ;
```

The built-in set Whitespace denotes any whitespace character and UppercaseAlpha any uppercase letter. String literals are enclosed in double quotation marks where Karttunen's FST uses curly braces [7]. For matching, Pmatch considers the regular expression with the special name TOP. Thus, to be able to tag the company names with the expression CorpSuffix, TOP must refer to it. In general, a Pmatch expression set (file) contains a list of named regular expression definitions of the form Define *name regex* ;.

The above expressions mark the company names in the following input:

```
Computer Systems Corp announced a merger with Home Computers Inc .
```

The output is:

```
<EnamexOrgCrp>Computer Systems Corp</EnamexOrgCrp> announced a merger
with <EnamexOrgCrp>Home Computers Inc</EnamexOrgCrp> .
```

Pmatch considers leftmost longest matches of TOP in the input and adds the tags specified in TOP or the expressions to which TOP refers. If several subexpressions have the same leftmost longest match in the input, it is unspecified (but deterministic) which one Pmatch chooses. To disambiguate between matches, context conditions can be added to the matching regular expressions. If a part of the input does not match TOP or only matches a subexpression without an EndTag or any transductions, Pmatch outputs it unaltered.

HFST Pmatch regular expressions may also contain transductions that can add extra output or discard specified parts of the input. Even though they are not in general used in tagging named entities, they can be used in correction expressions that modify tags added by previous sets of expressions. (Pmatch makes a single pass over its input, so a transduction cannot modify tags added by the same set of expressions.) If several different expressions have the same leftmost longest match but different transductions, Pmatch deterministically chooses one of them and issues a warning that there were other possible matches.

Context Conditions. An expression may be accompanied with a context condition specifying that a match should be considered only if the left or right context of the match matches the context condition. For example, the following expressions mark the capitalized words following *rörelseresultatet för* ('operating profit of') with EnamexOrgCrp:

```
Define CapWord2 UppercaseAlpha NSTag+ ;
Define OrgCrpOpProfit CapWord2 [" " CapWord2]*
    EndTag(EnamexOrgCrp) LC("Rörelseresultatet för ") ;
Define TOP OrgCrpOpProfit ;
```

For example:

```
Rörelseresultatet för <EnamexOrgCrp>Comp Systems</EnamexOrgCrp> ...
```

As in [7], the regular expression in LC() specifies a left context that must precede the actual match. Similarly, RC() specifies a right context that must follow the match. NLC() and NRC() specify negative left and right context, respectively, that may not precede or follow the match. Context conditions may be combined with conjunction and disjunction.

Conjunctive context conditions can also be specified at several stages in the expressions. For example, a name is marked as a sports event by the following expressions only if it is followed by a space and the word *spelades* ('was played') (right context expression from EvnAtlIntl) and preceded by a space or sentence boundary (#) (left context expression from TOP):

```
Define EvnAtlIntl [CapWord2 " "]+ "International "
    EndTag(EnamexEvnAtl) RC(" spelades") ;
Define TOP EvnAtlIntl LC(Whitespace | #) ;
```

In this case, the left context condition in TOP is considered for all the EndTag expressions contained or included in TOP. Karttunen [7] does not mention if his system can combine multiple context conditions in a similar way.

Converting a Swedish Named-Entity Recognizer to Use Pmatch. We have converted a Swedish named-entity recognizer [8] developed at the University of Gothenburg to use Pmatch. The Swedish NER tool works on tokenized running text input: punctuation marks are separated from words by spaces but the words are not annotated in any way. In contrast, the forthcoming Finnish NER tool will work on annotated text, which makes it easier to write more general rules, in particular for a morphologically rich language such as Finnish.

The original implementation of the Swedish NER tool [8] contained 24 different recognizers running in a pipeline and a correction filter run after each stage. 21 of the recognizers and the correction filter had been written using Flex[5] rules; the remaining three were Perl scripts recognizing names in gazetteers. The Flex rules recognize regular expression matches in the input, corresponding to names and their possible context, and the actions of the rules mark the name parts of the matches with XML tags in the output. The correction filter modifies, removes and adds new tags based on existing ones.

Motivations for reimplementing the Swedish recognizer in Pmatch included the slow compilation of some of the Flex rule sets, which hindered testing changes to the rules, and a desire to be able to use a single tool or formalism for all the components of the recognizer.

---

[5] http://flex.sourceforge.net/

Since both Flex and Pmatch are based on regular expressions and recognizing the leftmost longest match, we were able to automate a large part of the conversion from Flex rules to Pmatch rules. The conversion script analysed the Flex actions to split the recognized match into a name and its context. The correction filter was converted by hand, since its rules were more varied than those in the recognizers.

However, because of differences between the semantics of Flex NER rules and Pmatch, some Pmatch expressions generated by the automatic conversion had to be edited by hand to work correctly. Firstly, the Flex rules were written so that the matched regular expression covered the contexts in addition to the name to be recognized, whereas Pmatch excludes contexts from its leftmost longest match. Consequently, the leftmost longest match at a certain point in text may be found by different patterns in Flex and Pmatch.

Secondly, Flex rules are ordered whereas Pmatch expressions are not. Flex patterns can thus be ordered from the most specific to the most general, so the most specific pattern is chosen even if also a more general one would have the same leftmost longest match. In contrast, Pmatch cannot guarantee any specific order, so the ordering has to be replaced with more detailed context conditions or with regular language subtraction or both. For example, to prevent capitalized *järnväg* ('railway') from matching a more general expression marking street names, it is subtracted from the more general pattern:

```
Define LocStrSwe
    [Capword2 "väg" ("en")] - "Järnväg" EndTag(EnamexLocStr) ;
```

With some modifications to account for the lack of ordering, the Pmatch rules were able to recognize and classify the same names as the original Flex rules. However, many rules would be more natural if written from scratch to utilize the features of Pmatch, such as more powerful context conditions. A "native" Pmatch implementation could probably have been written without a correction filter.

The Pmatch implementation of the gazetteer lookup uses the construct @txt"*filename*" that treats the named file as a disjunction of strings, each line as one disjunct. The gazetteer has been divided into files by the type of the name:

```
Define LocStr @txt"LocStr.txt" EndTag(EnamexLocStr) ;
Define PrsHum @txt"PrsHum.txt" EndTag(EnamexPrsHum) ;
...
Define Boundary [" " | #] ;
Define TOP [LocStr | PrsHum | ...] LC(Boundary) RC(Boundary) ;
```

The context conditions in TOP allow a name to be recognized only at word boundaries. The name lists could be replaced with full-fledged morphological analyzers allowing the recognition of inflected words or names.

The original Swedish NER system marks named entities with XML elements encoding the precise type in attributes. The tags used by Pmatch can be converted to this format with Pmatch transductions or with a simple script. For example, the Pmatch-tagged text

```
<EnamexOrgCrp>Computer Systems Corp</EnamexOrgCrp>
```

is converted to

```
<ENAMEX TYPE="ORG" SBT="CRP">Computer Systems Corp</ENAMEX>
```

Performance. Compiling the Pmatch version of the Swedish NER was about ten times faster on the average than the Flex version, which we consider as a significant improvement. On our test machine[6], the average compilation time of a single recognizer was reduced from 53 minutes to 5.5 minutes, and the slowest one from 288 minutes (almost five hours) to 54 minutes. We will also investigate further ways to improve compilation speed. In contrast, at run time the Pmatch NER recognizers were about three times slower on the average than the Flex ones.

The total size of the current Pmatch FSTs for the Swedish NER is over three gigabytes, which is about eight times as large as the executables compiled from the Flex files. However, the FST sizes will be reduced as soon as expression caching is implemented in Pmatch. Using a recursive transition network feature similar to Karttunen's [7] Ins() will further reduce the FSTs and their compile times.

2.6 Spell-Checking

Using weighted finite-state methods for spell-checking and correction is a relatively recent branch of study in spell-checking research. The concept is simple: finite-state morphological analyzers can easily be transformed into spell-checking dictionaries providing a language model for the correctly spelled words in the spell-checking system. A baseline finite-state model for correcting spelling errors can be inferred from the language model by creating a Levenshtein-Damerau automaton based on the alphabetic characters present in the language. The language model can be trained to prefer more common words when the Levenshtein-Damerau distance between two suggestions is the same. This is done with a unigram language model that maximizes the frequency of the suggested word. In our experience, even relatively moderate amounts of training material will improve the quality, as the statistical training improves the discriminative power of the model due to the observation that the likelihood of random typing errors is greater in more frequent words.

The practical process of creating a finite-state spell-checker and corrector is simple: given an analyzer capable of recognizing correctly spelled word-forms of a language, make a projection to the surface forms to create a single-tape automaton. The automaton is trained with a corpus word-form list, for which the final state weight of each word-form is, e.g., $-\log \frac{c(wf)}{CS}$, where $c(wf)$ is the word-form count and CS is the corpus size. Words not found in the corpus are given a maximal weight $w_{max} > -\log \frac{1}{CS}$ to push them to the end of the suggestion list; this weighting can be done, e.g., in finite-state algebra by composition with a weighted Σ^* language.

The error model can be improved from the baseline Levenshtein-Damerau distance metric as well. For this purpose we need an error corpus, i.e., a set of errors with their frequencies. This can be semi-automatically extracted from weakly annotated sources, such as Wikipedia. From Wikipedia we get, among other things, word-to-word corrections by inspecting the commit messages from Wikipedia's logs. It is possible to use the specific word-to-word corrections to create an extension of common confusables to the error model. Another way is to re-align the corrections using the Damerau-Levenshtein algorithm and train the original character distance measure with frequencies of the character corrections in the same manner as we did for word-forms above.

---

[6] The test machine had Intel Xeon X7560 processors running at 2.27 GHz.

The application of the language and error model to spell-checking is a traversal or composition with a finite-state transducer. The checking of the correct spelling is a composition $w \circ L$, where w is a single path automaton containing the word-form and L is a single-tape automaton recognizing the correct word-forms of a language. The spelling correction is $(w \circ E \circ L)_1$, where E is a two-tape automaton containing the error model, and $_1$ is a projection to the surface language.

As an example of the simplicity of this process, we obtained an open-source German morphological analyzer morphisto[7] to generate a spell-checker, trained it with word-forms extracted from the German Wikipedia[8] and applied it to Wikipedia data to find spelling errors and correct them. The whole script for this can be found in our version control[9], and it took us no more than one work day by one researcher to implement this application. The resulting system does spell-checking and correction with a baseline finite-state edit distance algorithm [17] applying up to 2 errors per word-form at a speed of 77,500 word-forms per second. For further evaluations on other language and error models, refer to [16].

3 Examples for User Environments

In this section, we provide some examples of how to implement applications on top of the HFST library using Python. The HFST library and its Python bindings are readily installable in all major operating systems.

3.1 An Interface in Python

In addition to an API library and command line tools, the HFST library can also be used through SWIG-generated Python bindings. The bindings are offered for the Python programming language versions 2 and 3. All HFST functionalities are available via both versions, but the Python interpreters themselves have some differences. For example, Python 2 allows HFST exceptions to be caught directly, but Python 3 requires the use of a special wrapper function written as a part of the bindings. On the other hand, Python 3 has better support for unicode characters, so it is probably a better choice for most linguistic applications.

Below is an example of iterating through the states and transitions of an HFST transducer using Python bindings:

```
# Go through all states in fsm
for state in fsm.states():
    # Go through all transitions
    for transition in fsm.transitions(state):
        # do something
```

---

[7] http://code.google.com/p/morphisto/

[8] http://de.wikipedia.org

[9] svn://svn.code.sf.net/p/hfst/code/trunk/articles/sfcm-2013-article

And the same using the HFST API directly:

```
// Go through all states in fsm
for (HfstBasicTransducer::const_iterator it = fsm.begin();
     it != fsm.end(); it++ )
  {
  // Go through all transitions
  for (HfstBasicTransducer::HfstTransitions::const_iterator tr_it
       = it->begin(); tr_it != it->end(); tr_it++)
     {
     // do something
     }
  }
```

The Python bindings in particular make it easy to use language models developed for HFST in rapid prototyping of advanced tools. For example, a chunker for Finnish was developed by simply bracketing adjacent agreeing cases and a few other similar expressions with a few lines of code on top of an existing morphological analyzer. For example, given the Finnish sentence "miljoona kärpästä voi olla väärässä paikassa", we get a bracketing of all three phrases as illustrated in the following sentence with a gloss:

(1) *Miljoona$_1$ kärpästä$_1$ voi$_2$ olla$_2$ väärässä$_3$ paikassa$_3$*
     million-NUM   fly-PAR   can-AUXV   be-INFV   wrong-INE   place-INE

     'A million flies can be in the wrong place'

In this case the rules governing chunking are all about pairs of words: a measurement phrase is a numeral followed by a partitive nominal, a verbal phrase is an auxiliary followed by a lexical verb and a noun phrase is an adjective and a noun in an agreeing case. The three pairs of words can be identified as common chunks in Finnish and having specific rules for these pairs will give a reasonable baseline surface syntax for applications where a more elaborate syntactic structure is not required.

A Chatroom Morphology Tool. One example of rapid development and leverage of language resources is an IRC bot performing morphological analysis and synthesis on command. Originally written as a source of entertainment for linguistics students, it is usable as a learning resource and discussion facilitator for language learners. It also proved useful as a testing environment; requested analyses that were not found in the transducers can be written to a log file.

The pertinent Python code for performing lookup on an appropriate transducer is as simple as:

```
with libhfst
    transducer = HfstTransducer(HfstInputStream("transducer.hfst"))
    results = transducer.lookup(message)
    for result in vectorize(results):
        irc_message(result)
```

For more than just providing analyses of words, either the underlying transducer or the bot can be customized to allow specific queries:

```
<user> hfstbot: kintereellä
<hfstbot> user: kinner<N><Sg><Ade>
<user> hfstbot: gen kinner<N><Pl><Nom>
<hfstbot> user: kintereet
```

In this case, the user wants to see the analysis for "kintereellä", which translates to "on the hock". Being informed that it is a singular noun in the adessive case, the base or nominative form of which is "kinner", the user asks for the plural nominative, which is "kintereet".

3.2 HFST on Unix, Mac and Windows

Portability has been one of the design goals of the HFST system. The current versions are available or compilable on all POSIX-supporting systems, including Cygwin under Windows, Mac OS X and Linux. Compilation is also possible on MinGW under Windows.

Fresh versions of HFST source code can be fetched from our Subversion repository at Sourceforge[10]. We also offer, approximately twice a month, new release packages that include a source tarball (compilable on all the aforementioned platforms), Debian binaries (for Linux), a MacPort distribution (for MacOS X) and an NSIS installer (for Windows).

3.3 Other Usability Improvements

Four new command line tools have been added since 2011. The most important are the native XFST parser hfst-xfst and the tagging tool hfst-tagger. Also two functions that were earlier available only through the API can now be used as command-line tools: hfst-shuffle and hfst-prune-alphabet. The former is a special operation that freely interleaves the symbols of any two strings recognized by the respective transducers. The latter removes symbols that do not occur in the transitions of the transducer from its alphabet. Two existing tools that perform transducer-to-text conversion also have new features: hfst-fst2txt can write to dot/graphviz and PCKIMMO format and hfst-fst2strings has a new parameter that controls its output to achieve better interoperability with other command-line tools.

There is some additional control over special symbols as we have added a parameter for binary operators controlling whether unknown and identity transitions are expanded, the default being true. We also have a new special symbol, the default symbol matching any symbol if no other transition in a given state matches.

We have kept the number of dependencies in HFST as low as possible. All backends (SFST, OpenFst and foma) are now bundled with HFST. There is no longer a need to install them separately or worry about having the right version. We have also made modifications to the back-end libraries; for instance, some of the compile-time

---

[10] http://hfst.sf.net

warnings are now fixed or suppressed. GNU- and Bash-specific commands were also removed from the scripts to make them more portable.

4   Under the Hood

In the following section, we describe some of the technical choices made to implement the HFST library and the applications addressed in the previous sections, as well as some minor design differences with regard to XFST.

4.1   An Independent XFST Module

The HFST command-line tools include an XFST parser tool that can be used in interactive mode or to compile script files. The tool implements the same functionalities as the original XFST (Xerox Finite-State Tool) which is a general-purpose utility for computing with finite-state networks. There are over 100 commands in hfst-xfst, the same as those documented in the Xerox tool. In addition, there is an option to independently use the regular expression parser which the hfst-xfst module was built on through the hfst-regexp2fst tool for those who wish to parse regular expressions in Bash scripts.

Below is an example of using hfst-xfst in interactive mode where we define two transducer variables, use them in a regular expression and print random words recognized by the expression.

```
$ hfst-xfst2fst
hfst[0]: define Foo foo;
hfst[0]: define Bar bar;
hfst[0]: regex [[Foo|0] baz [Bar|0]];
424 bytes. 4 states, 4 arcs, 4 paths
hfst[1]: print random-words
baz
bazbar
foobaz
foobazbar
hfst[1]:
```

To test hfst-xfst2fst, we have compiled 17 out of the 22 XFST exercises that are found on the homepage of Beesley and Karttunen's book Finite State Morphology[11]. We have omitted the exercises that do not include an answer. We have compiled the exercises using both Xerox's XFST and HFST's hfst-xfst and compared the results for equivalence. We have also tested the functionality of the hfst-regexp2fst tool by rewriting the original exercises using HFST command line tools (other than hfst-xfst).

Although we are aiming at complete backward compatibility with XFST, we have noticed that in some borderline cases the results may differ when using replace rules in regular expressions. One example in which XFST and hfst-xfst2fst may give different results is the longest match.

---

[11] http://www.fsmbook.com

By definition, in left-to-right longest match:

```
A @-> B || L _ R
```

where A, B, L and R denote languages, the expression A matches input left-to-right and replaces only the longest match at each step.

Therefore, a left-to-right longest match is supposed to give exactly one output string for each input string. However, when compiled using XFST, both of the following left-to-right longest match rules result in transducers which for input aabbaax give two outputs: aaxx and xxx.

```
xfst[0]: regex a+ b+ | b+ a+ @-> x \\ _ x ;
3.1 Kb. 8 states, 31 arcs, Circular.
xfst[1]: down aabbaax
aaxx
xxx
xfst[1]: regex a+ b+ | b+ a+ @-> x \/ _ x ;
3.1 Kb. 8 states, 31 arcs, Circular.
xfst[2]: down aabbaax
aaxx
xxx
```

In the examples, the \\ sign denotes that the left context L is to be matched on the input side of the relation and the right context R is to be matched on the output side of the relation. The \/ sign denotes that both contexts are to be matched on the output side of the relation.

The same regular expressions compiled with hfst-xfst2fst will for the same input give only one output xxx, which we consider to be the only correct result.

It is likely that, in this case, the difference is caused by different compilation approaches. In hfst-xfst2fst, replace rules are compiled using the preference operator [4], which in this case successfully finds that the output string aaxx is less preferable in comparison with the output string xxx and is therefore excluded from the final result.

Furthermore, we have noticed that there are some differences in pruning the alphabet after performing certain operations. These two examples will give the same transition graphs, but different alphabet sets if compiled with XFST:

```
regex [a | b | c ] & $[a | b] ;
resulting alphabet: a, b

regex [a | b | c ] & [a | b] ;
resulting alphabet: a, b, c
```

HFST's hfst-xfst2fst always prunes the alphabet after the following operations: **replace rules** (contexts are also pruned before being compiled with the rule), **complement, containments, intersection, minus**. However, it seems that XFST prunes the alphabet only if at least one of the operands contains the unknown symbol and if the result does not contain the any symbol. Therefore, if the above commands were run in the hfst-xfst2fst environment, the resulting alphabet is different from that of XFST, being a, b in both cases.

In HFST, the alphabet pruning only removes symbols from the alphabet if the pruning has no effect on the function of the transducer. Therefore, we have not managed to find an example in which the above difference influences the correctness of the result, but pruning the alphabet results in a slightly smaller transducer.

4.2 Pmatch with Applications for NER

At the 2011 SFCM conference, it was remarked that the Pmatch system presented in [7], while of obvious practical interest, lacked a free implementation and certain useful features, such as flag diacritics. The idea of implementing something similar for an existing FST library became apparent, and ultimately the HFST team became motivated to design a rule-based named-entity recognizer (NER) by first implementing a subset of Pmatch deemed necessary for that purpose. Beyond the tagging concept, runtime contexts, named subnetworks and various utilities were most crucial and were implemented as need arose.

An overview of the relevant features is presented in Section 2.5. Building on an existing Xerox-oriented regex parser API (in `libhfst`) and a runtime-oriented transducer format with support for flag diacritics (`hfst-optimized-lookup`, see [18] and [9]), the remaining requisites were:

1. A mechanism for naming and retrieving transducers during compilation.
2. A scheme of control symbols to direct the runtime operation of the matching.
3. Logic for compiling new features.
4. A runtime tool that particularly needs to deal with the non-FST or state-preserving aspects of Pmatch.

We will first overview the details of some features.

Named-Entity Tagging. A straightforward way to accomplish tagging at the beginning and end of matches of first, last and complete names might look like this:

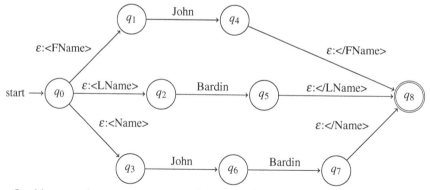

In this scenario, every new name is repeated in two places in the network. With large lists and multiple sources of this type of ambiguity, size inefficiencies can become serious.

One idea of Pmatch was to recognize the shared prefix in the first name "John" and the entire name "John Bardin" and to defer tag-writing until the entity has become unambiguous. In HFST, this is accomplished by detecting the tag directive during compilation and prefixing the subnetwork in question with an entry marker. After matching is complete, the entry marker is resolved in linear time with a simple position stack (in pseudocode):

```
for each symbol in result:
    if symbol == entry marker:
        push position into stack
    if symbol is end tag:
        insert corresponding start tag into position at stack top
        pop stack
        append end tag
    else:
        append symbol
```

With just the entry and end tags, the network simplifies to:

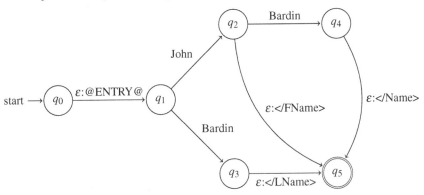

Contexts and States during Matching. Context markers trigger special runtime behavior and restrict progress during matching, very similarly to flag diacritics. There are two special considerations:

1. Left contexts are compiled to the left side of the network, in reverse (so that the first symbol to the left is at the end of the context).
2. Processing direction and position must be preserved during matching in a state stack.

Additionally, a stack for preserving the input tape position and the output tape content during each RTN (recursive transition network) invocation must be kept separately from the runtime context-checking stack. Otherwise, transition data is not duplicated, and these stacks are the only arbitrary amounts of memory reserved for accomplishing non-finite-state extensions.

Transduction. Each matching rule is by default compiled as an identity transduction. In many applications, however, it is useful to operate on input with some additional information, but give the output without such information. Matching is therefore not performed with automata, but with arbitrary transducers.

5   Future Work

The idea of combining linguistic rules and statistical models is intriguing but nontrivial. However, a pure finite-state left-to-right system is likely to be less efficient for syntactic parsing than a chart-based system, so the solution is probably to add linguistic constraints in the form of weighted finite-state constraints to a statistical parser before estimating the weights.

While existing statistical models like HMMs and PCFGs can incorporate a great deal of useful information for tasks like part-of-speech tagging and syntactic parsing, there are phenomena like non-local congruence which are too complex to estimate for these models. Probably because of this, there has been a growing interest in combining rule-based and statistical methods in core NLP tasks, such as part-of-speech tagging and syntactic parsing [11]. Such a combination presents challenges both for statistical estimation and inference methods and for the representation of linguistic information in a way which is compatible with a statistical system.

Finite-state transducers and automata can be used for expressing linguistically relevant phenomena for tagging and parsing as regular string sets. The validity of this approach is demonstrated by the success of parsing systems like Constraint Grammar [6], which utilizes finite-state constraints. Weighted machines offer the added benefit of expressing phenomena as fuzzy sets in a compact way. This makes them an excellent candidate for adding linguistic knowledge to statistical models.

6   Conclusion

The paper presented various NLP tools implemented with HFST and the minimal extensions they required to a pure finite-state system. In particular, the paper described an implementation of a full-scale named-entity recognizer for Swedish using Pmatch achieving a 10-fold compile-time speed-up compared with the original Flex implementation.

Acknowledgments. The research leading to these results has received funding from FIN-CLARIN, Langnet and the European Commission's 7th Framework Program under grant agreement n° 238405 (CLARA).

References

1. Bouma, G., Noord, G.V., Malouf, R.: Alpino: Wide-coverage computational analysis of Dutch. In: CLIN 2000, vol. 8, pp. 45–59. Rodopi (2000)
2. Brants, S., Dipper, S., Hansen, S., Lezius, W., Smith, G.: The TIGER treebank. In: Proceedings of the Workshop on Treebanks and Linguistic Theories. Sozopol (2002)
3. Cavnar, W.B., Trenkle, J.M.: N-gram-based text categorization. In: Proceedings of SDAIR 1994, 3rd Annual Symposium on Document Analysis and Information Retrieval, pp. 161–175 (1994)

4. Drobac, S., Silfverberg, M., Yli-Jyrä, A.: Implementation of replace rules using preference operator. In: Proceedings of the 10th International Workshop on Finite State Methods and Natural Language Processing, pp. 55–59. Association for Computational Linguistics, Donostia–San Sebastián (2012), http://www.aclweb.org/anthology/W12-6210

5. Einarsson, J.: Talbankens skriftspråkskonkordans. Lund University (1976)

6. Karlsson, F.: Constraint grammar as a framework for parsing running text. In: Karlgren, H. (ed.) Proceedings of the 13th Conference on Computational linguistics, COLING 1990, vol. 3, pp. 168–173. Association for Computational Linguistics, Stroudsburg (1990), http://dx.doi.org/10.3115/991146.991176

7. Karttunen, L.: Beyond morphology: Pattern matching with FST. In: Mahlow, C., Piotrowski, M. (eds.) SFCM 2011. CCIS, vol. 100, pp. 1–13. Springer, Heidelberg (2011)

8. Kokkinakis, D.: Swedish NER in the Nomen Nescio project. In: Holmboe, H. (ed.) Nordisk Sprogteknologi – Nordic Language Technology 2002, pp. 379–398. Museum Tusculanums Forlag, Copenhagen (2003)

9. Lindén, K., Axelson, E., Hardwick, S., Pirinen, T.A., Silfverberg, M.: HFST—framework for compiling and applying morphologies. In: Mahlow, C., Piotrowski, M. (eds.) SFCM 2011. CCIS, vol. 100, pp. 67–85. Springer, Heidelberg (2011)

10. Lindén, K., Pirinen, T.: Weighted finite-state morphological analysis of Finnish compounds. In: Jokinen, K., Bick, E. (eds.) Nodalida 2009. NEALT Proceedings, vol. 4 (2009), http://www.ling.helsinki.fi/~klinden/pubs/linden09dnodalida.pdf

11. Manning, C.D.: Part-of-speech tagging from 97% to 100%: Is it time for some linguistics? In: Gelbukh, A.F. (ed.) CICLing 2011, Part I. LNCS, vol. 6608, pp. 171–189. Springer, Heidelberg (2011)

12. Marcus, M.P., Santorini, B., Marcinkiewicz, M.A.: Building a large annotated corpus of English: The Penn Treebank. Computational Linguistics 19(2), 313–330 (1993)

13. McDonald, D.D.: Internal and external evidence in the identification and semantic categorization of proper names. In: Boguraev, B., Pustejovsky, J. (eds.) Corpus Processing for Lexical Acquisition, pp. 21–39. MIT Press, Cambridge (1996)

14. Nadeau, D., Sekine, S.: A survey of named entity recognition and classification. Lingvisticae Investigationes 30(1), 3–26 (2007)

15. Pirinen, T.: Suomen kielen äärellistilainen automaattinen morfologinen analyysi avoimen lähdekoodin menetelmin. Master's thesis, Helsingin yliopisto (2008), http://www.helsinki.fi/~tapirine/gradu/

16. Pirinen, T., Silfverberg, M., Lindén, K.: Improving finite-state spell-checker suggestions with part of speech n-grams. In: IJCLA (2012)

17. Pirinen, T.A., Lindén, K.: Finite-state spell-checking with weighted language and error models. In: Proceedings of the Seventh SaLTMiL Workshop on Creation and Use of Basic Lexical Resources for Less-Resourced Languagages, Valletta, Malta, pp. 13–18 (2010), http://siuc01.si.ehu.es/

18. Silfverberg, M., Lindén, K.: HFST runtime format—a compacted transducer format allowing for fast lookup. In: Watson, B., Courie, D., Cleophas, L., Rautenbach, P. (eds.) FSMNLP 2009 (July 13, 2009), http://www.ling.helsinki.fi/~klinden/pubs/fsmnlp2009runtime.pdf

19. Silfverberg, M., Lindén, K.: Combining statistical models for POS tagging using finite-state calculus. In: Nodalida 2011, Riga, Latvia (2011)

A System for Archivable Grammar Documentation

Michael Maxwell

University of Maryland, College Park MD 20742, USA
mmaxwell@umd.edu

Abstract. This paper describes a number of criteria for archivable documentation of grammars of natural languages, extending the work of Bird and Simons' "Seven dimensions of portability for language documentation and description." We then describe a system for writing and testing morphological and phonological grammars of languages, a system which satisfies most of these criteria (where it does not, we discuss plans to extend the system).

The core of this system is based on an XML schema which allows grammars to be written in a stable and linguistically-based formalism, a formalism which is independent of any particular parsing engine. This core system also includes a converter program, analogous to a programming language compiler, which translates grammars written in this format, plus a dictionary, into the programming language of a suitable parsing engine (currently the Stuttgart Finite State Tools). The paper describes some of the decisions which went into the design of the formalism; for example, the decision to aim for observational adequacy, rather than descriptive adequacy. We draw out the implications of this decision in several areas, particularly in the treatment of morphological reduplication.

We have used this system to produce formal grammars of Bangla, Urdu, Pashto, and Persian (Farsi), and we have derived parsers from those formal grammars. In the future we expect to implement similar grammars of other languages, including Dhivehi, Swahili, and Somali. In further work (briefly described in this paper), we have embedded formal grammars produced in this core system into traditional descriptive grammars of several of these languages. These descriptive grammars serve to document the formal grammars, and also provide automatically extractable test cases for the parser.

1 Introduction

I will take it as given that one of the goals in language documentation is to create descriptions which will be usable as long as possible—preferably for hundreds, if not thousands, of years. This paper discusses design criteria for computer-supported morphological analysis in support of that goal.

The earliest morphological parsers were written in ordinary programming languages for specific languages. Hankamer's *keçi* [10], for example, was written in the C programming language, primarily to parse Turkish.[1] One implication of this sort of design is software obsolesence; the knowledge about the grammar is encoded in a format

---

[1] Hankamer suggests that the program might be useful to parse other agglutinating languages, but as far as I can determine, it was never used in that way.

C. Mahlow and M. Piotrowski (Eds.): SFCM 2013, CCIS 380, pp. 72–91, 2013.
© Springer-Verlag Berlin Heidelberg 2013

(the C programming language) which is destined to some day be obsolete. Moreover, the language-specific linguistic aspects of the analysis are intermingled with language-general aspects (what a suffix is, for example), not to mention information which has nothing to do with linguistics, such as the way for-loops are encoded in the C programming language.

The use of language-independent parsing engines for morphological parsing was the first step beyond programs designed from the ground up for a particular language. Programs like AMPLE (developed by SIL in the 1980s: [26]) and the Xerox XFST finite state transducer [1], along with many other such tools provide language-general knowledge about many aspects of morphology and phonology. AMPLE, for example, allows one to build a database of allomorphs conditioned by phonological environments. XFST allows in addition the statement of various kinds of phonological alternations or processes, which can generate allomorphs from underlying forms.

Such language-independent parsing engines represent an important step towards linguistically motivated computational descriptions, in that they release the writer of a language description from the necessity of building programming tools to treat morphotactics, phonotactics, phonological environments, and phonological processes. This is a necessary step, but not a sufficient one. A further step is needed to ensure the longevity of those linguistic descriptions, so that they may be consulted by future generations of linguists, and used for morphological parsing long after any particular parsing engine is obsolete and unusable. This paper describes a framework with those characteristics: it supplies a linguistically based notation, one which will be familiar to most linguists; and the notation, being stated in XML, is stable and (as much as such a notation can be) self-documenting.

2   Criteria for Grammatical Descriptions

In this section I motivate criteria for archivable grammatical descriptions, and use these criteria to argue for a way of describing grammars which is computationally implementable and at the same time indepenent of any particular parser implementation. I begin with a seminal document in the language description literature, *Seven dimensions of portability for language documentation and description*.

2.1   Seven Pillars for Language Description

Bird and Simons [2] discuss the requirements for producing archivable descriptions of languages.[2] Among these requirements are the following:[3]

---

[2] Bird and Simons make a distinction between "documentation," that is primary language data such as recordings and transcriptions, as opposed to "description," that is a linguistic analysis of the primary language data. Since these terms are easily confused, I will use "description" in the same sense as Bird and Simons, to refer to the linguistic analysis, but "data" to refer to what Bird and Simons call documentation.

[3] I omit some of Bird and Simons' criteria which seem less relevant to the discussion here, namely *discovery, access, citation, and rights*.

1. Content: Among content-based requirements, Bird and Simons include:

   Accountability: By "accountability," they mean the ability to verify the description against actual language data.

   Terminology: The terminology used in a language's description should be defined, e.g., by pointing to standardized ontologies.

2. Format: This refers to the structure of the file in which the description is housed.

   Openness: Linguistic descriptions should use formats which conform to open standards.

   Encoding: Unicode is preferable.

   Markup: Bird and Simons call for plain text markup formats. They further argue that the markup should be descriptive, not presentational, with XML as the standard for such markup.

   Rendering: There needs to be a method to render linguistic documents in human-readable form.

3. Preservation: This desideratum refers to the need for linguistic descriptions to be archivable, as well as to be archived. Bird and Simons emphasize the need for *longevity*, that is, planning for the use of the resource for periods of decades (or, one may hope, centuries).

2.2   More on Pillars for Grammatical Descriptions

Bird and Simons are not explicit about the sorts of language descriptions for which these criteria are relevant, but they discuss textual descriptions of languages, annotated corpora, and lexical resources. It may not be at first glance clear how the above criteria apply to grammatical resources, and specifically to morphological descriptions. I will therefore elucidate in this section specific ways in which grammatical resources must be created if they are to support the general goals of *content, format,* and *preservation* which Bird and Simons outline. I will also discuss some additional criteria which are more specific to grammatical descriptions.

To begin, in order for a grammatical description to meet their criterion of accountability—the ability to validate a description against primary language data—it must be possible to test such a description on actual language data. While it may seem that this can be done by pure thinking (aided, perhaps, by pencil and paper), the last decades of computational linguistics have shown nothing if they have not demonstrated that grammatical descriptions are hard to debug. While this has long been clear in syntax, it has also become clear in morphology and phonology (e.g., [3,16,27,28]). These last two references describe problems arising in the interpretation of Newman's [22] description of Yokuts (= Yawelmani, or Yowlumne). As Weigel [27,28]) and Blevins [3] make clear, the misinterpretations have resulted in something of a disaster for theoretical phonology, in that fundamental claims in generative phonology turn out to have been supported by misunderstandings of Newman's work.

It is not the case that Newman's description was unintelligible or inherently faulty; no less a linguist than Zellig [12, p. 196] described it in glowing terms:

Newman's long-awaited Yokuts grammar is [...] a model contribution to descriptive linguistic method and data. It is written clearly and to the point, in a matter that is aesthetically elegant as well as scientifically satisfactory. It is sufficiently detailed [...] to enable the reader to become familiar with the language and to construct correctly his own statements about the language. Phonology and morphology are treated fully [...] students and workers in linguistics should read [this] with close attention to the method of handling descriptive and comparative data.

Nevertheless, Weigel [28] writes:

Newman's explanations and descriptive rules of Yokuts morphology are often not completely clear. Indeed, no less a linguist than Charles Hockett had to admit (in Hockett 1973) that he had misapplied some of Newman's rules in an earlier published piece (Hockett 1967).

One might ask why linguists mis-construe the output of grammars. Certainly complexity is one aspect; for any non-trivial grammar, it is difficult to think through all the implications of all the rules on all the lexical items and affixes. But there is another reason. One may view a grammar as the description of a piece of software. In this case, the "software" is originally implemented as "wetware," that is in people's brains; the task is to describe that program (or at least generate its outputs) clearly and unambiguously.[4] The problem of grammatical description is thus an issue of software documentation. And as is well known, verbal descriptions of software are inherently and nearly unavoidably ambiguous. Thus, in addition to the complexity of natural language grammars themselves, we have the ambiguity of their descriptions.

If then a model grammar such as Newman's can be so misinterpreted, what hope is there for the average grammar? The hope, I contend, is that we should use computers to help us validate and understand grammars. But it is obvious that computers cannot interpret descriptive grammars, written in English or any other natural language—computers are actually worse at this task than humans are. We therefore require computationally implementable and testable grammars. By implementing such a grammar, we can arrive at a description which can unambiguously answer the questions we put to it, such as "What is the complete paradigm of verb X?", a question which (as Weigel notes) is difficult to answer from Newman's description.

We thus arrive at the first of several criteria for adequate morphological descriptions:

Criterion 1. *A morphological (or more generally, grammatical) description must be computationally implementable.*

This criterion in support of Bird and Simon's pillar of *accountability* immediately raises questions. In particular, what description language should we use? Obvious candidates are the programming languages used by modern morphological parsing engines. But the problem with this answer should be clear from the plural suffix on "candidates":

---

[4] It is possibile that mental grammars are inherently "fuzzy," that is that there is no black-and-white grammar to be described. The same is true, only more so, of languages as they are spoken by communities, where questions of individual and dialectal variability arise. But I assume for this paper that there is some definite body of knowledge to be described, even if statements of variability must form a part of the description.

which one of the many parsing engines should we use as *the* standard? SIL's AMPLE has the longest history, however it is incapable of describing real phonological rules. The Xerox finite state transducer, XFST, was developed in the late 1990s as proprietary software, and can describe phonological rules.[5] Another finite state transducer is the Stuttgart SFST program [24].[6]

The problem is that while these programs are useful, and certainly capable of creating testable grammars, none represents a real standard.

Moreover, none of these programs' notations looks to a linguist quite like a linguistic notation. Linguists are used to thinking in terms of phonological representations, parts of speech, morphosyntactic feature systems, declension or conjugation classes, allomorphs and phonological rules, and perhaps exception features. While all of these constructs *can* be represented in most modern morphological parsing engines, the *appropriate* representation is not always clear. For example, how should allomorphs and their conditioning environments be represented? The answer is clear in AMPLE (indeed, this is the only way in AMPLE to represent allomorphy), but it is not at all clear for the finite state transducers.

This brings us to my second criterion for morphological description:

Criterion 2. *There must be obvious formalisms which make it easy to handle the phenomena required for linguistic analysis.*

Again, the question arises as to what kind of formalism should be provided. It is a slight exaggeration to say that for nearly any mechanism which has been used in languages descriptions, there are proposals from theoretical linguists to do away with that mechanism. Phonological rules, for example, have been disposed of in Optimality Theory approaches to phonology. So what *is* the appropriate linguistic theory that a morphological parsing framework should implement?

It is safe to say that there is no consensus among linguists as to the One True Theory of morphology or phonology. This is in part an indication of our ignorance; we don't know enough yet to choose among the possibilities, and indeed the correct theory may not have appeared yet. But it is also the case that the term "correct" is part of the problem. In fact, linguists have explored several possible meanings of this term, using the terms *Observational Adequacy, Descriptive Adequacy*, and *Explanatory Adequacy* [5]. A description of a language can be considered observationally adequate if it generates all and only the sentences of the language—or, if one's interests are confined to morphology and phonology, then it is capable of generating all and only the possible inflected word forms of the language.[7] A theory of linguistics would meet this standard if it allowed observationally adequate descriptions of the grammars (or of the morphology and phonology) of all languages.

---

[5] A free implementation with most of the functionality of XFST exists as the Foma program, see https://code.google.com/p/foma/.

[6] http://www.ims.uni-stuttgart.de/projekte/gramotron/SOFTWARE/SFST.html

[7] As compilers and users of corpora know, it is not clear that the set of all possible word forms of some language is a well-defined notion. Proper names, loan words in the process of being assimilated, and other boundary cases make this a dubious concept. For our purposes, however, I will assume that it is at least an approximation. Alternatively, one may conceive of a grammar which generates all and only the inflected forms of some static dictionary of words.

Given that for most languages, the number of inflected word forms is finite and (relatively) small, it would in principle be possible to create observationally adequate grammars by simply listing all the word forms. That is almost certainly not what humans do, at least not for languages which have any degree of inflectional or derivational morphology. The next step in Chomsky's hierarchy of adequacy is descriptive adequacy. The description of a language meets this standard if its analysis accounts for the intuitions that an adult native speaker has about the language; for example, that a *writer* is someone who *writes*, whereas a *grammar* does not mean someone who **gramms*. Determining those intuitions can be difficult; for example, it is not easy to know which inflected forms are memorized and which are derived by rule (or in some other way). Analogously, a descriptively adequate theory would allow descriptively adequate grammars to be written of all natural languages.

Finally, an explanatorily adequate *theory* would allow the selection from among candidate grammars of the correct descriptively adequate grammar.

As practiced by generative linguists, the science of linguistics is the search for an explanatorily adequate theory, based on descriptively adequate grammars. Until such a theory exists, and indeed until linguists have determined what a possible descriptively adequate grammar is, it would be inadvisable—not to mention impossible—to create a computational model for morphology and phonology which allowed for only descriptively adequate grammars. We simply don't know the range of possible variation, so trying to limit the range of what can be modeled could prevent the description of phenomena in some language. In other words, it is better to err on the side of excess descriptive power (potentially allowing the modeling of grammars which do not represent possible human languages) than on the side of insufficient power (thereby preventing the modeling of some languages).

An additional motivation for not attempting to attain the level of descriptive adequacy is that any such attempt would face a choice among several targets, all of which are moving. Not only are there multiple theories from which we could choose, but today's theories of morphology and phonology are not the same as those of ten or twenty years ago—and there is little reason to think that any theory in existence today will survive unaltered over the next ten or twenty years. Choosing one putatively descriptively adequate theory would therefore be very unlikely to result in a model which would stand the test of time.

In view of these facts, we have elected to create a model which gives observational adequacy only. The implications of limiting the scope in this way will become more apparent later, when I discuss the modeling of morphological reduplication; for now, I will state this point as the following criterion:

Criterion 3. *The model should allow for observational adequacy, not (necessarily) for the level of descriptive adequacy, even if this enables the description of grammars which may not correspond to any human language.*

Even if we did know what constituted a descriptively adequate grammar, our knowledge of the structure of a particular language at some point in time, while sufficient to describe that language's morphology to some satisfying level of detail, might be insufficient to create a descriptively or even observationally adequate grammar of the language. This is commonplace among field linguists, who wish to describe a language based on limited field data; but it may also be true of comparatively well-known languages, where crucial data may be missing due to defects in previous descriptions, data which is unavailable, insufficient corpora, etc. An example of this is the notion of defective paradigms. It is known that for some languages, one form or another in the paradigm of particular verbs may not exist for various reasons [8, 23]. But it is nearly impossible to distinguish this situation in a corpus (particularly in a corpus of the size most field linguists will have) from the situation where a form is accidentally missing from the corpus.

While missing (or incorrectly assuming) paradigm gaps may be a relatively minor problem, there are many other situations where it will not be clear which analysis captures the facts of a native speaker's grammar better, particularly in less documented languages. Moreover, there may be disagreement among linguists as to the correct description; for instance, whether semi-regular forms are to be captured by special allomorphs of the stem or affix, or by rules governed by exception features (see section 3.2), or even whether such forms are memorized as entire words: Halle and Mohanan [9] argue for a rule-based analysis of English past tense verbs like *wept, kept,* and *slept,* while most linguists would be happy to treat those as being listed in the mental lexicon as irregular forms.

The point here, however, is not that linguists may disagree, or that they may have insufficient evidence to decide particular cases; rather, a morphological parsing system intended for use by real linguists should not force them into an analysis that they are not comfortable with, or which the evidence does not support. If it does, it will not be used. This point may be summarized by the following criterion:

Criterion 4. *If there is disagreement among linguists about the correct analysis of a particular language, the model should, where possible, allow for alternative analyses.*

The need for allowing the modeling of alternative analyses also may arise in the course of grammar development. It is especially unclear at the beginning of analysis of a previously undocumented or under-documented language what the phonological rules are by which allomorphs are derived. Usually only after observing a number of allomorphs conditioned by similar phonological environments does the linguist realize that a generalization can be made, allowing the allomorphs of distinct morphemes to be derived by a single set of rules.

This brings us to another point about modeling grammars, having to do more with the development of grammars than with the model itself: the need for testing, visualization and debugging methods. As with software development, grammar development is a process. Generalizations which seemed clear initially may turn out to be incorrect, while some correct generalizations may not become clear until much later. Finding out where a derivation is going wrong requires the ability to test a sequence of rules individually.[8] I summarize this point as follows:

---

[8] I assume here a model in which phonological rules are applied in a linear sequence, or possibly cyclically. But the same point—the need to visualize the application of grammar components, and to tease out the interaction among such components—applies to other models as well, e.g., to Optimality Theory models.

Criterion 5. *A grammar development environment must allow linguists to easily see the effects of individual grammar rules or other components of the grammar.*

This same point is also true for the reader of the grammar: it should be possible to visualize the derivation of individual forms. Moreover, it will be helpful to the reader (and also to the writer) if the components of the grammar can be displayed in some familiar form. While XML is a suitable format for archiving and transmission of grammars and other structured data (addressing Bird and Simons' concern for preservation, in particular that the need for longevity of the data), it does not lend itself to easy editing or even comprehension. Anyone who has looked at an XML-tagged textual document, and at the same document as a formatted PDF, will surely agree. This suggests two criteria; the first refers to static views of the grammar, the second to the ability to edit the grammar:

Criterion 6. *A grammar must be visualizable in a format which is familiar to linguists.*

Criterion 7. *A grammar development environment must allow easy editing of components of the grammar, in some format which is likely to be familiar to a linguist.*

There are several final criteria which are of a more practical nature. The first of these is connected with the fact that linguist must sometimes deal with written forms which do not represent all the phonemic contrasts of the language, or—worse—may even omit certain phonemes entirely. Languages written in Arabic scripts, for example, frequently omit short vowels. In many Brahmi-based scripts, consonants are assumed to be followed by a default vowel, unless there is an overt vowel letter following, or there is a mark indicating that no vowel follows. In practice, however, the mark representing no vowel is frequently omitted, which makes for ambiguity in the text representation. In sum, orthographies are seldom ideal, but they are what corpora are written in, and a linguist looking to create a practical morphological parser must deal with them. At the same time, the linguist may wish to have a more principled analysis, one which corresponds more closely to the phonological facts of the spoken language. While one could simply write two formal grammars, one for the orthographic form and one for the linguist's phonemic form, the two are likely to be quite similar. Certainly morphosyntactic features of affixes will be identical, as will many other features. A practical grammar development system should therefore allow parts of the description to be tagged for particular writing scripts; parts of the description which are not so tagged will be assumed to apply to all scripts. I capture this requirement as follows:

Criterion 8. *A grammar formalism must allow a single grammar description to be used with multiple scripts, with those parts of the description which apply only to a particular script being tagged for that script.*

Similarly, languages may have dialects which share most features, but differ in small ways. Again, it would be undesirable to have to write separate grammars for each dialect; rather, it should be possible to tag the differences:

Criterion 9. *A grammar formalism must allow a single grammar description to be used with multiple dialects, with those parts of the description which apply only to a particular dialect being tagged for that dialect.*

Finally, it is important in language documentation that the grammar description not suffer obsolescence. While the use of open-source software as a parsing engine partially alleviates this problem, since one can presumably re-compile the source code in the future, it is not a complete answer. First, there is no guarantee that the source code of such a parsing engine *will* re-compile; programming languages change, and so do libraries that the parsing engine may require.[9] In principle, such problems could be overcome by running old versions of all the software; in practice, this solution is too complex for use.

A second issue with the use of open-source software for preventing obsolesence is that even this may not suffice for the long term. What will the computing landscape be in a hundred years, or five hundred? Imagine if we had to reconstruct programs which were written for Babbage's mechanical computers. It is safer to assume much less about what facilities will be available; and text (Unicode) data in plain text markup formats is far safer than untagged data in the programming langauge of a present-day parsing engine (cf. Bird and Simons' point about "Markup," specifically their calls for the use of plain text markup, as well as their point about "Openness," their term for the avoidance of proprietary formats). I represent this criterion as follows:

Criterion 10. *A plain text with markup representation of the grammar is to be preferred to a representation in the programming language of some particular software.*

While one could no doubt add criteria for grammatical modeling and the development of grammatical analyses, the above list will suffice for now. I will now describe a methodology which we have developed and are using, and how it satisfies these criteria.

3   Satisfying the Criteria for Grammatical Descriptions

At the University of Maryland, we have developed a technology which allows the statement of language-specific aspects of morphological and phonological descriptions in a transparent, parser-independent and linguistically motivated formalism. This technology has allowed us to satisfy many of the criteria outlined in the previous section. Planned extensions will further increase the ability to satisfy these criteria, but the existing system is robust enough to have been used for constructing descriptions from which (along with XML-based dictionaries) parsers for five languages have been built and tested automatically.

In broad overview, descriptions are written in an XML-based formal grammar format and validated against an XML schema. These descriptions are then read into a converter program, along with lexicons. The converter functions in a way analogous to a modern programming language compiler: it converts the XML-based description into a corresponding internal representation, which is in turn output in the form required by

---

[9] The author experienced this with a parser he wrote in the 1990s. The parser and its user interface was written in three programming languages: C, Prolog, and Smalltalk. Within one year, all three languages changed in ways which broke the parser. While changing the parts written in C would not have been difficult (it involved a change from 16 bit integers to 32 bit integers), the changes in Prolog (having to do with calling the C code from Prolog) were extensive, and the Smalltalk vendor went out of business, leaving only another vendor's incompatible version.

an external parsing engine (currently the Stuttgart Finite State Tools, SFST). Running the parsing engine's "compiler" over this output results in a form usable by the parsing engine for morphological analysis.

For three of the five languages that we have worked on, we have additionally employed Literate Programming [17]: we embed the formal grammar as XML fragments into an XML-based (DocBook, [25]) descriptive grammar. Each fragment appears in the text of the overall document next to the description of the grammar construction that the fragment instantiates, allowing the descriptive grammar to explain the formal grammar, while at the same time allowing the formal grammar to disambiguate the descriptive grammar where necessary. The fragments appear in an order which is useful for expository purposes; e.g., fragments having to do with nominal affixes appear in the nouns chapter, while fragments containing verbal suffixes appear in the verbs chapter. The fragments can be extracted by an XSLT transformation and placed in the correct order for computational processing in a file to be read by the converter program mentioned above.

In addition, the interlinear and in-line examples found in our descriptive grammars are extracted and used for parser testing. (Additional testing is done by running the parser over corpora.)

The use of Literate Programming and the extraction of examples from the descriptive grammar is discussed elsewhere [6, 19, 21]. The remainder of this document discusses the formal grammar and converter implementation, plus planned enhancements.

3.1   Formal Grammar Implementation

As mentioned above, the formal grammar of a language is a linguistically-based description of the morphology and phonology of that language, written in XML and validated against an XML schema. After briefly describing this schema, I show how this approach accomplishes most of the design goals outlined in the earlier sections of this paper.

The XML schema, to be documented in [20], organizes information about the grammar into five general categories:

1. Morphosyntactic Feature System
2. Grammatical Data
3. Morphological Data
4. Phonological Data
5. Lexical Data

The Morphosyntactic Feature System specification is slightly simplified from the model given in [4, 13, 15], and defines the possible morphosyntactic features including both simple features (e.g., binary features) and feature structures (features whose values consist of other features).

The Grammatical Data module supplies information about parts of speech (typically just those that accept affixes). This information includes which of the morphosyntactic features defined in the Feature System are possible for each part of speech. It also points to the affixes that each part of speech takes (these are defined in the Morphological Data module), and specifies their morphotactics.

The Morphological Data module defines the derivational and inflectional affixes of the language. They are defined here, rather than in the Grammatical Data module, so that they can be shared across parts of speech. For example, in Tzeltal (an ergative language of Mexico), transitive and intransitive verbs share absolutive agreement suffixes. If these two verb classes are defined as different parts of speech in the grammatical module, the shared absolutive suffixes can be defined once in the Morphological Data module, and used for both parts of speech.[10]

As will be discussed in greater detail below, the model allows for "ordinary" prefixes, suffixes and infixes; these may be defined either as underlying forms, with any allomorphs derived by phonological rules, or as allomorphs which appear in particular phonological environments. In addition, there is allowance for affixes defined as processes, that is, as morphological rules which may attach constant phonological material (as with ordinary affixes), but may also copy or delete parts of the base, and which can therefore model processes such as reduplication.[11] Allowing affixes to be represented as either a set of allomorphs, or as underlying representations with allomorphs derived by phonological rule, and allowing affixes to also be represented as processes, are two examples of the way the model allows for multiple analyses of a language's grammar (criterion 4).

In addition, the Morphological Data module allows for the definition of inflectional classes (declension and conjugation classes); since they are defined here, they can be shared by multiple parts of speech, as in Pashto, where nouns and adjectives have more or less similar declension classes. Finally, any "stem names" are defined in the Morphological Data module. These allow the implementation of irregular stems for certain lexemes, such as the diphthongized forms of Spanish verbs.[12]

The Phonological Data module defines the phonemes and/or graphemes of the language, boundary markers (used to delimit morpheme boundaries), and phonological rules. The latter come in three varieties: rules which change input phonemes (or graphemes) to other phonemes (graphemes); rules which epenthesize phonemes (or graphemes); and rules which delete phonemes (graphemes).

Notice that the model does *not* define phonological features. While the model could be extended to allow this (as well as the definition of phonological rules using such features), this omission is intentional. First, the nature of phonological features is still in doubt; it is not clear whether they are hierarchically structured, for example. Second, the use of phonological features in parsing would preclude the use of most present-day

---

[10] The ergative agreement prefixes on Tzeltal transitive verbs are homophonous with the possessive prefixes on nouns. Depending on how their morphosyntactic features are defined, it would also be possible to define these prefixes once in the Morphological Data module, and use them for both nouns and transitive verbs.

[11] This is discussed further below; however, this has not yet been implemented in the converter program.

[12] An alternative analysis would derive some or all irregular stems by phonological rules, probably conditioned on lexeme-specific rule exception features; this can also be modeled.

parsing engines. [13] In generative phonology, the principle use of phonological features is to define natural classes of phonemes, which are then used in the inputs and environments of phonological rules. Such a definition may be termed intensional. The approach taken in our model may be described as extensional: natural classes are instead defined by listing their member phonemes (or perhaps graphemes).

It is sometimes convenient to define natural classes, contexts (regular expressions over phonemes, graphemes and natural classes), and environments (the combined left and right context of some phonological process) once, and re-use these definitions for multiple rules or allomorph environments. These elements can therefore be defined in the Phonological Data module, and referred to where used (by their XML ID); but they may also be simply written out in rules or allomorph environments, which is convenient when such an element is needed only once.

As discussed above, the linguist must sometimes deal with scripts which differ in their ability to represent the phonology (criterion 8). The phonology module is frequently the locus of such differences; such differences are handled by tagging affected elements for the script for which they are relevant. Script-specific elements are therefore tagged with a 'script' attribute; they can then be included, or not, by removing or retaining them during a pre-processing stage, prior to their being read by the converter program. Dialect-specific elements are handled in the same way (cf. criterion 9).

The Lexical Data specification is derived from the ISO Lexical Markup Framework standard [14], supplying just the information about suppletive word forms and stem allomorphs required for morphological parsing. Words which require no special treatment (i.e., "regular" words) could be loaded in this module, but they are usually handled more quickly by pre-processing a dictionary into whatever form is required by the parsing engine, and them loading them into the parser directly, during the parser compilation phase.

Affixes as Processes. As discussed earlier, the goal of this framework is to attain the level of observational adequacy (cf. criterion 3). This is perhaps nowhere more apparent than in the treatment of affixes as processes, particularly reduplication. Reduplicative morphology in real languages ranges from complete reduplication, where an entire word is pronounced twice (used for a sort of pluralization in Bahasa Indonesian), to forms in which a single phoneme of the base is copied, perhaps augmented by some constant phoneme or sequence of phonemes (as was found in the perfect of some Ancient Greek verbs). Complications abound; for example, it is not unheard of for both the reduplicant and its correspondent in the base (the input to the reduplication process) to undergo some phonological process for which only one or the other is in the appropriate phonological environment.

Among theoretical linguists, it has become a cottage industry to develop theories which limit the possible forms of reduplication to all and only forms which are attested in languages of the world. In contrast, the model described here makes no attempt at limiting the power of reduplication; the formalism is sufficiently powerful allows almost anything to happen, even for the phonemes of a (fixed length) word to be reversed,

---

[13] One exception is the Hermit Crab parser, described in `http://www-01.sil.org/computing/hermitcrab/` . This parser was originally developed by the author in the 1990s, but it has been re-implemented more recently in SIL's FLEx tool.

something which has never been observed in real languages. That is, the formalism is observationally adequate, but probably not descriptively adequate.

The formalism is based on [18]. It involves matching an input word (the base) with a regular expression over phonemes, graphemes and natural classes. The output is formed by concatenating copies (possibly altered) of the parts of the base which matched the regular expression in some pre-defined order, possibly combined with other strings or phonemes.

An example may help; for ease of exposition, I will use a notational formalism, rather than the XML formalism.

Suppose we have a rule of reduplication which copies the first consonant (if any) of the base, adds the vowel 'e', and appends this to the base. Conceptually, we may capture this with the input regular expression '(C) X', where 'C' is assumed to have been defined as the natural class of consonants, 'X' is a variable matching any sequence, and the parentheses around the 'C' represent optionality. The content parts are implicitly numbered; the 'C' as part 1, the 'X' as part 2. The output may then be specified as '1 e 1 2'. Note that if the base is vowel-initial, the optionality of the '(C)' in the regular expression means that part 1 would be a null match, giving what is presumably the desired result.[14] Had the input regular expression been 'C X' (with the consonant obligatory), the rule would not match a vowel-initial base, meaning that this affix process would not apply to such a base.

In addition to copying part of the base to the output or adding specific strings (represented as phonemes, graphemes, and boundary markers), process affixes allow modification of input parts which are copied over. Suppose for example the grammar defines phonemes /p/, /pʰ/, /t/, /tʰ/, /k/ and /kʰ/, and suppose further that the output of the above process had been defined conceptually as

$$[1 \ (/p^h/{\rightarrow}/p/,/t^h/{\rightarrow}/t/,/k^h/{\rightarrow}/k/)] \ e \ 1 \ 2$$

where the square brackets are used here for grouping the phonological process of deaspiration with the output part to which the process applies. Applied to a base beginning with an aspirated consonant such as /phu/, this would give the reduplicated form /pe-phu/; applied to a base which began with an unaspirated consonant such as /grap/, the result would be /gegrap/.[15]

The use of this process affix formalism is not limited to rules of reduplication; it can also be used to describe the situation where an affix simply modifies its input, without copying or adding additional phonemes. For example, the following rule describes an

---

[14] The parsing of the base into the parts which correspond with the regular expression must prioritize contentful parts of the regular expression (like the part in the example which matches a consonant) over less contentful parts (like the variable matching any string), lest the output be ambiguous. One can imagine regular expressions which would remain ambiguous even under such prioritization, such as '(C)(C)X' matched against a base beginning with a single consonant followed by a vowel; presumably what would be intended in such a case would be '((C)C)X' or '(C(C))X'. Some error checking will therefore be required, to avoid such ambiguous regular expressions.

[15] This is known to linguists as Grassmann's Law, and the examples given are from Ancient Greek (ignoring vowel length for purposes of exposition).

affix formed by palatalizing the stem-final consonant, under the assumption that the phoneme inventory has been defined as including /p/, /p^y/, /t/, /t^y/, /k/ and /k^y/:[16]

```
X C
1 2 →
1 [2 (/p/→/pʸ/,/t/→/tʸ/,/k/→/kʸ/)]
```

We are now in a position to understand why this system achieves only the level of observational adequacy, not (probably) descriptive adequacy. Consider the following description of a putative process affix process ('C' and 'V' are assumed to have been defined as the natural classes of consonants and vowels respectively):

```
C V C C V C
1 2 3 4 5 6 →
6 5 4 3 2 1
```

This rule takes a six phoneme input and reverses it. It is highly unlikely that such a process exists in any human language, but it can be easily described in the notation used here (or in its XML equivalent). Most generative linguists would prefer a theory which disallowed (or at least made highly unlikely) statements of such nonexistent processes. The problem is that we don't have such a theory, but we still wish to be capable of writing grammars—which is wy we have settled for the level of observational adequacy; that is, we are content to describe *all* languages, but make no attempt to limit possible descriptions to *only* natural languages.[17]

3.2   Converter Implementation

This section describes how the converter takes as input a formal grammar stated in XML, and outputs the grammar in the form required by a parsing engine.

There are several reasons for using a formalism which requires a converter in order to be usable by a parsing engine, rather than a formalism which is directly interpretable by the parsing engine. First, criterion 2 in section 2.2 dictates that the formalism needed to handle linguistic structures should be (relatively) obvious. By constructing our linguistically based formalism in XML, we hope that the formal grammar mechanism will be more easily learned by most working linguists, and grammars written in that formalism will be more easily understood by linguists.

Another reason for using a formalism such as the one described here, rather than the programming language of some parsing engine, is to prevent the formal grammar from becoming obsolete when the parsing engine becomes obsolete, as it (like any software) inevitably will. This is another of the criteria given above (10), as well as helping answer Bird and Simons' points about "Markup" and "Openness."

---

[16] This rule is based on Oaxacan Mixe, as described by Dieterman [7, p. 39].

[17] It is at least possible that the explanation for the non-existence of processes reversing their input is due to factors other than the human language capability, e.g., the fact that such systems have no plausible diachronic source. The fact that certain reversals do occur in language games, e.g., the reversal of two consonants across a vowel, might be taken as such evidence. Thus, the search for a formalism which prevents such unattested processes might be misguided.

As discussed above, we are currently using the Stuttgart Finite State tools (SFST) as our parsing engine. Given that a formal grammar written in XML cannot be directly interpreted by SFST, there is a need for converting the XML representation into the representation required by SFST. In principle, this could be done using Extensible Stylesheet Language Transformations (XSLT). In practice, it has been easier to do the transformation in Python. The converter is written as an object-oriented program, where the classes correspond one-for-one to the elements defined in the XML schema. The conversion takes place in two phases. In the first phase (corresponding roughly to the "front end" of a modern programming language compiler), the XML representation is converted into the internal representation as Python objects. References from some objects to definitions made elsewhere (e.g., from natural classes to the phonemes they are composed of) are converted into pointers to the corresponding definitions (analogous to "object binding" in modern compilers). Most errors and warnings are issued at this stage.

In the second phase, corresponding to the "back end" in a modern compiler, the converter writes the parsing engine's code to output. Some optimization is done at this point, in the sense that the output code is optimized for "compilation" by the parsing engine.[18]

Since the first phase maps between two fairly congruent representations, it makes use of a mostly declarative format for the individual classes; most of the non-declarative code for converting from XML to the internal format is contained in an abstract superclass.

The second phase, however, can be more complex, since it maps between two representations which at times diverge strongly. Where these representations are similar, the conversion is fairly straightforward. Consider for example the following code:

```
def SFSTOutput(self, sFormat, ExtraArg=None):
    """

    Output this context in the form expected by SFST, i.e.,
    ( X | Y | Z )
    """

    if sFormat == 'AsRegex':
        self.SFSTOutputList("PhonologicalContexts",
                            "(",
                            "|",
                            ")",
                            sFormat)
    else:
        AbstractClasses.LangClass.SFSTOutput(sFormat, ExtraArg)
```

This SFSTOutput() function is defined for the class AlternativeContexts, which encodes a set of alternative phonological contexts forming part of the

---

[18] There is no attempt to ensure that the final transducer as compiled by the parsing engine will be optimal, e.g., by tweaking the alignment of lexical and surface sides of lexical items. This might have significant effects if the citation form of lexemes includes a prefix, which is removed to form the stem.

environment of a phonological rule (or a phonologically determined allomorph); for example, the context of a long vowel or a vowel plus consonant. The function is called with an argument list specifying a format (and an optional extra argument). The only format this particular function knows about is called 'AsRegex'; any other format is referred by the 'else' clause to the superclass of AlternativeContexts, here AbstractClasses.LangClass. For this 'AsRegex' format, the function needs to output the alternatives in the format which SFST expects for a regular expression, namely a parenthesized list with list members separated by the character '|'. Since outputting of lists with various delimiters is a common task in the converter, the details of outputting the list (such as the need to output the separator character after every member of the list except the last) is here delegated to a more generic function, SFSTOutputList(), which takes as additional arguments the character which starts the list (here an open parenthesis), the separator character ('|'), and the character which marks the end of the list (a close parenthesis).

The XML elements which constitute the alternatives (represented by X, Y and Z in the quoted comment) will be recursively output by SFSTOutput() functions defined on whatever classes these individual contexts belong to. This is the general pattern for how the SFSTOutput() function is written on all classes: there may be several cases, depending on the purpose for which the element is being output (although here there is only one case, the 'AsRegex' case). Within each such case, the class specifies some of the output (here, the open and close parentheses, and the pipe symbol '|'), while the output of elements which may be contained by an element of the specified class are delegated to those classes (here, the classes of the embedded contexts).

A more complex conversion is needed for other constructs. The code for converting Affix Allomorphs, for example, has four cases. One of these cases constrains the allomorph to appear in its required environment. This requires outputting the allomorph itself, as well as calling the environment class to output the phonological environment, in essence creating a rule which blocks the allomorph if this environment is not satisfied. The mechanism for accomplishing this is that all allomorphs are initially inserted in the transducer bracketed by marks which would block a derivation containing them from appearing at the end of the derivation. The marks are erased for allomorphs whose environment is satisfied; finally, any words still containing marks are removed from the network. This is precisely the sort of non-obvious solution that is one of our motivations for the use of a linguistically informed formalism, which must be automatically converted into the parsing engine's formalism.

Another example of a non-obvious solution concerns rule exception features. These are lexical features (that is, features assigned to particular roots or stems in the lexicon) which either trigger the application of particular rules (positive exception features) or prevent the application of certain rules (negative exception features). Consider for example diphthongization in Spanish verb paradigms. For a certain set of verbs (those which had a long stem vowel in Latin), the vowel /e/ diphthongizes to /ye/ (spelled 'ie') when stressed, while the vowel /o/ diphthongizes to /we/ (spelled 'ue') when stressed.[19] There is no phonological indication of which verbs undergo this rule and which do not;

---

[19] There are exceptions to this generalization, chiefly where an 'n' becomes an 'ng', for example: tiene "he/she has", tengo "I have", both with stress on the first syllable.

hence this information must be stored in the lexicon, either in the form of listed allomorphs, or—for a rule-governed analysis—in the form of positive exception features. Thus, contar~ cuento "to count/ I count" (a diphthongizing verb) vs. montar~ monto "to mount/ I mount" (a non-diphthongizing verb).

Linguists often conceive of such exception features as being part of the phonological material, and therefore visible to the phonological rules which may require them. The obvious solution would then be to assign such features to the "surface" side of the transducer representing the word of the language, and to apply phonological rules on this side so that rules which need to refer to exception features can "see" them. However, exception features must be invisible to phonological rules which do not require them, since the features might otherwise appear to be phonemes, and such rules would therefore not match the lexical entries containing these phoneme-like exception features.

The problem is that phonologists really conceive of words not as strings composed of sequences of phonemes and exception features, but rather as sequences of phonological features representing such properties as voicing, nasalization, and place and manner of articulation, with each such feature on a different plane;[20] exception features are on yet other planes. The voice features of two adjacent phonemes are therefore adjacent on the voice plane, regardless of any exception features, so that the problem that adjacency between phonological features would be blocked by exception features or other phonological features is avoided.

But practical finite state transducers, such as XFST and SFST, have only two planes (or levels): a lexical side and a surface side. In such a model, exception features on the surface side would block adjacency between phonological features as seen by phonological rules composed on that side (indeed, distinct phonological features would get in each other's way, if they were to be represented in such transducers).

There are several ways that this issue of adjacency could be treated in a transducer with only two levels. One way would be to construct phonological rules such that exception features (and other grammatical information relevant to rule application) are allowed to intervene between any two phonemes in the regular expressions representing the rule environments. While tools such as SFST allow rules to be constructed in this way, in practice it tends to make compilation very inefficient. Our converter therefore handles exception features in a different way, which may be less obvious at first sight. When lexical entries are imported from a machine-readable dictionary, the conversion process constrains any exception features to appear on the lexical side of lexical entries.[21] At the beginning of the derivation, the converter collects these lexical entries into a lexical transducer L, to which the phonological rules are applied in sequence by composing each rule on the surface side of L. When translating a rule which is sensitive to an exception feature, the converter first outputs SFST code which composes a filter on the lexical (underlying) side of L, thereby selecting a subset $L1$. This filter is a regular expression accepting all paths through the lexical transducer which contain the relevant exception feature. The converter also outputs SFST code to create the complement of

---

[20] I abstract away here from questions of the typology of features, which are generally held to have still more structure than what is described here.

[21] A given lexical entry may have several such exception features; see for instance Harris's [11] analysis of Spanish verbal morphology.

this subset—call this *L2*—by subtracting *L1* from *L*.[22] The sensitive rule is then applied to *L1* by composing the rule on the surface side of *L1*. Finally, *L1* and *L2* are unioned to form a new lexical transducer *L*, to which the remaining phonological rules will be applied. At the end of the derivation, when the exception features have done their work, they are removed from the underlying side of *L*.

Linguists also occasionally find the need to write phonological rules which are sensitive to particular parts of speech, or to certain morphosyntactic features. Allowing this sensitivity can be done in a way analogous to that used for rule exception features: splitting the lexicon into two halves allows for rules which do not display such sensitivity (usually the vast majority of such rules) to implicitly ignore the part of speech or morphosyntactic features.

3.3   Further Work

The description of the work we have done thus far leaves several of the criteria for a morphological and phonological description system unsatisfied. In particular, the criterion that there be a debuggging environment (5); that the formal grammar be in a form that is easily visualized by linguists (cf. Bird and Simons' point about rendering linguistic documents in human-readable form, and my criterion 6 that the grammar be visualizable); and the criterion calling for a grammar editing environment (7), have not been addressed, unless one considers viewing and editing XML to be something the average linguist will enjoy, and that editing the SFST code is a suitable means of debugging.

In addition, while the XML schema supports all the elements described above, not all such elements are supported by the converter as yet. In particular, the support for affixes as processes is missing, and the support of listed stem allomorphs is not complete. We plan to address these shortcomings in future work; I outline the plans here.

First, conversion support for the remaining elements needs to be added.

Secondly, when a descriptive grammar (which we write using a slightly modified version of the DocBook XML schema) is converted to PDF presently, the formal grammar is output in its native XML form. Needless to say, linguists have a hard time interpreting this. For instance, rather than outputting a phonological rule as some complex XML structure, most linguists would prefer to see it in something like this format:

$z \rightarrow s$ / VoicelessC ___

We produce the descriptive grammars by converting the XML source into LaTeX (or more precisely, XeLaTeX), and then producing a PDF from that. The conversion from XML to LaTeX format is done by XSLT transformations, using the `dblatex` program.[23] We therefore need to add XSLT transformations to convert our formal grammars into LaTeX format; alternatively, we could process them using another program (such as our existing Python-based converter).

A grammar development environment which knows what elements are possible at any point would also be an improvement over editing the XML formal grammar in a programmer's editor. Displaying the elements of the formal grammar in something like

---

[22] Alternatively, by composing the converse of the filter on the underlying side of *L*.

[23] The dblatex program is open source; see `http://dblatex.sourceforge.net`

the format a linguist expects (probably an approximation of the planned PDF format) would also help make grammar editing accessible to more linguists. We currently edit the DocBook descriptive grammars in the XMLMind editor.[24] This program uses Cascading Style Sheets (css) to display DocBook structures in a semi-wysiwyg editable fashion, and XML schemas (in the Relax NG, or RNG, format), to determine what elements can be added at any place in the structure. We already have an RNG schema for our formal grammar, so the remaining work would be to specify CSS styles for the elements.

Thirdly, we intend to build a grammar debugging environment, which will allow linguists to generate and view paradigms, and help determine why expected forms are not being produced. This will involve automatically compiling subsets of the grammar—e.g., compiling the grammar for a single part of speech, using a single lexical item for the sake of speed. To show the steps in a derivation, the debugging system would compile the transducer multiple times, with one additional phonological rule applied each time.

Finally, I have not said anything about Bird and Simon's call for linguistic descriptions to support the need for terminology to be defined. To some extent, this can be done in the descriptive grammars associated with our formal XML-based grammars. However, we also plan to add a simple enhancement to our current XML schema for tagging appropriate elements, such as morphosyntactic features, by linking to their definition, e.g., in the ISOcat data category registry of linguistic terminology (http://www.isocat.org/).

4   Conclusion

I have laid out a number of design critera for a morphological and phonological system to be used in language documentation, and shown how the system our team has developed satisfies most of those criteria. I have also described how we plan to further develop this system to satisfy the remaining criteria.

A few aspects of the system are still in flux; specifically, the representation and conversion of lexically listed stem allomorphs, and the conversion of process affixation into the form needed by a parsing engine. Satisfying the remaining design criteria—for example, by providing a debugging system—would make the system still more usable. As the system becomes stable and more usable, we expect to make it freely available through an open source license (which one is yet to be determined).

References

1. Beesley, K.R., Karttunen, L.: Finite State Morphology. University of Chicago Press, Chicago (2003)
2. Bird, S., Simons, G.: Seven dimensions of portability for language documentation and description. Language 79(3), 557–582 (2003)
3. Blevins, J.: A reconsideration of Yokuts vowels. International Journal of American Linguistics 70(1), 33–51 (2004)

---

[24] This is a commercial program; see http://www.xmlmind.com/xmleditor. A similar program is the oXygen XML Editor, see www.oxygenxml.com.

4. Burnard, L., Bauman, S.: TEI P5: Guidelines for electronic text encoding and interchange (2013)
5. Chomsky, N.: Aspects of the Theory of Syntax. MIT Press, Cambridge (1965)
6. David, A., Maxwell, M.: Joint grammar development by linguists and computer scientists. In: IJCNLP, pp. 27–34. The Association for Computer Linguistics (2008)
7. Dieterman, J.I.: Secondary palatalization in Isthmus Mixe: a phonetic and phonological account. SIL International, Dallas (2008),
   http://www.sil.org/silepubs/Pubs/50951/
   50951_DietermanJ_Mixe_Palatalization.pdf
8. Halle, M.: Prolegomena to a theory of word formation. Linguistic Inquiry 4, 3–16 (1973)
9. Halle, M., Mohanan, K.P.: Segmental phonology of modern english. Linguistic Inquiry 16(1), 57–116 (1985)
10. Hankamer, J.: Finite state morphology and left to right phonology. In: Proceedings of the Fifth West Coast Conference on Formal Linguistics. pp. 29–34 (1986)
11. Harris, J.W.: Two theories of non-automatic morphophonological alternations. Language: Journal of the Linguistic Society of America 54, 41–60 (1978)
12. Harris, Z.: Yokuts structure and Newman's grammar. International Journal of American Linguistics 10, 196–211 (1944)
13. ISO TC37: Language resource management — Feature structures — Part 1: Feature structure representation (2006)
14. ISO TC37: Language resource management — Lexical markup framework, LMF (2008)
15. ISO TC37: Language resource management — Feature structures — Part 2: Feature system declaration (2011)
16. Karttunen, L.: The insufficiency of paper-and-pencil linguistics: the case of Finnish prosody. In: Kaplan, R.M., Butt, M., Dalrymple, M., King, T.H. (eds.) Intelligent Linguistic Architectures: Variations on Themes, pp. 287–300. CSLI Publications, Stanford (2006)
17. Knuth, D.E.: Literate Programming. Center for the Study of Language and Information, Stanford (1992)
18. Marantz, A.: Re reduplication. Linguistic Inquiry 13, 435–482 (1982)
19. Maxwell, M.: Electronic grammars and reproducible research. In: Nordoff, S., Poggeman, K.-L.G. (eds.) Electronic Grammaticography, pp. 207–235. University of Hawaii Press (2012)
20. Maxwell, M.: A Grammar Formalism for Computational Morphology (forthcoming)
21. Maxwell, M., David, A.: Interoperable grammars. In: Webster, J., Ide, N., Fang, A.C. (eds.) First International Conference on Global Interoperability for Language Resources (ICGL 2008), Hong Kong, pp. 155–162 (2008), http://hdl.handle.net/1903/11611
22. Newman, S.: The Yokuts Language of California. Viking Fund, New York (1944)
23. Rice, C., Blaho, S. (eds.): Modeling ungrammaticality in Optimality Theory. Advances in Optimality Theory. Equinox Press, London (2009)
24. Schmid, H.: A programming language for finite state transducers. In: Yli-Jyrä, A., Karttunen, L., Karhumäki, J. (eds.) FSMNLP 2005. LNCS (LNAI), vol. 4002, pp. 308–309. Springer, Heidelberg (2006)
25. Walsh, N.: DocBook 5: The Definitive Guide. O'Reilly, Sebastopol, California (2011), http://www.docbook.org/
26. Weber, D.J., Black, H.A., McConnel, S.R.: AMPLE: A Tool for Exploring Morphology. Summer Institute of Linguistics, Dallas (1988)
27. Weigel, W.F.: The interaction of theory and description: The yokuts canon. Talk Presented at the Annual Meeting of the Society for the Study of the Indigenous Languages of the Americas (2002)
28. Weigel, W.F.: Yowlumne in the Twentieth Century. Ph.D. thesis, University of California, Berkeley (2005)

A Rule-Based Morphosemantic Analyzer for French for a Fine-Grained Semantic Annotation of Texts

Fiammetta Namer

UMR 7118 ATILF - CNRS & Université de Lorraine, Nancy, France
fiammetta.namer@univ-lorraine.fr

Abstract. We describe DériF, a rule-based morphosemantic analyzer developed for French. Unlike existing word segmentation tools, DériF provides derived and compound words with various sorts of semantic information: (1) a definition, computed from both the base meaning and the specificities of the morphological rule; (2) lexical-semantic features, inferred from general linguistic properties of derivation rules; (3) lexical relations (synonymy, (co-)hyponymy) with other, morphologically unrelated, words belonging to the same analyzed corpus.

Keywords: NLP, morphosemantic approach, rule-based, French, derivation, neoclassical compounding, lexical-semantic feature, neologism, automatic definition, synonymy, hyponymy, co-hyponymy.

1 Introduction

In the domain of morphology, Word Formation (WF) is the branch that studies the process or result of forming new words. When it comes to computational morphology, the question becomes that of generating or analyzing unknown - and thus, new- morphologically complex words. We are interested here in morphological analysis. Usually, morphological analyzers aim to decompose complex words in order to isolate their stems and affixes; word decomposition may also result in their classification, where they are grouped in families (when they share a common stem), or in series (when they start or end with the same affix).

In this paper, we want to describe a morphological analyzer the main purpose of which is not only that of decomposing (new) words according to bases and affixes, but also and most importantly, that of providing them with a morphologically-driven semantic description. The original purpose of this analyzer emerges form the following observation: most of state-of-the-art computational morphology tools are assessed according to to their ability to process existing words, as evidenced in the many competition campaigns in this field (e.g. MorphoChallenge). However, these tools are not assessed according to their robustness with respect to the issue of the linguistic meaning of (new) complex words, even though it plays a key-role in the development of semantic lexica. This is precisely what DériF, the morphological analyzer presented here, is designed for. This tools has been developed for French, it has been partially

C. Mahlow and M. Piotrowski (Eds.): SFCM 2013, CCIS 380, pp. 92–114, 2013.
© Springer-Verlag Berlin Heidelberg 2013

extended for English, and its fundamental working principles result from the adaptation of linguistic knowledge belonging to the so-called Word-Based Morphology framework (for an outline, see e.g., [1]). Once shown the originality of DériF' results, with respect to other up-to-date morphological parsing systems, we will come back briefly to its disadvantages, intrinsic to its design, and the way they can be corrected.

The paper is structured as follows. First we present the context in which DériF was developed, with respect to past and current related works in the field of morphological parsing (§2), then we give an outline of DériF's fundamental mechanisms and results (§3). Next, we present in detail two of its original aspects: an annotation system, assigning semantic features to general language derived words and their base (§4.1), and a predicting module, providing medical domain language compound words with synonymy and (co-)hyponymy relationships with other, morphologically unrelated, compound words (§4.2). The paper ends with a summary of the main advantages and drawbacks of DériF, as well as its most recent improvements (use of notations pertaining to formal logic to encode semantic relationships, and creation of an hybrid morphological analyzer by merging DériF with an analogy-based system) (§5).

2 Related Work

Morphological parsing is a crucial task in the NLP chain, and morphological resources serve several purposes: build (multilingual) lexicographic data [2] or large-scale lexica [3, 4], optimize question-answering [5] or expand queries in IR applications (for an overview, [6]). Morphological parsers are often distinguished according to the implication of human knowledge: un- or supervised learning techniques are opposed to rule-based approaches.

Unsupervised morphological parsing systems allow performing language-independent morphological analyses. Several algorithms have been developed to achieve this goal. As [7] points out, unsupervised morphological parsing involves two tasks: "(1) a morpheme induction step in which morphemes are first automatically acquired from a vocabulary consisting of words taken from a large, un-annotated corpus, and (2) a segmentation step in which a given word is segmented based on these induced morphemes". A high-performance tool parser, then, must be able to induce morphemes correctly without prior linguistic knowledge. This has been successfully achieved for several European languages (e.g. [8, 9]).

Gradually stepping away from unsupervised systems, other language-independent morphological parsers are based on **semi-supervised methods**. Like unsupervised ones, they do not rely on linguistic knowledge, but on the other hand, a human expert is made available to provide supervision on specific tasks. For instance, [10] and [11] make use of semi-supervised technique to discover morphological relations within medical corpora; and [12] developed an algorithm for automatic lexical acquisition relying on statistical techniques applied on raw corpora, and whose results are manually assessed.

Finally, **supervised learning tools** require annotated data for their training task, as described, for instance, in [13], which is devoted to inflection phenomena of non-concatenative languages.

In short, when based on **machine learning** techniques, morphology analysis tools train on real (annotated or raw) data in order to automatically decompose words into their constituents by learning the rules for representing permissible sequences of word constituents and the rules that change the orthographic shape of the constituents. Machine-learning approaches to morphological parsing are optimal candidates to the many competitions (TREC, CLEF, MorphoChallenge, SIGMORPHON) aiming to rank tools according to their performances with respect to parsing efficiency, and to precision and recall measures (for a recent comparison of evaluation methods in these competitions, see e.g., [14]). These systems are primarily intended to decompose words into prefixes, suffixes and roots. Therefore, best results are achieved on morphologically poor languages, as well as on agglutinative ones. However, thanks to improvements such as analogical learning [15] good results are achieved with both inflectional and non-concatenative languages. Making use of analogy-based devices, [16] proposes a morphological resource for French, resulting from a paradigmatic conception of derivational morphology, while [17] develop an analogy-based algorithm to expand queries in IR.

As opposed to the previous ones, **rule-based systems** necessarily involve linguistic knowledge, and, consequently, are often (at least partly) language–dependent devices. According to the nature and the complexity of the required knowledge, rule-based systems go from stemmers [18] to morphosemantic analysis tools. As [5] points out, *stemmers*, consisting in stripping away affixes from a word until an indecomposable stem is obtained, are particularly suitable for IR (see e.g., [19]) especially for languages with clear morpheme boundaries. *Finite state transducers* [20] are network-based techniques, which rely on a deeper level of linguistic knowledge. Therefore, unlike stemmers, they are capable of accounting for irregular inflected or derived forms. Extensions have been proposed for the description of non-affixal morphology: for instance, template morphology, which is typical of Semitic languages such as Hebrew [21] or reduplication, a morphological construction observed in almost every languages of the world (e.g., the stemmer described in [22] deals with an Asian language).

For some rule-based tools, their segmentation task is completed by a semantic annotation of word constituents; we call such devices *morphosemantic approaches*. Usually, these tools have a finite-state algorithm base, with deep modifications in order to account for (sub-)lexical semantic knowledge. Most of the time, morphosemantic approaches are language-dependent and designed for specialized languages (medicine, biology), especially in the fields of information extraction and text mining (e.g., [23, 24]), sometimes from a multilingual perspective [25, 26]. Some morphosemantic tools applied to biomedical corpora provide in addition a definition to morphologically complex words [27, 28]. We will come back later on the results to these applications.

To sum up, there are various morphology parser types, and all aim to segment words into smaller parts in order to recognize and link them together when they share the same root. Such systems are either rule-based or machine learning based. Some are language independent, while others are not. But none of them is primarily interested in the semantic content of morphologically complex words, with a few exceptions, e.g., [10, 11, 29, 30]. As far as morphosemantic approaches are concerned, they certainly use semantic knowledge, but none of them do make use of this knowledge to compute additional semantic information (e.g., the meaning of neologisms). However, morphosemantic information proves to be useful. For instance [31] has measured how significant WorldNet improvement is in text understanding after its extension with morphosemantic relations.

The main purpose of DériF ("Dérivation en Français"), the parser presented below, is precisely to annotate corpora with semantic knowledge. This knowledge is predicted from the linguistic content of word formation rules that are used to segment derivatives and compounds. Thus, DériF is able to guess the meaning of unknown words. Following similar linguistic principles, DériF predicts the semantic and syntactic features of words from their morphological relationship. Finally, when applied on a medical lexicon, it can be used to infer lexical relationships between morphologically unrelated compounds words.

3   Description of DériF

DériF's first development dates back to 1999 [32], and some key-aspects of its evolution are given in [33]. This system[1] is a rule-based, morphological parser for French complex (i.e., derived and compound) words. This linguistically-motivated tool implements a word-based framework to Word Formation, where, basically, affixes are not lexical components, but rule markers, and where a rule application takes the form of a relation between two words (for a detailed comparison of Word-based versus Morpheme-based approaches to morphology, see e.g., [1]). The reason why DériF does not implement and/or extend a stemming algorithm, and adapts linguistic constraints instead is based upon two facts:

- **Typological Adequacy:** English is largely used to experiment stemming algorithms. On top of the many reasons of this (besides the supremacy of this language) is the place of English in the morphological typology continuum. According to the literature (see e.g., [34]) morphological typology involves two parameters. The first one is based on the transparency of morphological boundaries between the constituents of a word, and the second one relates to the degree of internal complexity of words. As shown in Figure 1, borrowed from [35], p.8, languages are ranked from analytic to polysynthetic when the dimension under consideration is that of word complexity, whereas the way stem-affixes boundaries are realized allows to divide them according to the isolating/agglutinating/fusional tripartition.

---

[1] DériF is distributed free of charge for research purposes; an online version is available at the URL: www.cnrtl.fr/outils/DeriF/

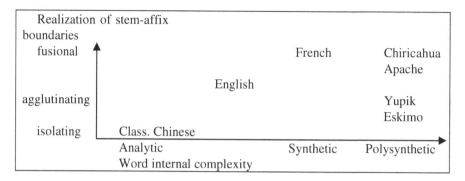

Fig. 1. Two-Dimension Classification of Languages

Languages classification results from the integration of these two parameters. So, English morphology, like that of European languages in general, is predominantly synthetic, and makes use of rather agglutinating techniques in word formation. On the other hand, French belongs to the group of both synthetic- and fusional-morphology world's languages, with Italian, Russian, or Spanish. Namely, stem-affix boundaries are the scene of many kinds of formal variations (1): vowel alternation (a), epenthesis (b), truncation (c), etc. resulting from arrays of constraints the mere application of general phonological adjustment rules is not sufficient to account for.

(1)   a: floral$_A$ [floral] **derives from** fleur$_N$ [flower]
      b: lionceau$_N$ [young lion] **derives from** lion$_N$;
      c: mathématiser$_V$ [mathematize] **derives from** mathématiques$_N$ [mathematics]

- **Usefulness:** word segmentation into morphemes is a task of limited use, if not accompanied by the discovery of a dependency relation between these identified morphemes. This pure segmentation task is particularly irrelevant in the unknown-words meaning prediction. As [36] shows, followed by [37], complex word interpretation is generally far from resulting from a simple combination of the meanings of the identified stem and affixes (2):

(2)   a   *scolariser*$_V$ [put in school] **derives from** *école*$_N$ [school] (and not *scolaire*$_A$ [pertaining to school])
      b   *sous-marin*$_A$ [sub-marine] **derives from** *mer*$_N$ [sea] (and not *marin*$_A$ [pertaining to the sea])

In short, DériF's mechanism performs a deep analysis on complex words: beyond simple affix stripping, its purpose consists in realizing a linguistically motivated word analysis, in order to acquire new semantic knowledge originating in Word Formation principles.

3.1 Mechanisms and Results

DériF takes as an input a POS tagged lemma. If this lemma is morphologically complex, DériF provides it with an output including its direct morphological family, grouping its entire ascendancy up to a non-analyzable lexical unit. The family second element is the base of the parsed lemma (3). DériF calculates also the definition of the analyzed lemma, according to both the meaning of its base (4) or bases (5), and the word-formation rule at play. Additional semantic information is produced during each analysis step, cf. (§4). Each derivative/base or compound/bases rule forms an independent module; a given module is activated according to the lemma formal and POS properties, and retrieves the lemma's base(s). The appropriate module in turn supports the base in question, which is also a POS-tagged lemma. In other words, DériF operates in a recursive way, which enables the system to associate any analyzed lemma with its morphological family (cf. 3). The loop stops as soon as an indecomposable unit is acknowledged: (a) it contains neither affix nor compounding form and (b) its part-of-speech makes it an unlikely converted word, so that no analysis module is activated. Analysis modules can be subdivided into four interacting types, according to the morphological structure of the lemma to be parsed: suffixation, prefixation, conversion and compounding. Updating DériF is equivalent to adding a new module to process a new kind of derivation or compounding. The activation of concurrent modules, i.e., that can apply to a word both suffixed and prefixed (e.g., _déverrouillage_ in (3), is hierarchized according to the relative scope of each rule. For instance, for the above example, the age-module is activated prior to the dé-module: _déverrouillage_ < _déverrouiller_ < _verrouiller_ < _verrou_. Here, the system accounts for the fact that dé-prefixation rule derives verbs (from verbs, adjectives and nouns), which prevents dé-module to be activated on the noun _déverouillage_.

(3) déverrouillage$_N$: (déverrouillage$_N$, déverrouiller$_V$, verrouiller$_V$, verrou$_N$)
     [unlocking$_N$: (unlocking$_N$, unlock$_V$, lock$_V$, lock$_N$)]

(4) _déverrouillage$_N$_: 'action de _déverrouiller$_V$_' [action of unlock]

(5) _hydromassage$_N$_: '_massage$_N$_ utilisant l'_eau$_N$_' [massage with water]

The only information required by DériF as input to analyze a lemma is its POS. DériF has no previous knowledge about words and it provides them with a definition calculated according to the morphological relation between the analyzed word and its base, and making use of this base meaning.

3.2 Semantic Relationship

The way in which DériF has been designed entails three implications dealing with the analysis mechanism. First, as we said, DériF produces for each analyzed lemma a semantic relationship between this lemma and its base(s). In other words, this system contributes to the establishment of a semantic network between lexical units, by supplying morphosemantic knowledge. In the current DériF distribution, definitions are in natural language; in recent developments [38] they are expressed by means of a logic formula (6).

The second implication is methodological: with a functioning based on (weighted) rules/exception oppositions, DériF affects each examined lemma with the most suitable analysis rule(s). A default rule is always available. Moreover, when two morphological analyses are equally probable, then two results are provided (7). Exception lists are used to prevent formally complex but actually simple words to be wrongly analyzed as derived or compound words. For instance, noun-based -age suffixed nouns denote collections of what is referred to by the base noun (*plume* [feather] > *plumage* [feathering]): as a member of the –age module exception list, the noun *orage* [storm] will not be (wrongly) related to *or$_N$* [gold]. The same principle is applied in order to block multiple analyses of a complex word, when various decompositions are available from a formal point of view, but only one is semantically suitable.

(6) *lavable$_A$* [washable] (*lavable$_A$, laver$_V$* [wash])
   "y / exists(x), ◊(laver(e, x, y))"

(7) a *importable$_A$* [unwearable] : (*importable$_A$, portable$_A$* [wearable], *porter$_V$* [wear])
   "Not wearable"
   b *importable$_A$* : (*importable$_A$, importer$_V$* [import$_V$])
   "Which can be imported"

Finally, DériF's linguistic principles lead to a third consequence, developed in what follows: the production of two types of lexical semantic annotations, as an integral part of derived lemmas analysis rules for the former type, and of compound ones for the latter.

4   Morphology for the Semantic Annotation of Lexica

In this section, we present two distinct results in term of acquisition of semantic features: one is illustrated by the analysis of general language derivatives; the other one, by the analysis of neoclassical compounds within biomedical specialized corpora.

Linguistic descriptions of Word Formation Rules (WFR) may include semantic, syntactic and phonological constraints that are typical of the rule under study, and that the rule exerts on both words it links to each other.

NLP draws immediate advantage from these linguistic studies. Linguistic constraints are adapted in order to be reused for the automatic labeling of analyzed words with lexical information. When applied on corpora, this word tagging contributes to the enrichment of these corpora lexical annotation. This is what is discussed in §4.1.

Section §4.2 is about another remarkable DériF's result, dealing with the analysis of neoclassical compounds [39]: the edification of a list of terms sharing a lexical relation (synonymy, hyponymy...) with the analyzed compound. This constitution of such "lexical families" is a valuable result for the annotation task of medical corpora and the exploration of terminological bases for this specialty domain.

4.1   Predicting Semantic Properties to Bases and Derivatives

Recall that a first way morphology is exploited to acquire lexical-semantic knowledge is by the semantic relationship the analysis rule establishes between the word to be analyzed and its base (§3). Other pieces of information, expressed as attribute-value pairs, are assigned to words by the appropriate analysis rules.

Basic Predictions. The definition of these features takes advantage of the most frequently observed morphological constraints on rules, according e.g., to productivity measures [40]. A sample is given in Table 1 (for further examples, see [41, 42]). We call these features 'basic predictions', because they emanate directly from linguistic studies on WFR. As Table 1 shows, feature structures are provided by feature-prediction rules, each of them being correlated to a derivation analysis rule (col1), a feature structure can be assigned to the parsed word (col2) as well as to the base calculated by the rule (col3). For each prediction (and analysis) rule, the last raw recalls the semantic pattern defining derived words according to the meaning of their base. All examples follow the same principle.

Table 1. Feature Predictions on Derivatives and Bases

Feature-prediction rule ($W_{DER.} < W_{BASE}$)	Feature structures on the analyzed Word	Feature structures on the base
(1) é- pref: V2 < N1	*épulper* [remove pulp], *émiette* [crumble]	*pulpe* [pulp], *miette* [crumb]
	[aspect=telic, subcat= <NPagent,NPpatient>, NPagent=[concrete=yes, count=yes], NPpatient=[concrete=yes, natural=yes]]	[concrete=yes, hum=no, natural=yes]
	V2 = Deprive smne/smth of N1	
(2) -able suff: A2 < V1	*lavable* [washable], *lançable* [throwable], *périssable* [perishable], *tombable* [fall-able]	*laver* [wash], *lancer* [throw], *périr* [perish], *tomber* [fall]
	[adj_type = property, inherent=no, init_boundary=no]	[subcat= <(NPagent), NPpatient]
	A2 = (<Prep> that) one can V1	
(3) -eur suff: N2 < V1	*danseur* [dancer], *interrupteur* [switch]	*danser* [dance], *interrompre* [interrupt]
	[concrete=yes, hum=yes, count=yes] or [concrete=yes, anim=no, natural=no, count=yes]	[aspect=dynamic, subcat=<NPagent, ...>]
	N2 = (Agent who – Instrument which) V1	

In (1), é- prefixed verbs are noun-based. These prefixed verbs have a telic lexical aspectual value, and they are agentive, transitive predicate; in addition, agents are concrete and countable, and patients denote natural entities. Base nouns are concrete, natural, and non-human.

In (2), derived words are verb-based adjectives suffixed with –able. These adjectives denote acquired properties, and base verb predicates necessarily have a patient argument, regardless of the other arguments.

Finally, in (3), -eur suffixed nouns refer either to (male) human beings, or to concrete entities. Base verbs are dynamic agentive predicates.

Property Self-assessment. As a lemma may undergo several analysis steps, more than one feature-prediction rule can apply, and at a given step, several feature-structures can be assigned to the same word by different feature-prediction rules. Consequently, these pieces of information can be compared with each other in a sort of self-assessment. For instance, consider the case of *évaporateur$_N$* [evaporat-er]. Its complete analysis chain results in the morphological family (8):

(8) (*évaporateur$_N$*, *évaporer$_V$*, *vapeur$_N$*) [evaporator$_N$, evaporate$_V$, vapor$_N$]

The first step of this analysis is performed by the -eur suffix module and leads to the base *évaporer$_V$*. This analysis task triggers the feature-prediction rule (3, Table 1), resulting in a first feature-structure, cf. Table 2, raw 1; then, the second morphological parsing step, realized by the é- prefix module, causes the activation of the feature-prediction rule (1, Table 1), which provides *évaporer$_V$* with a second feature-structure, cf. Table 2, raw 2. So, *evaporer$_V$* has two sets of annotations, and their unification results in the more precise of the two, i.e., that provided by the é- rule.

Table 2. *évaporer$_V$* feature-structures self-assessment

(3) évaporer$_V$: [subcat = < NPagent, ... >]
(1) évaporer$_V$: [aspect = telic, subcat = < NPagent, NPpatient >, NPagent = [concrete = yes, hum = yes, count = yes], NPpatient = [concrete = yes, anim = no, natural = yes]] ;
(1) + (3) évaporer$_V$: [aspect = telic, subcat = < NPagent, NPpatient >, NPagent = [concrete = yes, hum = yes, count = yes], NPpatient = [concrete = yes, anim = no, natural = yes]] ;

Property Combination. Another consequence of multiple feature assignment is the possibility for these pieces of information to be automatically combined to obtain a more precise knowledge. For instance, consider the case of *laver$_V$* [wash$_V$]. This sequence is the base of several derivatives. From DériF's point of view, it is obtained by means of –eur module, from *laveur$_N$* [wash-er$_N$], so that rule (3, Table1) provides *laver$_V$* with the appropriate features accordingly (cf. raw 1, Table 3). Since *laver$_V$* also originates from *lavable$_A$* [wash-able$_A$], the corresponding feature prediction rule (2, Table 1) produces another feature set (cf. raw 2, Table 3). Eventually, *laver$_V$* has two distinct sets of annotations, hence their unification (cf. raw 3, Table 3) results in a more precise information, taking advantage of both sources: namely it amount to

Table 3. *laver*$_V$ feature-structures combination

(3) laver$_V$: [aspect = dynamic, subcat = <NPagent, ...>]
(2) laver$_V$: [subcat = < (NPagent), NPpatient, ... >]
(2) + (3) laver$_V$: [aspect=dynamic, subcat = < NPagent, NPpatient, ... >]

determine that, on the one hand, *laver* is an agentive dynamic predicate, on the other hand, it subcategorizes for a patient argument.

The way DériF directly exploits WF descriptions and analyses gives very satisfactory results in terms of acquisition of lexical knowledge. This knowledge is produced during analysis process, in conjunction with this parsing task. Annotations can be displayed according to various formats (e.g., the SIMPLE formalism, cf. [43], close to the Generative Lexicon model [44]). A manual assessment on prediction features has been performed on 338 *–eur* suffixed nominal neologisms found in the newspaper *Le Monde*, which have been used to enhance the French SIMPLE lexicon [45], with almost 70% of fully satisfying results (the remaining 30% having idiosyncratic characteristics making them fail to at least one feature value). As far as self-assessment and feature combination devices are concerned, potential usefulness is very high, considering the following factors:

1. The amount of feature prediction rules currently implemented in DériF is of 26.
2. Every time the morphological family of an analyzed lemma is of a size over two elements (e.g., (4)), then any family member, excepted both the starting lemma and the final stem, is likely to undergo self-assessment (e.g., *évaporer*$_V$ in (4), cf. Table 2). An experiment was carried out, consisting in analysing and automatically annotating 338 unknown *–eur* suffixed nouns and 453 unknown *-able* suffixed adjectives collected from *Le Monde 1999* newspaper corpora. Given that *–able* and *–eur* parsed lemmas may have different internal structures, we end up with 30 different ways to perform self-assessment.
3. As soon as two morphological families share a common ascendant (e.g., *laver*$_V$, Table 3, belonging to both *lavable*$_A$ and *laveur*$_N$ families), feature combination can be activated.

The annotation system, tested on *-able* and *-eur* analysis and prediction rules, seems a very promising technique for word (especially neologisms) semantic annotation, where semantic information originates from linguistic knowledge inferred by word formation rules. In §4.2, we describe another DériF's ability: that of deducing lexical relationships (synonymy, hyponymy, etc) between morphologically unrelated words, based on their morphological parsing results.

4.2 Lexical Family of Biomedical Neoclassical Compounds

We have seen (§2) that the biomedical field is very demanding in NLP tools and resources: among others, detecting lexical-semantic relations between terms is a task that proved useful in many respects: improvement of IR and IE tasks, in particular specialized document ranking according to the intended audience [46] or terminological extension of specialized lexica [47]. DériF's contribution aims to a multilingual identification of biomedical terms surfacing as nominal and adjectival neoclassical compounds. DériF gathers compound terms occurring in a medical text, which are morphologically unrelated but semantically close. This recognition task involves two stages, which implies for the text content to be browsed twice. The first stage takes place during morphological parsing. For each compound word, it consists in drawing up a list of its potential synonyms, hyponyms and co-hyponyms, based on its morphological parsing result, i.e., on its components value. The compilation of this list is realized by 4 rules, thanks to elementary information taken from a database of Greek- and Latin-based stems, we call hereafter combining forms (CF). In the second stage, compound words occurring in the corpus and having been labelled with these primary annotations are retrieved and linked to each other according to the appropriate lexical relationship. For instance, the neoclassical compound noun *gastralgie* [gastralgy] ("pain 'algie' in the stomach 'gastr'") forms links with 14 nouns and adjectives appearing in the same corpus, and belonging to the same conceptual domain, that of digestive system pathologies (Table 4). The corpus used here is the set of compound terms contained in the Systematized Nomenclature of Medicine-Clinical Terms (SNOMED-CT) dataset[2]. In raw 3, the label 'semantic neighbourhood' is meant to gather co-hyponyms and co-meronyms essentially.

Table 4. *gastralgie* and its links with its lexical family members in SNOMED-CT

Synonym of	*gastrodynie$_N$*, [gastrodyny] *stomacalgie$_N$*, [stomacalgy] *stomac(h)odynie$_N$*, [stomac(h)odyny] *gastralgique$_N$* [gastralgic]
Hyponym of	*abdominalgie$_N$* [abdominalgy]
Other semantic neighbourhood	*entéralgie$_N$*, [enteralgy] *entérodynie$_N$*, [enterodyny] *gastrite$_N$*, [gastritis] *hépatalgie$_N$*, [hepatalgy] *hépatodynie$_N$*, [hepatodyny] *pancréatalgie$_N$*, [pancreatalgy] *gastrose$_N$*, [gastrosis] *antigastralgique$_N$* [antigastralgic]

In what follow, we briefly recall the main properties to neoclassical compounds, because they are of a great importance for the rest of the procedure. Then, we outline the tasks involved in stages 1 (description of the CF database and the 4 rules) and 2 (compound terms identification and linking).

Neoclassical Compounds. In Romance languages, neoclassical compounds are formed from two lexical units, as are standard compounds, whereas derived words have only one base (on compounding in general, see [48], on a discussion about the nature of compounding units, see [49]) (9). But unlike standard compounds' components (9a), CFs in neoclassical compounds are very often bound stems, inherited from Latin or Greek form, e.g., *gastr* or *algie* in (9b). Moreover, interpreting a neoclassical

---

[2] http://www.nlm.nih.gov/research/umls/Snomed/snomed_main.html

compound with respects to its CFs proceeds from the right to the left, following Ancient Greek word-order constraints in WF[3].

(9) a $porter_V$ [carry] + $monnaie_N$ [coin] > $porte\text{-}monnaie_N$ [purse]
    "object   which   is   used   to   carry   coins   "
    b $gastr$ 'estomac$_N$' [stomach] + $algie$ 'douleur$_N$' [pain] > $gastralgie_N$
    "pain in the stomach"

Neoclassical compounds have been massively and simultaneously created
throughout Europe from the 18th century onwards, in order to meet denomination
needs due to scientific and technical discoveries started during Enlightenment. Therefore these compounds are nearly identical in almost every West-European languages,
the differences relying on small spelling variants: e.g., *gastragie* in French, *gastralgy*
in English, and *gastralgia* in Italian. Assuming with [50] that CF are suppletive stems
of contemporary nouns, adjectives or verbs, they can be assigned both a POS and a
meaning (those of the word they substitute for). As a result, parsing a neoclassical
compound includes the identification of its CFs, as well as both POS and meaning for
each CF, which are used to calculate the definition of this compound (for a brief
typology of neoclassical compounds and related analysis issue see [51]; for an illustration, cf. Table 9). The list of compound words likely to be lexically related to a
neoclassical compound is drawn up from the value and properties of the CFs obtained
at the end of the analysis process of this compound. This compilation task takes advantage of a CF database content, which is based on (French versions of) international
terminology classifications (SNOMED-CT[2], MeSH[4], CIM-10[5]).

CF Database. As Table 5 shows, each entry of the base is a CF representation, including its graphic value (col. 1), POS (col. 3) and meaning (col. 2). Other features,
such as the CF's position within a compound (e.g., assuming that compounds have a
YX structure, *ectomie* never occupies the Y position) are not displayed in Table 5.
The current version of the CF database contains more than 1,600 CF descriptions for
French. Moreover, each CF points to another table (cf. Table 6) containing its equivalent forms in 4 other West European languages. Therefore, the CF base can be reused
for the morphological analysis of medical words in these languages, as the experiment
in [28] and outlined below shows for English. For each CF description, the most relevant database field for the task described here is that illustrated in col. 5. It contains
other CFs, which have synonymy (symbol =), hyponymy (<<), meronymy (←), or
neighbourhood (~) links with the entry. As said before, with neighbourhood relationship we mean either co-meronymy (both *hépat* and *gastr* refer to parts of the abdo-
men) or co-hyponymy (both *ite* and *algie* are sorts of symptoms). This information is
extracted from the SNOMED-CT hierarchical system, as well as the chapter it comes
from (col. 4).

---

[3] In Romance languages, strandard compounds' interpretation goes from the left to the right.
[4] http://www.ncbi.nlm.nih.gov/mesh
[5] http://www.med.univ-rennes1.fr/noment/cim10/

Table 5. Sample of the CF database

CF (1)	Meaning (2)	POS (3)	SNOMED Chapter (4)	Primary Lexical Relation (5)
gastr	stomach	N	anatomy	=stomac, ←abdomin, ~hépat, ~enter , ~pancréat
algie	pain	N	symptom	=odynie, ~ite
ite	inflamma-tion	N	symptom	~algie, ~odynie
phléb	vein	N	anatomy	=vén, << angi, <<vascul
angi	blood vessel	N	anatomy	=vascul, ~vas
ectomie	ablation	N	surgery act	~tomie, ~stomie

Table 6. `ectomie' variations across languages

French	English	German	Italian	Spanish
ectomie	ectomy	ektomie	ectomia	ectomía

Lexical relations at play between neoclassical compounds can be inferred from these primary relationships between the CFs contained in these compounds, by the implication rules system presented below.

Lexical Relationship Implication Rules. Four rules are used to group neoclassical compounds according to synonymy, hyponymy and neighbourhood relationships. They are based on three principles: (1) neoclassical compounds having the YX structure denote almost always a subtype of X (a *gastralgy* is a type of pain=*algy*), much less often a set containing X and Y (the *rhinopharynx* is a body part pertaining to both the nose=*rhino* and the *pharynx*); (2) discovering primary relationships between CFs enables to infer relationships between compounds containing these CFs; (3) implication rules must be language-independent. These principles are translated into 4 language-free rules:

1. **R1:** two compounds YX_1 and YX_2 share the same lexical link than X_1 and X_2;
4. **R2:** two compounds Y_1X and Y_2X share the same lexical link than Y_1 and Y_2, unless Y_1 is a meronym of Y_2. In this case, Y_1X is hyponym of Y_2X;
5. R1 (resp. R2) implication remains valid when Y components (resp. X components) are synonyms: **R3** (resp. **R4**).

Rules R1-R4 apply on the morphological parsing result of YX nominal compounds, as well as YXsuf compound adjectives (e.g., *gastralgique*). The effect of these rules is illustrated in Table 7. Examples are given here in French, but R1-R4 rules work exactly in the same way for the other languages represented in the database.

Table 7. From CF relations to relations between compounds

Rule	Example		
	Y	X	$[Y_AX_A] R [Y_BX_B]$
R1	bactér	oïde = forme	bactéroïde = bactériforme [bacteroid = bacteriform]
	oto	rragie <<rrhée	otorrhagie << otorrhée [otorragy << otorrhea]
	arthr	algie ~ ite	arthralgie ~ arthrite [arthralgy ~ arthritis]
R2	proct ← colo	rragie	proctorrhagie << colorrhagie [proctorragy << colorrhagia]
	abdomin=lapar	scopie	abdominoscopie = laparoscopie [abdominoscopy = laparoscopy]
	albumin << protéin	émie	albuminémie << protéinémie [albuminemia << proteinemia]
	xér ~ sclér	ophtalmie	xérophthalmie ~ sclérophthalmie [xerophtalmy ~ sclerophtalmia]
R3 (Y_a syn. of Y_b)	orth = rect	dont = dent	orthodonte = rectident [with straight teeth]
	métr = hystér	rragie<<rrhée	métrorragie << hystérorrée [metrorragy << hysterorrhea]
	lip = adip	matose ~ ome	lipomatose ~adipome [lipomatosis ~ adipoma]
R4 (X_a syn. of X_b)	entér←abdomin	algie = odynie	entérodynie << abdominalgie [enterodynia << abdominalgia]
	mort = thanat	fère = gène	mortifère = thanatogène [mortiferous = thanatogenous]
	api << entom	vore = phage	apivore << entomophage [apivorous << entomophagous]
	bacill ~bacter	forme = oïde	bacilliforme ~ bactérioïde [bacilliform ~ bacterioid]

Rule Activation, and Actual Relationships between Compounds. When a YX neoclassical compound is parsed, the identification of Y and X triggers the application of rules R1 to R4. The result is a set of potential lexical relationships (Table 8). Their assessment depends on the actual content of the medical corpus the lexical units of which undergo morphological parsing. For instance, you can see that only a subset of the *gastralgie* potentially related compounds (Table 8) is actually found in the

SNOMED-CT lexicon, as Table 4 above shows. To calculate the relationship between two terms belonging to the same corpus, a mapping rule compares the value of the CFs identified for one parsed compound (e.g., *hépat* 'liver' and *odynie* 'pain' CFs for *hépatodynie*) with the potential relation list of the other parsed compound (e.g., for *gastragie*). If these CF values are found in the list (this is what happens for *hépatody-nie*, whose CFs occur in ~:hépat/odyn), then the semantic relationship between the two compounds is that indicated by the symbol '~'. Hence, *gastralgie* and *hépa-todynie* are in a neighbourhood relationship.

Table 8. Discovering the lexical relationship between *gastralgie* and *hépatodynie*

gastralgie/NOM==> " pain in the stomach "
Constituants = /gastr/algie/
Potential relations = (=:gastr/odyn, =:stomac/algie, =:stomac/odyn, =:stomach/algie, =:stomach/odyn, <<:abdomin/algie, <<:abdomin/odyn, ~:entéro/algie, ~:entéro/odyn, ~:gastr/ite, ~:gastr/ose, ~:hépat/algie, **~:hépat/odyn,** ~:pancréat/algie, ~:pancréat/odyn, ~:stomac/ite, ~:stomac/ose, ~:stomach/ite, ~:stomach/ose)
hépatodynie/NOM==> " Pain in the liver "
Constituants = **/hépat/odyn/**
Potential relations = (=:hépat/algie, <<:abdomin/algie, <<:abdomin/odyn, ~:gastr/odyn, ~:gastr/algie, ~:hépat/ose , ~:stomac/algie, ~:stomac/odyn, ~:stomach/algie, ~:stomach/odyn, ~:entéro/algie, ~:entéro/odyn, ~:pancréat/algie, ~:pancréat/odyn)

Results and Assessment. 29,137 terms from the UMLS Metathesaurus[6] have been used as training lexicon for the DériF parsing. In particular, this analysis task has been performed on the French SNOMED-CT, namely 5,800 nouns and adjectives from the chapter *Disorders*, 1.645 from *Procedures* and 766 from *Anatomy*. From these 29,137 terms, lexical relations have been established between 6,710 YX(suf) compound adjectives and/or nouns. The gap between these two numbers is due to the fact that a medical lexicon contains a large amount of compounds with a structure different from YX, and of course, a large amount of derived words. While DériF provides all of them with both a valid analysis and definition, the relationship assignment task currently works only for YX compounds. The other compound types have various structures (see some of them in Table 9, col.1) and their constituents are either free words or CFs. For each example in Table 9, col. 2, num.1, the size of the compound's morphological family indicates how many analysis steps have been required to perform its complete analysis. Notice that cutting a compound into components leads to a given components linear order (col. 2, num.2) which does not presuppose the right definition pattern (col. 2, num. 3): compare, for instance, the *anti-* prefix scope in *antiandrogène*, where it applies on the *gène* ('generate') predicative CF, and that of *mono-* in *monochromophile*, where the affix has scope over *chrom* ('colour'). One of DériF's ability is to envisage various interpretative patterns, as illustrated below.

---

[6] http://www.nlm.nih.gov/research/umls/

Table 9. Different types of neoclassical compounds, and their analysis

Comp. Struct.	Compounds analysis : 1. morphological family, 2. constituents' linear order, 3. definition with respect to its base
ZYX : acarodermatite$_N$ [acarodermatitis]	1. (acarodermatite/N, dermatite/N, ite/N*) 2. acarN*/dermatN*/iteN* 3. 'Type of [dermatitis] related to [acar: mite]'
YPfxX colpohyperplasie,$_N$ [colpohyperplasia]	1. (colpohyperplasie/N, hyperplasie/N, plasie/N*) 2. colpN*/hyperPfx/plasieN* 3. 'Type of [hyperplasia] related to [colp: vagina]'
YXSfx brachiocéphalité,$_N$ [brachiocephal-ity]	1. (brachiocéphalité/N, brachiocéphale/A, céphal/N*) 2. brachioN*/céphalN*/itéSfx 3. 'Property of what is [brachiocephalous]'
PfxYX antiandrogène$_A$ [antiandrogenous]	1. (antiandrogène/A, gène/V*) 2. antiPfx/andrN*/gèneV* 3. 'against that what [gène: causes] [andr: masculine character]'
monochromophile$_A$ [monochromatophil]	1. (monochromophile/A, phile/V*) 2. monoPfx/chromN*/phileV* 3. 'which [phile: is attracted] by a unique [chrom: colour]'
PfxYXSfx interthoracoscapulaire$_A$ [interthoracicoscapular]	1. (interthoracoscapulaire/A, scapul/N*) 2. interPfx/thoracN*/scapulN*/aireSfx 3. 'which is between thorax and scapula'

Neoclassical compound analysis, definition-guessing, and relationship-assignment tasks have undergone two assessment experiments.

- The purpose of the former [27] was to validate both definitions and relationships, and to weight their usefulness in the biomedical IR domain. Therefore a quantitative evaluation of DériF's results against a Gold Standard has been realized. Two blind manual assessments (the first one by a linguist, the second one by a medical expert) have been performed in order to check results validity. Assessment results show that DériF is able to produce up to 77.3% correct definitions to unknown terms, and reaches a prediction of almost 70% percent of correct synonymy links. As for neighbourhood relationships however, they have raised a problem of interpretation between the experts, who did not reach a common understanding of what means to be neighbour for lexical entries; such a linguistic notion is indeed largely dependant of the intended use of neighbourhood links, therefore, assessment of this point has been postponed, as it requires a more concise basis.
- The second validation experiment has to do with cross-linguistic transferability of the relationship prediction system, which has been attempted with English [28]. This adaptation of DériF methods to analyze English medical neoclassical

compounds was tested on a set of 859 YX compounds extracted from the WHO-ART[7] terminology. 675 could be successfully decomposed and defined.

4.3   Synthesis

We have described two original functionalities characterizing the DériF system. They allow co-operation to take place between NLP, word formation and lexical semantics. First, DériF provides parsed derived words and calculated bases with lexical features, informing upon syntactic or semantic properties. Second, DériF allows biomedical neoclassical compound nouns and adjectives to be grouped according to lexical-semantic relationships, thanks to a multilingual database containing 1,600 CF (for each represented language) enhanced and completed from the content of medical international terminologies. A few language-free rules are used to propagate the CFs' primary relationship encoded in the database, in order to infer lexical relationship between the compounds containing these CFs.

5   Discussion and Conclusion

Evaluating a morphosemantic analyzer is a difficult task. In fact, beside the assessment experiments described above, concerning the quality of semantic features (§. 4.1) or that of semantic relationships (§. 4.2), global evaluation tasks have been performed on DériF's results in two respects.

5.1   Task-Based Assessment

First, a task-based evaluation experiment involving DériF has been carried out, and is described in [5]. The authors aimed to measure the coverage of several French lexical resources and tools for a Question Answering task performed on three previously annotated corpora: Quareo [52], EQueR-Medical [53] and Conique [54]. Compared to the heuristic-based Snowball stemmer[8], DériF results show the following characteristics (for a detailed presentation of DeriF's assessment, see [5]):

- DériF is better than Snowball for the EQueR corpus (which is made of medical specialized documents); in particular, it is quite efficient for the treatment of compounding.
- When checked against the other two corpora, and as far as derivation is concerned, DériF and Snowball show complementary scores, because these tools do not cover the same morphological constructions.
  - Snowball results are better as far as conversion is concerned.
  - DériF coverage being affix-dependent, this tool is very efficient for some processes, and fails for other ones (see §.5.2, Table 10).

---

[7] http://www.umc-products.com/DynPage.aspx?id=4918
[8] http://snowball.tartarus.org/download.php

— DériF proves to be better when it comes to the analysis of both verb-based nouns and relational adjectives, which appear to be the most frequent derivational phenomena occurring in both these general-language corpora. However, evaluation results show that DériF's coverage is still poor and has to be improved, in order to address such a frequent issue in a more effective way.

Evaluation also focused on the quality of analysis: only a few errors were found with DériF, in the general-language corpora, and none within EQueR.

5.2   Evaluation with Respect to a Reference Lexicon

Second, general language evaluation tasks are regularly achieved, where DériF is always applied on the same reference lexicon: the vocabulary of the "Trésor de la Langue Française" (a French general language multivolume dictionary), that is about 99,000 nouns, adjectives and verbs. Updated parsing results are automatically compared to the previous ones, in order to perform differential evaluation.

Currently, 43.2% of the 99,000 words are successfully analyzed and defined, according to this assessment method. This apparently small percentage of satisfying results has at least two main reasons. The first one is a matter of DériF coverage, and is detailed below. The second one has to do with the tested vocabulary: the meaning of many complex words recorded in dictionaries is no longer compositional. In other words, successful rates with DériF are much higher on corpora with an important density of new-coined words, e.g., when DériF is applied on newspaper corpora.

63% of the 29,137 analyzed medical terms of the SNOMED French version produce a correct base and definition. Several experiments, reported in §4, enabled the assessment of three aspects of this morphological parsing system:

1. When it comes to the general language lexicon, feature structures on derived words and on their base have been both manually and automatically (self-assessment and cross-annotation) checked,
2. As for the biomedical corpus, a quantitative evaluation of both the neoclassical compounds definition and the lexical relations has been performed against a Gold Standard. Assessments confirm that the system main drawback lies in the delta that may occur between linguistic predictions and real meanings or lexical links. For instance, the current, lexicalized interpretation of *microstomie* [stenostomia] i.e., "congenital pathology characterized by an abnormal narrowness of the mouth"), is no longer computable from that of *stomie* ("opening"), unlike e.g., *périnéostomie* ("surgical opening = *stomie* of pelvic floor = *périnée*").
3. Again, for biomedical compounds, the portability of the analysis system to another West-European language has been successfuly checked for English: 78,5% of YX compounds can be analyzed, defined and lexically related to each others by a simply transposition of the method used for French.

Table 10 provides a qualitative summary of DériF current coverage. Col.1 indicates the analysis module applied, named after the recognized affix and the POS involved, in the Derived-Word < Base order. An illustration is given in col. 2.

Table 10. Dérif's coverage

Derivation or compounding rule (analyzed-word$_{CAT}$ < BASE$_{CAT}$)	Examples (derived/comp. word < base)
-able suff (A < N, A < V), -age suff (N < V, N < N)	abaissable$_A$ < abaisser$_V$ [lower-able$_A$ < lower$_V$]
-ais, -eux, -ien , -iste, -al, -el, -aire, -ique, anti- suff (A < N, A < Nam), Quantifying pref. : a-, mono-, bi-, di-, tri-,... (N < N, A < N)	écossais$_A$ < Ecosse$_{NPR}$ [scottish$_A$ < Scotland$_{NPR}$]
avant-, après-, anté- pref (N < N)	avant-bras$_N$ < bras$_N$ [forearm$_N$ < arm$_N$]
auto- pref (N < N, A < N, V < V)	auto-financer$_V$ < financer$_V$ [selffinance$_V$ < finance$_V$]
co- pref (V < V, N < N, A < A, A < N)	coexister$_V$ < exister$_V$ [coexist$_V$ < exist$_V$]
contre- pref (V < V, N < N, A < N)	contre-nature$_A$ < nature$_N$ [counter-nature$_A$ (*unnatural$_A$*) < nature$_N$]
dé-, en-, é- pref (V < V, V < N, V < A)	désherber$_V$ < herbe$_N$ [un-grass$_V$ (*weed$_V$*) < grass$_N$]
exo-, infra-, inter-, ... locative pref (A < N, N < N, A < Nam, V < V), in- pref (A < A, N < N, V < N)	impur$_A$< pur$_A$ [impure$_A$ < pure$_A$]
-if suff (A < N), -ie suff (N < N , N < A)	sportif$_A$< sport$_N$ [sportive$_A$ < sport$_N$]
-ifier, -iser suff (V < N, V < A, V < Nam)	momifier$_V$ < momie$_N$ [momify$_V$ < mummy$_N$]
-ion, -ment suff (N < V)	libération$_N$ < libérer$_V$ [freedom$_N$ < free$_V$]
-ité suff (N < Nam, N< A), non- pref (N < N, A < A)	accessibilité$_N$ < accessible$_A$ [accessibility$_N$ < accessible$_A$]
re- pref (N < N, V < V, A< A, V < N, V < A)	réenfoncer$_V$ < enfoncer$_V$ [re-press$_V$ < press$_V$]
Other X < X pref (alpha-, bêta-, gamma-, dis-, iso-, kilo-, macro-, micro-, etc)	malchance$_N$ < chance$_N$ [badluck$_N$ < luck$_N$]
Conversion (N < V ; V< N ; N < A), Neoclassical Compounding (see table 9)	vol$_N$ < voler$_V$ [flight/theft$_N$ < fly/steal$_V$]
Neoclassical Compounding (see Table 9)	thalassothérapie$_N$ < thérapie$_N$ [thalassotherapy$_N$ < therapy$_N$]

5.3   Current Improvements and Further Research

Like morphosemantic systems in general, DériF suffers from lack of coverage, insofar as it relies on detailed linguistic analyses that are often restricted to limited linguistic phenomena. Of course, DériF current coverage can be easily updated with the insertion of missing morphological modules, for instance the analysis rule of –*ure* suffixed nouns (*blessure* > *blesser*). For two sets of morphological constructions, however, DériF improvements are more complex to achieve.

- The analysis of standard compounds is tricky to envisage given its structural similarity with neoclassical compounding. The issue is namely that of their correct definition: given e.g., the standard compound noun *poisson-chat* [cat-fish], DériF current analysis (based on that of neoclassical compounds) defines it as a "sort of cat", whereas it should be interpreted as a "sort of fish". There is one distinctive feature that can be used by DériF to detect standard compounds and define them accordingly: they never contain CF components. With this clue, a morphological parsing module for standard compounds can be developed in a near future.
- Many derived word have no base to be directly related to. For some of them, the only existing parenthood relation is an indirect one, e.g., *communisme/communiste*: such morphological relations, called cross-formations, are obtained by affix mutual truncation. Other non standard derivational structures are the so-called back-formations: the derivative is formally shorter than its base. Because of its conception principles, DériF is primarily designed to deal with oriented rules, which makes not trivial its analysis of these morphological constructions. However, a specific module is proposed in this respect in [55].

Other well-known DériF defaults are inherent to its methodological foundation and common to rule-based linguistically motivated systems: it is language-dependant, and its maintenance and updating tasks are time-consuming. Most recent DériF developments are meant to address these coverage and conceptual issues. They consist in coupling DériF with Morphonette, an analogy-based system [16]. This combination results in a lexical network, called Daemonette, which takes advantage of both systems. First, thanks to Morphonette analogy-based technology, a broad coverage is ensured, and so are indirect lexical relationships, such as with the agent and process nouns pair {*prédateur$_N$* [predator], *prédation$_N$* [predation]}, where the common verbal ancestor (which would be otherwise °*prédater*) is lacking in French.

Second, words of a same morphological family are combined into sub-networks which instantiate types of n-tuples, where words share both the same internal structure and the same semantic annotations, the latter resulting from (combinations of) basic predictions (see §. 4.1). For instance, each network in (10) is an instance of the n-tuple type in (11), grouping a dynamic durative verbal predicate, an agent or instrument noun suffixed by –eur, a process or result noun, suffixed by –ion, and a property adjective, suffixed by -if. As in (10c), a network slot may be empty: is this case, the lack of member indicates a lexical gap in the family.

(10)   a   {*produire*[product], *producteur*[productor], *produc-*
tion[production], *productif*[productive]}

b   {*diriger*[direct], *directeur*[director], *direction*[direction],
directif[directive]}

c   {*adapter*[adapt], *adaptateur*[adapter], *adapta-*
tion[adaptation], --}

(11)   {V [accomplishment/activity], N-eur [agent/instrument], N-ion
[process/result], A-if [property]}

This tool merging task is a work in progress [38], with already promising results, which will certainly be confirmed in future developments.

References

1. Plag, I.: Word-formation in English. Cambridge University Press, Cambridge (2003)
2. Cartoni, B., Lefer, M.-A.: Improving the representation of word-formation in multilingual lexicographic tools: the MuLeXFoR database. In: XIV EURALEX, pp. 581–591. Fryske Academy, Leeuwarden (2010)
3. Creutz, M., Lagus, K.: Inducing the Morphological Lexicon of a Natural Language from Unannotated Text. In: AKRR 2005, pp. 106–113. Pattern Recognition Society of Finland, Helsinki (2005)
4. Sagot, B.: The Lefff, a freely available and large-coverage morphological and syntactic lexicon for French. In: LREC 2010, pp. 2744–2751. ELRA, La Valetta (2010)
5. Bernhard, D., Cartoni, B., Tribout, D.: A Task-Based Evaluation of French Morphological Resources and Tools. Linguistic Issues in Language Technology 5, 2 (2011)
6. Bilotti, M.W., Katz, B., Lin, J.: What Works Better for Question Answering: Stemming or Morphological Query Expansion? In: Proceedings of the Information Retrieval for Question Answering (IR4QA) (Workshop at SIGIR 2004), Sheffield (2004)
7. Dasgupta, S., Ng, V.: Unsupervised morphological parsing of Bengali. Language Resources and Evaluation 40(3-4), 311–330 (2006)
8. Goldsmith, J.: An algorithm for the unsupervised learning of morphology. Computational Linguistics 27(2), 153–198 (2001)
9. Cavar, D., Rodriguez, P., Schrementi, G.: Unsupervised morphology induction for part-of-speech-tagging. In: Proceedings of the 29th Annual Penn Linguistics Colloquium, vol. 12(1), pp. 29–41. University of Pennsylvania, Philadelphia (2006)
10. Claveau, V.: Unsupervised and semi-supervised morphological analysis for Information Retrieval in the biomedical domain. In: COLING, Mumbai, India, pp. 629–646 (2012)
11. Bernhard, D.: Automatic Acquisition of Semantic Relationships from Morphological Relatedness. In: Salakoski, T., Ginter, F., Pyysalo, S., Pahikkala, T. (eds.) FinTAL 2006. LNCS (LNAI), vol. 4139, pp. 121–132. Springer, Heidelberg (2006)
12. Clément, L., Sagot, B., Lang, B.: Morphology based automatic acquisition of large-coverage lexica. In: LREC, pp. 1841–1844. ELRA, Lisbon (2004)
13. Wicentowski, R.: Multilingual Noise-Robust Supervised Morphological Analysis using the WordFrame Model. In: Proceedings of 7th Meeting of the ACL Special Interest Group on Computational Phonology (SIGPHON), pp. 70–77. ACL, Barcelona (2004)
14. Virpioja, S., Turunen, V.T., Spiegler, S., Kohonen, O., Kurimo, M.: Empirical Comparison of Evaluation Methods for Unsupervised Learning of Morphology. TAL 42(2), 45–90 (2011)

15. Stroppa, N., Yvon, F.: An Analogical Learner for Morphological Analysis. In: CoNLL, pp. 120–127. ACL, Ann Arbor (2005)
16. Hathout, N.: Morphonette: a paradigm-based morphological network. Lingue e Linguaggio 2, 245–264 (2011)
17. Moreau, F., Claveau, V., Sébillot, P.: Automatic morphological query expansion using analogy-based machine learning. In: Amati, G., Carpineto, C., Romano, G. (eds.) ECiR 2007. LNCS, vol. 4425, pp. 222–233. Springer, Heidelberg (2007)
18. Porter, M.F.: An algorithm for suffix stripping. Program 14(3), 130–137 (1980)
19. Hull, A.D.: Stemming Algorithms - A case study for detailed evaluation. Journal of the American Society of Information Science 47(1), 70–84 (1996)
20. Juravsky, D., Martin, J.: Speech and Language Processing. Prentice Hall, New Jersey (2000)
21. Cohen-Sygal, Y., Wintner, S.: Finite-State Registered Automata for Non-Concatenative Morphology. Computational Linguistics 32(1), 49–82 (2006)
22. Walther, M.: Temiar reduplication in one-level prosodic morphology. In: Proceedings of SIGPHON, Workshop on Finite-State Phonology, Luxembourg, pp. 13–21 (2000)
23. Pacak, M.G., Norton, L.M., Dunham, G.S.: Morphosemantic Analysis of -ITIS Forms in Medical Language. In: Methods of Information in Medecine, pp. 99–105 (1980)
24. Schulz, S., Hahn, U.: Morpheme-based, cross-lingual indexing for medical document retrieval. International Journal of Medical Informatics 58-59, 87–99 (2000)
25. Markó, K., Schulz, S., Hahn, U.: MorphoSaurus – design and evaluation of an interlingua-based, cross-language docuyment retrieval engine for the medical domain. Methods of Information in Medecine 44(4), 537–545 (2005)
26. Cartoni, B.: Lexical Morphology in Machine Translation: A Feasibility Study. In: Proceedings of the 12th EACL, pp. 130–138. ACL, Athens (2009)
27. Namer, F., Baud, R.: Defining and relating biomedical terms: towards a cross-language morphosemantics-based system. International Journal of Medical Informatics 76(2-3), 226–233 (2007)
28. Deléger, L., Namer, F., Zweigenbaum, P.: Morphosemantic parsing of medical compound words: Transferring a French analyzer to English. International Journal of Medical Informatics 78(suppl.1), 48–55 (2009)
29. Bernhard, D.: Apprentissage de connaissances morphologiques pour l'acquisition automatique de ressources lexicales. Université Joseph Fourier, Grenoble (2006)
30. Wilbur, W.J.: BioNLP: Biological, Translational and clinical language processing, pp. 201–208. ACL, Prague (2007)
31. Clark, P., Fellbaum, C., Hobbs, J.R., Harrison, P., Murray, B., Thompson, J.: Augmenting WordNet for deep understanding of text. In: Proceedings of Semantics in Text Processing, pp. 45–57. ACL, Venezia (2008)
32. Dal, G., Hathout, N., Namer, F.: Construire un lexique dérivationnel: théorie et réalisations. In: TALN 1999, pp. 115–124. Université Paris 7, Cargèse (1999)
33. Namer, F.: Morphologie, Lexique et TAL: l'analyseur DériF. Hermes Sciences Publishing, London (2009)
34. Sapir, E.: Language. Harcourt, Brace and Company, New York (1921)
35. Aikhenvald, A.Y.: Typological distinctions in word-formation. In: Shopen, T. (ed.) Language Typology and Syntactic Description. Grammatical Categories and the Lexicon, vol. III, pp. 1–65. Cambridge University Press, Cambridge (2007)
36. Corbett, G.: Canonical Derivational Morphology. Word Structure 3(2), 141–155 (2010)
37. Hathout, N., Namer, F.: Discrepancy between form and meaning in Word Formation: the case of over- and under-marking in French. In: Rainer, F., Dressler, W.U., Gardani, F., Luschützky, H.C. (eds.) Morphology and Meaning (Selected Papers from the 15th International Morphology Meeting), Vienna. John Benjamins, Amsterdam (2010)

38. Hathout, N., Namer, F.: Règles et paradigmes en morphologie informatique lexématique. In: TALN 2011, pp. 215–220. LIRMM/ATALA, Montpellier (2011)
39. Lüdeling, A.: Neoclassical word-formation, 2nd edn. Encyclopedia of Language and Linguistics, pp. 580–582. Elsevier (2006)
40. Baayen, R.H.: Quantitative aspects of morphological productivity. Yearbook of Morphology 1991, 109–149 (1992)
41. Namer, F., Bouillon, P., Jacquey, E.: Un lexique Génératif de référence pour le Français. In: TALN 2007, pp. 233–242. ERSS, Toulouse (2007)
42. Namer, F., Jacquey, E.: Word Formation Rules and the Generative Lexicon: Representing noun-to-verb versus verb-to-noun Conversion. In: Pustejovsky, J., Bouillon, P., Isahara, H., Kanzaki, K., Chungmin, L. (eds.) Advances in Generative Lexicon Theory, pp. 385–414. Springer, Heidelberg (2012)
43. Ruimy, N., Monachini, M., Distnte, R., Guazzini, E., Molino, S., Uliveri, M., Calzolari, N., Zampolli, A.: CLIPS, A Multi-level Italian Computational Lexicon. In: LREC, pp. 792–799. ELRA, Las Palmas de Gran Canaria (2002)
44. Pustejovsky, J.: The Generative Lexicon. MIT Press, Cambridge (1995)
45. Namer, F., Bouillon, P., Jacquey, E., Ruimy, N.: Morphology-based enhancement of a French SIMPLE Lexicon. In: 5th International Conference on Generative Approaches to the Lexicon, pp. 153–161. ILC-CNR, Pisa (2009)
46. Chmielik, J., Grabar, N.: Détection de la spécialisation scientifique et technique des documents biomédicaux grâce aux informations morphologiques. TAL 52(2), 151–179 (2011)
47. Cartoni, B., Zweigenbaum, P.: Extension of a specialised lexicon using specific terminological data: the Unified Medical Lexicon for French (UMLF). In: Proceedings of 14th EURALEX, pp. 892–905. De Skriuwers, Leeuwarden (2010)
48. Lieber, R., Štekauer, P.: Introduction: status and definition of compounding. In: Lieber, R., Štekauer, P. (eds.) The Oxford Handbook of Compounding, pp. 3–18. Oxford University Press, Oxford (2009)
49. Montermini, F.: Units in compounding. In: Scalise, S., Vogel, I. (eds.) Cross-Disciplinary Issues in Compounding, pp. 79–82. Benjamins, Amsterdam (2010)
50. Dal, G., Amiot, D.: La composition néoclassique en français et ordre des constituants. In: Amiot, D. (ed.) La composition dans une perspective typologique, pp. 89–113. Artois Presse Université, Arras (2008)
51. Namer, F.: Guessing the meaning of neoclassical compound within LG: the case of pathology nouns. In: 3d Workshop on Generative Approaches to the Lexicon, pp. 175–184. Université de Genève, Geneva (2005)
52. Quintard, L., Galibert, O., Adda, G., Grau, B., Laurent, D., Moriceau, V.R., Rosset, S., Tannier, X., Vilnat, A.: Question Answering on Web Data: The QA Evaluation in Quæro. In: LREC 2010, pp. 2368–2374. ELRA, La Valletta (2010)
53. Ayache, C., Grau, B., Vilnat, A.: EQueR: the French Evaluation campaign of Question-Answering Systems. In: LREC 2006, pp. 1157–1160. ELRA, Genova (2006)
54. Grappy, A., Grau, B., Ferret, O., Grouin, C., Moriceau, V.R., Robba, I., Tannier, X., Vilnat, A., Barbier, V.: A Corpus for Studying Full Answer Justification. In: LREC 2010, pp. 2361–2367. ELRA, La Valletta (2010)
55. Namer, F.: Analyse automatique des noms déverbaux composés: pourquoi et comment faire intéragir analogie et système de règles. In: TALN 2009, pp. 1–10. ATALA, Senlis (2009)

Implementing a Formal Model
of Inflectional Morphology

Benoît Sagot[1] and Géraldine Walther[2,3]

[1] Alpage, INRIA & Univ. Paris-Diderot, 75013 Paris
[2] Laboratoire de Linguistique Formelle, CNRS & Univ. Paris-Diderot, 75013 Paris
[3] UFR de Langue Française, Univ. Panthéon-Sorbonne, 75005 Paris
benoit.sagot@inria.fr, geraldine.walther@linguist.jussieu.fr

Abstract. Inflectional morphology as a research topic lies on the crossroads of many a linguistic subfield, such as linguistic description, linguistic typology, formal linguistics and computational linguistics. However, the subject itself is tackled with diverse objectives and approaches each time. In this paper, we describe the implementation of a formal model of inflectional morphology capturing typological generalisations that aims at combining efforts made in each subfield giving access to every one of them to valuable methods and/or data that would have been out of range otherwise. We show that both language description and studies in formal morphology and linguistic typology on the one hand, as well as NLP tool and resource development on the other benefit from the availability of such a model and an implementation thereof.

1 Introduction, Motivation and Related Work

Contrarily to syntax and derivational morphology, inflectional morphology has the advantage of dealing, for a given language, with a finite range of data. Given a set of lexical units, it is possible to list all their inflected forms. From a theoretical point of view, one can therefore expect any formal approach to inflectional morphology to account not only for the data, i.e., inflectional paradigms in a given language, but also for the regularities and irregularities found within them.

Because of its finiteness, inflectional morphology also readily lends itself to typological approaches, where regularities and irregularities can be studied in a contrastive way. Among those approaches, the corpus of work carried out in the framework of **canonical typology** [12] aims at modeling and explaining inflectional phenomena across languages, including **non-canonical** phenomena such as syncretism, suppletion, heteroclisis or defectivity.

The confined set of data underlying inflectional morphology makes for the perfect place to combine approaches as different as computational linguistics, formal linguistics, linguistic typology, and descriptive linguistics, i.e., approaches that seldom get to combine in a global enterprise of precise language description, analysis and effective processing. The work described in this paper aims at furthering the combination of those complementary approaches. We describe the development of a lexical framework redesigned for implementing a theoretical and formal approach to inflectional morphology as well as improving the quality and speed of lexical resource and tool development.

C. Mahlow and M. Piotrowski (Eds.): SFCM 2013, CCIS 380, pp. 115–134, 2013.
© Springer-Verlag Berlin Heidelberg 2013

As a framework designed for all of the subfields cited above, it entails specific benefits for each one of them, but its main advantage lies in the combination of its possible different outcomes.

More specifically, this paper describes Alexina$_{PARSLI}$, a formalism for encoding inflectional descriptions (lexicon and grammar) that aims at filling the gap between morphologically and typologically motivated approaches on the one hand and implemented approaches on the other hand, as will be discussed in the remainder of this section. Indeed, Alexina$_{PARSLI}$ is both:

- an **implementation formalism for** PARSLI, a formal model of inflectional morphology [30,31] that accounts for concepts underlying the canonical approach of morphological typology.[1] We briefly describe the last version of PARSLI, on which Alexina$_{PARSLI}$ relies, in Section 2. In particular, we point out the major innovations with respect to earlier versions of PARSLI [30,24];
- an **extension of the Alexina lexical framework** [22] used in the field of Natural Language Processing (NLP) for modeling lexical information and developing lexical resources. The morphological layer of the (original) Alexina formalism is sketched in Section 3.

In Section 4, we show how we extended the morphological components of Alexina for turning it into an implementation formalism for PARSLI, namely Alexina$_{PARSLI}$. Finally, in Section 5, we show why the Alexina$_{PARSLI}$ formalism and tools have been greatly beneficial to works both in descriptive and formal morphology, in particular in studies about Latin passivisation and Maltese verbal inflection and in studies comparing the compacity of morphological descriptions, as well as in NLP, for the efficient development of a large-scale and linguistically sound morphological lexicon for German.

1.1 A Tool for Enhancing Studies in Theoretical Linguistics

From the point of view of theoretical linguistics in general and linguistic typology in particular, the main goal in the study of inflectional morphology lies in the description and comparison of inflectional systems belonging to different languages. As mentioned above, joint efforts therefore entail the following advantages. In order to simply generate paradigms from a morphological description of a given language, to describe and measure regularities and irregularities in these paradigms, or even to perform cross-linguistic comparisons, only formal and computational approaches can lead to reliable results: Formalisation allows for guaranteeing the consistency of an analysis, in particular within a full morphological system; Implementation allows for concretely verifying the validity of the analysis; In addition, large-scale implementation allows for a verification of the quasi-exhaustivity of the proposed analysis. In particular, it is a way to assess the overall relevance of a complete morphological description and the relative importance of a given phenomena within the full morphological system.

---

[1] We use here the term 'implementation' for expressing the fact that Alexina$_{PARSLI}$ provides a way to create and manipulate electronic resources (lexicon, grammar) that follow morphological analyses developed within the PARSLI formal model of inflectional morphology. Alexina$_{PARSLI}$ is both a language and a set of tools that can process a morphological description written in this language, e.g., for generating an automatic inflection tool.

Yet, this formalisation and implementation approach is still rarely used in theoretical morphology. In many cases, formalisations are somewhat approximative, and sometimes only concern the modeling of one particular phenomenon, often independently of the overall morphological system it has been extracted from [31]. Few models exist for which real implementations are available, that make it possible to validate theoretical assumptions. Among these few models are PFM [27] and *Network Morphology* [8], together with Finkel's *Cat's Claw* for the former[2] and the DATR formalism for the latter [13] and its extensions such as KATR [14]. Still, large-scale implementations in these frameworks remain rare. For example, analyses available on the *Cat's Claw* web site rarely involve more than fifty lexical entries. One exception is Brown and Hippisley's analysis of Russian nouns [8], which involves 1,500 lexical entries.[3]

On the other hand, computational approaches, most of them based on finite-state automata [5], have no difficulty for efficiently generating correct paradigms. As a matter of fact, it has been shown by Karttunen [16] that if one reduces morphological theories, including PFM and *Network Morphology*, solely to their ability to generate paradigms, they come down to realisational systems equivalent to finite-state automata [5]. However, even if computational approaches perfectly achieve this goal, they are often criticised, in the eyes of theoricists, for lacking what is the most interesting aspect from the theoretical point of view, namely explicitly modeling regularities and irregularities within paradigms. We introduce a means to easily implement formal analyses in a typologically sound framework that benefits from the data processing power available through computational approaches alone. [4] On an experiment carried out on modelling Maltese verbal inflection, we show the benefit for formal approaches to rely on computational approaches.

1.2   Improving the Quality and Efficiency in NLP Resource Development

On the other side of the scope, the issue for computational linguistics, and in particular NLP tool and resource development, lies in rapidly building high quality resources. We show on experiments on German, that Alexina_PARSLI also allows for quickliy setting up new NLP ressources that are theoretically sound.

2   The PARSLI Model of Inflectional Morphology

As indicated by its acronymic name, PARSLI [30,31], 'PARadigm Shape and Lexicon Interface', is a formal model of inflectional morphology in general and of the interface

---

[2] *Cat's Claw*: http://www.cs.uky.edu/~raphael/linguistics/claw.html

[3] This analysis is avaiable at http://networkmorphology.as.uky.edu

[4] As a result, our contribution does not rely in the computational aspects *per se*, and are complementary to standard finite-state morphology tools. Drawing a parallel with syntax, one could compare Alexina_PARSLI with the LKB plateform [11], PARSLI corresponding to the HPSG theoretical model of syntax [19]. On the other hand, finite-state tools such as XFST [5] or FOMA [15] would correspond to optimised and generic parser generators for context-free grammars such as the Lex/Yacc pair (http://dinosaur.compilertools.net).

between the shape of a lexeme's paradigm and the structure of its lexical entry in particular. This **inferential-realisational** model in the sense of Stump [27] has been built as a formalisation of the notions developed within the typological framework of canonical typology [12]. It explicitly models regularities and irregularities within a paradigm and/or an inflectional system, so called **non-canonical phenomena** as defined within canonical typology. Among those are suppletion [7], heteroclisis [26], deponency (or morphosyntactic mismatches) [2], defectiveness [4], overabundance [29], etc. It relies on the explicit representation of each non-canonical phenomenon as pieces of information directly encoded within the structure of a specific lexical entry. Moreover, the extent of the non-canonical phenomenon can be quantified with specific non-canonicity measures developed within the framework [31].

A preliminary version of the framework had been introduced in [30] and used in experiments described in [24]. The version described here is the one presented in [31]. Compared to the version in [30], it contains many innovations, among which the formal representation of the lexical entry itself, including the specification of an entry's morphosyntactic feature structure set, the formalisation of an **inflectional category**, the layered representation of inflection and the encoding of the full range of non-canonical phenomena defined within canonical typology.

2.1   Representation of a Lexical Entry

ℙ𝔸ℝ𝕊𝕃𝕀 explicitly formalises the notion of inflectional lexical entry. As shown in Figure 2, each entry (or lemma) is defined through a phonological base input I-PHON for the realisation rule sequences, its inflectional category I-CAT (such as *verb*, *transitive verb*, *noun*, etc.), a set of expressable morphosyntactic feature sets, a set of suppletive stems S-STEM or forms S-FORM and an inflectional pattern I-PAT consisting of a set of subpatterns.

2.2   Morphosyntactic Feature Sets and Inflectional Categories

Each lexical entry is defined through its membership within a specific inflectional category. Each one of those categories *canonically* expresses a certain set of morphosyntactic feature sets. Latin nouns, for example, will express two number values (SG and PL) as well as five differents case values (NOM, ACC, GEN, DAT and ABL). If a lexeme belongs to a specific category, it will canonically express the same set of features and be marked as *standard* in its lexical entry (see the feature set under MSF for French BALAYER 'swipe' at Figure 2). Sometimes, lexemes will express more or less features than expected. These deviations will be noted under MSF in their lexical entry. They are then considered to display the non-canonical phenomena of **overabundance** [29], resp. **deficiency** [31].

2.3   Realisation Zones

One of ℙ𝔸ℝ𝕊𝕃𝕀's major innovations with respect to comparable models [27,28,8] is the generalisation of the notion of paradigm partition in the sense of Pirelli and Battista's 'partition spaces' [18] or Bonami and Boyé's thematic spaces [6] to the exponence [17] level by stipulating so called **realisation zones**, illustrated by the different colours in Figure 1. Instead of associating lexical entries with a complete inflection class, ᏢᏗᏒᏕᏞᏗ associates every entry with realisation zones that contain the realisation rules allowing for the construction of specific partitions of this lexeme's paradigm. These realisation rules can thus be combined in different ways to account for the realisation of different types of paradigms. In particular, heteroclite paradigms as illustrated by the Slovak data in Table 1, can be accounted for by the combination of zones usually used by lexemes belonging to two different inflection classes. The Slovak data shows how some animal nouns use the singular inflection zone of animate nouns to build their singular forms, and the plural zone of inanimate nouns to build their plural forms. ᏢᏗᏒᏕᏞᏗ defines realisation classes, such as inflection class Z_{anim}^{exp} for masculine animate nouns in Table 1, as default combinations of realisation zones: classes are thus a derived notion built from the clustering of realisation zones that are observed in the construction of a significant number of paradigms. The significance itself is derived from a notion of decriptive economy: classes are only stipulated if this allows for a more compact representation of the whole system.

The set of morphosyntactic feature sets expressed by the realisation rules of a given realisation zone is called this zone's **partition space**.

Table 1. Heteroclite Slovak animal nouns

	Z_{anim}^{exp}: MASC. ANIMATE CHLAP 'guy'		Z_{inan}^{exp}: MASC. INANIMATE DUB 'oak tree'		MASC. HETEROCLITE OROL 'eagle'	
	$z_{anim,sg}^{exp}$: SG	$z_{anim,pl}^{exp}$: PL	$z_{inan,sg}^{exp}$: SG	$z_{inan,pl}^{exp}$: PL	$z_{anim,sg}^{exp}$: SG	$z_{inan,pl}^{exp}$: PL
NOM	chlap	chlap-i	dub	dub-y	orol	orl-y
GEN	chlap-a	chlap-ov	dub-a	dub-ov	orl-a	orl-ov
DAT	chlap-**ovi**	chlap-om	dub-u	dub-om	orl-**ovi**	orl-om
ACC	chlap-a	chlap-ov	dub	dub-y	orl-a	orl-y
LOC	chlap-**ovi**	chlap-och	dub-e	dub-och	orl-**ovi**	orl-och
INS	chlap-om	chlap-mi	dub-om	dub-mi	orl-om	orl-ami

2.4 A Layered Representation of Inflection

ᏢᏗᏒᏕᏞᏗ relies on a highly structured representation of form realisation by specifying various inflectional layers as illustrated in Figure 1. Every realisation zone belongs to a specific layer. Among these layers is at least one stem layer dealing with potential stem alternations (allomorphy). But other, optional theme (green) or exponence (blue) layers can also be stipulated. Figure 1 illustrates a realisational architecture containing three layers – one of each type. The theme and exponence layers could also further be split into several layers if needed.

The realisation of a given form thus consistst in the application of one realisation rule per layer. For example, inflecting the French verb BALAYER 'swipe' consists in applying realisation rules of two different layers, one stem layer and one exponence layer.

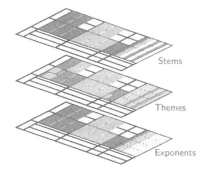

Stems

Themes

Exponents

Fig. 1. Inflectional layers

$$\begin{array}{ll} \text{BALAYER} & \\ \text{I-PHON} & balayer \\ \text{I-CAT} & verb \\ \text{MSF} & \{\,standard\,\} \\ \text{S-STEM} & \mid (empty) \\ \text{S-FORM} & \mid (empty) \\ & \mid (z_{ay}^s, \text{id}), (z_{v1,1}^{exp}, \text{id}) \\ \text{I-PAT} & \mid (z_{ay}^s, \text{id}), (z_{v1,2}^{exp}, \text{id}) \\ & \mid (z_{ai}^s, \text{id}), (z_{v1,2}^{exp}, \text{id}) \end{array}$$

Fig. 2. French BALAYER 'swipe'

One specificity of French verbs in -*ayer* like BALAYER is that they are overabundant [29] for half of their paradigm, i.e., half of their paradigm's cells display two different forms for expressing the same morphosyntactic feature set: *balayent* and *balaient* are both valid for expressing the features 3.PL.PRS.IND, whereas only *balayons* holds for 1.PL.PRS.IND. More precisely, each of the overabundant cells can be filled using one of two different stems (*balay-* and *balai-*) but the same exponents. As a result, we use two different stem zones, corresponding to two different realisation rules, and split the set of realisation rules into two exponence zones: zone $z_{v1,1}^{exp}$ corresponding to overabundant cells and $z_{v1,2}^{exp}$ for non-overabundant cells.[5] For example, building the form *balayent* for 3.PL.PRS.IND involves the application of the stem realisation rule in stem zone z_{ay}^s, which builds the stem *balay-*, followed by a form realisation rule from zone $z_{v1,1}^{exp}$ that adds the suffix -*ent*. Generating the alternate form *balaient* involves the other stem realisation rule from stem zone z_{ai}^s, which builds the stem *balai-*, followed by the same inflection zone $z_{v1,1}^{exp}$ at the exponence layer. On the other hand, *balayons* obtains its 1.PL.PRS.IND suffix -*ons* from a rule in $z_{v1,2}^{exp}$, applied on the stem *balay-* generated by the stem realisation rule in z_{ai}^s. The combination of z_{ai}^s with $z_{v1,2}^{exp}$ is not allowed, therefore *balaions is not generated.

The licit associations of realisation zones across layers are stated in a lexeme's inflectional subpatterns grouped together in the inflectional pattern I-PAT, as indicated in the lexical entry for BALAYER illustrated by Figure 2.

2.5 Suppletive Stems and Forms

Lexical entries can also specify suppletive stems or forms. In the canonical case, the list of suppletive stems S-STEM or forms S-FORM will be marked as empty (see the example of BALAYER). But in the case of a verb like French ALLER 'to go', suppletive stems can be specified along with a stem index corresponding to the stem zone's partition space in which the suppletive stem is used. The three suppletive stems *v-*, *aill-* et *ir-* of ALLER

---

[5] In the name $z_{v1,1}^{exp}$, 'v1' stands for 'First group verb', whereas the final '1' is the index of the exponence zone.

$$\begin{bmatrix} \text{ALLER} \\ \text{I-PHON} \quad aller \\ \text{I-CAT} \quad verb \\ \text{MSF} \quad \{\ standard\ \} \\ \text{S-STEM} \quad \begin{vmatrix} z_2^s\colon & v- \\ z_7^s\colon & aill- \\ z_{10}^s\colon & i- \end{vmatrix} \\ \text{S-FORM} \quad |\ (empty) \\ \text{I-PAT} \quad \Big| (Z_{def}^s, \text{id}), (Z_{aller}^{exp}, \text{id}) \end{bmatrix}$$

Fig. 3. French ALLER 'to go'

$$\begin{bmatrix} \text{BRAT} \\ \text{I-PHON} \quad brat \\ \text{I-CAT} \quad noun \\ \text{MSF} \quad \{\ standard\ \} \\ \text{S-STEM} \quad |\ (empty) \\ \text{S-FORM} \quad |\ (empty) \\ \text{I-PAT} \quad \begin{vmatrix} (Z_{reg}^s, \text{id}), (z_{M\text{-}A,SG}^{exp}, \text{id}) \\ (Z_{reg}^s, \text{id}), (z_{F\text{-}A,SG}^{exp}, t_{NB}) \end{vmatrix} \end{bmatrix}$$

Fig. 4. Serbo-croatian BRAT 'brother' (data from [3])

are listed under S-STEM in Figure 3. Suppletive forms are listed under S-FORM along with the feature set they express.

2.6 Realisational Couples and Transfer Rules

For each lexical entry, the inflectional pattern I-PAT specifies a certain number of subpatterns consisting of realisational couples, such as the couple (Z_{reg}^s, id) in the entry of Serbo-croatian BRAT 'brother'. These couples themselves consist in a realisation zone or class such as Z_{reg}^s and a **transfer function**. Transfer functions are identity functions in the canonical case. However, there are cases where a feature expressed by a lexeme's form differs from the feature canonically expressed by a given realisation rule. Such a case arises for example in nouns like BRAT who build their plural form by using realisation rules usually used for building singular forms. Such nouns specify a particular transfer function such as t_{NB} that allows for specifying the morphosyntactic mismatch between the features expressed (PL) and the features realised (SG).

This summary presentation of the ℙⅯℝⅼ model will be extended while showing how we implemented the formal notions within Alexina℗ℝℒ (section 4).

3 The Original Alexina Formalism

We have based our implementation of the ℙⅯℝⅼ model on the Alexina lexical formalism [20,23,21,22]. Alexina covers both the morphological and the syntactic level, only the former being relevant here.[6] Alexina's original morphological layer, although significantly different, shares some fundamental properties with ℙⅯℝⅼ. These include in particular an explicit interface between the inflectional lexicon and the inflectional grammar.

Alexina already has a good track record as a lexical formalism, as there exist a number of medium- and large-scale lexicons for diverse languages (see Table 2), among which the first, largest and richest is the French lexicon L*efff* [23,22]. Indeed, the development of Alexina lexicons is facilitated by the availability of associated development, maintenance, validation and extension tools and interfaces. Moreover, all Alexina

---

[6] Alexina also entails a means to represent derivational morphology, but this also lies beyond the scope of this paper.

Table 2. Alexina lexicons. Darker lines correspond to Alexina$_{\text{PARSLI}}$ lexicons. References for each of these resources can ben found in [22,31].

LEXICON	LANGUAGE	#LEMMAS	#LEXEMES	#FORMS	#DISTINCT FORMS
Lefff[7]	français	120,000	125,000	550,000	460,000
Leffe	espagnol	180,000	180,000	1,500,000	700,000
Leffga	galicien	70,000	70,000	750,000	500,000
Leffla	latin	2,200	2,200	115,000	96,000
EnLex	anglais	350,000	350,000	580,000	510,000
DeLex	allemand	63,000	63,000	2,100,000	405,000
PolLex	polonais	240,000	240,000	1,400,000	360,000
SkLex	slovaque	50,000	50,000	470,000	250,000
PerLex	persan	30,000	30,000	550,000	460,000
KurLex	kurde kurmanji	22,000	22,000	410,000	240,000
SoraLex	kurde sorani	520	520	30,000	25,000
MaltLex	maltais	560	560	9,000	7,200

lexicons are freely available (including Alexina$_{\text{PARSLI}}$ lexicons). This guarantees that morphological analyses and lexical data can be checked and used by anyone, be it for typological, morphological or NLP studies.

The way Alexina encodes morphology explicitly relies on a paradigmatic approach. Each lexical entry is associated with an inflection class, as illustrated in the upper part of Figure 5 with five verbal lexical entries from the Lefff.[8] Each **intensional entry** consists of a citation form (respectively *accoutumer* 'accustom', *appeler* 'call', *enrichir* 'enrich', *dormir* 'sleep', *admettre* 'admit') and an **inflection class**. In the morphological grammar, each inflection class is explicitly defined through the realisation rules that describe how it will build paradigms. In Figure 5, the inflection classes involved are v-er for the regular and productive class of first group verbs, v-ir2 for the regular and virtually non-productive class of second group verbs, v-ir3 for third-group verbs in -*ir* and v55 for one of the irregular third-group inflection classes. For some lexical entries, the inflection class is associated with inflection class **variants**, which allow for selecting specific rules for generating some of the forms in the paradigm. For example, in Figure 5, variants dbl and std respectively apply to first-group verbs which double their stem-final consonant in some cells (cf. *appeler / appelle*) and to first-group verbs which do not (cf. *peler* 'peel' / *pèle*). The lower part of Figure 5 shows a few inflected entries, or **extensional entries**, generated by the lexical entries of the upper part. The lexemes' morphological categories are displayed next to the inflected form, along with their citation forms and a morphological tag encoding the feature sets expressed by the inflected form.

An Alexina morphological grammar contains two main sections: (1) a set of morphonological rules — or rather, as all Alexina lexicons to date are orthographic, morphographemic rules that simulate morphonological rules; and (2) the morphological part proper, i.e., the description of each inflection class.

---

[7] The Alexina$_{\text{PARSLI}}$ version of the Lefff's morphological description is called NEW in [24]. Its original ("official") version relies on the original Alexina formalism [22].

[8] For the sake of simplicity, syntactic information is not displayed.

accoutumer	v-er:std		
appeler	v-er:dbl		
enrichir	v-ir2		
dormir	v-ir3		
admettre	v55		

accoutuma	v	accoutumer	J3s
accoutume	v	accoutumer	PS13s
accoutumant	v	accoutumer	G
appela	v	appeler	J3s
appelle	v	appeler	PS13s
appelant	v	appeler	G
enrichit	v	enrichir	J3s
enrichit	v	enrichir	P3s
enrichissant	v	enrichir	G
dormit	v	dormir	J3s
dort	v	dormir	P3s
dormant	v	dormir	G
admit	v	admettre	J3
admet	v	admettre	P3
admettant	v	admettre	G

Fig. 5. Lexical entries from the L*eff*: intensional entries in the upper part, a few corresponding extensional entries in the lower part

The morphonological part usually starts by the definition of graphemes (including digraphs or trigraphs) and grapheme classes (e.g., the set of back vowels). These classes can then be used when defining morphonological rules.

In the original Alexina formalism, the strictly morphological part of the grammar defines inflection classes by specifying realisation rules for inflected forms associated with the corresponding feature tag. These rules can only involve suffixation and/or prefixation. Any other morphological operation must therefore be simulated in two steps, namely first an affixation rule that inserts the necessary information for the subsequent application of dedicated "morphonological" rules that produce the correct output.[9] A realisation rule can also simply stipulate the form for a given morphological tag to be realised in the same way that the form for another tag (this corresponds to Stump's [27] "rules of referral"). This constitutes a simple (and directional) modeling of the notion of syncretism. An inflection class can also inherit all or some rules from another inflection class. Thus, in the L*eff*, the inflection class adj-4 for adjectives that inflect both in gender (-e for the feminine) and in number (-s in the plural) inherits all rules from the inflection class nc-4 for masculine nouns inflecting in both gender and number using the same suffixes (e.g., *doctorant/doctorante* 'PhD student'). All types of

---

[9] Cf., producing *appelle* from *appeler* and *jette* from *jeter* in a unified way entails using a non-strictly concatenative operation: the duplication of the stem-final consonant. There, one can use an affix such as *-2e* followed by a "morphonological" rule that rewrites *t_2* as *tt_* and *l_2* as *ll_* ("_" indicates a morph boundary).

realisation rules (explicit or inheritance) can be restricted based on their input, using positive (`rads=`) or negative (`rads_except=`) regular-expression-like **constraints**.[10]

At the technical level, an Alexina morphological grammar is an XML document. A dedicated tool can then compile into an inflection script (which can inflect the associated intensional lexicon), a "disinflection" (ambiguous lexicon-free lemmatisation) tool and a derivation tool (that produces all possible derived lexemes based on regular derivation patterns, sketched above but not described here). This technical architecture is preserved in Alexina_PARSLI.

4   Adapting Alexina to PARSLI: Alexina_PARSLI

Our development of an implementation formalism for PARSLI is based on the orignal Alexina formalism, which we adapted for it to take into account PARSLI-specific concepts. The notions of inflection class variant, classes of letters, morphonological rules and constraints on realisational rules have been retained from Alexina, and sometimes generalised.

As already mentioned, a partial Alexina implementation of a preliminary version of PARSLI was used in [24]. However, the work presented in this section goes far beyond, for at least two reasons.

First, the PARSLI formalism itself has been heavily enriched since [24]. The first version of PARSLI was for example restricted to one stem level and one exponence level, and was not able to deal with the full range of non-canonical phenomena. Because this was sufficient for encoding French verbal inflection, it allowed for carrying the compacity experiments described in [24]. The latest version of PARSLI, whose implementation within Alexina is described here, has proven adapted to a large variety of typologically diverse languages since, such as Sorani Kurdish (Indo-European, western Iranian), German (Indo-European, Germanic, see Section 5.2) Latin (Indo-European, Italic), Maltese (western Semitic), Khaling (Sino-Tibetan, Kiranti), and others.

Second, the implementation of the preliminary version of PARSLI used in [24] only covered those PARSLI notions that were required for implementing the four morphological descriptions of French verbal inflection used in the compacity study. Notions such as transfer rules were already in PARSLI but not implemented. Moreover, Alexina_PARSLI offers many ways to simplify morphological grammars, that are also new to the work presented here. This includes for example (1) various factorisation mechanisms; (2) a mechanism for specifying, for each category the inventory of morphological attributes, their values, and their incompatibilities, thus specifying the inventory of cells in the paradigms; (3) a novel and generic way to model morphological (realisational) operations; (4) the possibility to encode realisation rules using *rule blocks*, in a way similar to Stump's [27] Paradigm Function Morphology.

---

[10] For example, it is possible to posit two rules for the same tag, and specify that one applies only to stems ending with a consonant or a glide, the other only to stems ending with a vowel or a glide. As a result, the corresponding cell will be overabundant for lexical entries whose stem ends in a glide, yet for those lexical entries only.

4.1 Morphological Operations

As mentioned above, the only available operations for expressing realisation rules in the original Alexina formalism were prefixation and suffixation operations, and more complex operations had to be simulated via morphonological rules. Alexina_{Pꝶꝶℒꝰ} now allows for modeling non-concatenative operations. More specifically, it is now possible to define in the morphological grammars all morphological operations required by realisation rules, including non-concatenative ones. Indeed, such morphological operations are considered as specifically belonging to the morphological system of the language at hand. Suffixation (written as `append=`) and prefixation (`left_append=`) are retained from Alexina as basic morphological operations. In addition, `insert` operations allow for inserting segments, while `replace` allows for replacing one segment by another. These basic operations can be used for defining more complex operations, as illustrated in Figure 7, which we explain below. The definition of morphological operations, just as morphonological rules in the original Alexina, often makes use of the notion of *letter class*, sketched above and retained within Alexina_{Pꝶꝶℒꝰ}. Two letter class definitions from MaltLex are snown in Figure 6.

```
<letterclass name="C" letters="b␣ċ␣d␣f␣ġ␣g␣għ␣ħ␣ħ␣h␣j␣k␣l␣m␣n␣p␣q␣r␣s␣t␣v
    ␣w␣x␣ż␣z␣'␣"/>
<letterclass name="V" letters="a␣e␣i␣o␣u␣ie"/>
```

Fig. 6. Two letter classes from MaltLex

Based on letter classes and on the primitive operations (`append`, `left_append`, `insert` and `replace`), operations such as shown in Figure 7 can be defined. In this Figure, the operation `deleteV1` defined for Maltese stems stipulates for example that for a given stem construction rule input (`source=`) with a CVCVC structure, applying `deleteV1` produces a new stem (`target=`) with a CCVC structure. A `replace` operation keeps the occurrences of a letter class c unchanged if it is written `[:c:]` on both sides of the rule, as is the case for all consonants `[:C:]` in the definition of `deleteV1`, and deletes it if it is written `[0:c:]`, as is the case for the first vowel `[0:V:]`. Within an operation definition, the first applicable rule is applied, and the following rules are ignored (except if the applied rules specifies explicitly the opposite, with `stop="0"`). If none of the rules can be applied on a particular input, the operation fails.

Erasing segments is not the only option when using `replace`. Not preserving a segment can also be used as the first part of a real replacement operation. Thus, any occurrence of the symbol "_" in the output of a rule will be replaced by an argument given to the operation in addition to its input, as is the case in the second operation definition in Figure 7. For example, one can invoke the `deleteV1changeV2` operation in a realisation rule by writing `deleteV1changeV2(i)`, in order to replace the second vowel by an *i*. Note that each occurrence of "_" in the output of a rule corresponds to a different argument to be given to the operation at invocation time.

```
<!-- Maltese (MaltLex) -->
<operation_definition name="deleteV1">
  <replace source="[:C:][O:V:][:C:][:V:][:C:]"
           target="[:C:][:C:][:V:][:C:]" />
  <replace source="[:C:][O:V:][:C:][:V:]" target="[:C:][:C:][:V:]" />
</operation_definition>
<operation_definition name="deleteV1changeV2">
  <replace source="[:C:][O:V:][:C:][O:V:][:C:]"
           target="[:C:][:C:]_[:C:]" />
  <replace source="[:C:][O:V:][:C:][O:V:]" target="[:C:][:C:]_" />
</operation_definition>

<!-- Latin (Leffla) -->
<operation_definition name="redup-initial">
  <replace source="#[1:C:][O:V:]" target="#[1:C:]_[1:C:]_"/>
</operation_definition>
```

Fig. 7. Morphological operations in Alexina_PARSLI (data from MaltLex and Leffla)

Finally, it is also possible to duplicate segments, as necessary for encoding reduplication. The last operation definition in Figure 7 is an example of a reduplication operation, used for producing several Latin verbal stems. The initial consonant is indexed by a numeric identifier, here 1 in [1:C:], which allows for invoking it more than once anywhere in the rule. In this operations, it is reduplicated in the output. In addition, the initial vowel is dropped. This operation is also an illustration of a two-argument operation: the first, respectively second occurrence of "_" in the output of the rule will be replaced by the first, respectively second argument provided to redup-initial upon invocation. For example, calling redup-initial(e,e) on the stem *fall-* from the verb FALLO 'deceive' outputs the stem *fefell-*.

4.2   Stem Allomorphy, Stem Suppletion and Form Suppletion

In the original Alexina formalism, each lexical entry is meant to have one unique stem. Accounting for **stem allomorphy** requires to circumvent this limitation by using available mechanisms in ways that are both very *ad hoc* and not linguistically sound.[11] In Alexina_PARSLI, stem allomorphy is directly handled by two distinct mechanisms, one for regular stem allomorphy (as in Iranian languages, for example) and one for irregular stem allomorphy (as for the verb *aller* 'go' in French, illustrated in Figure 3.[12]

Regular allomorphy is modeled using realisation rules at the stem level within the grammar. Figure 8 provides two such rules for modeling Maltese regular stem allomorphy, which is illustrated the two paradigms in Table 3. Within Maltese paradigms, stem

---

[11] For example, one can define "morphonological" rules that play the role of stem generators. In that case, the realisational rule can suffix the stem with a special marker that will later be interpreted by these "morphonological" rules. This temporary solution was used, for example, for simulating stem allomorphy Persian.

[12] We refer the reader to [31] for a discussion on why and how regular and irregular stem allomorphy should be distinguished from one another.

Table 3. Paradigms for the Maltese verbs RASS and MESS

		RASS 'press'	MESS 'touch'
RAD2	PFV 1.SG	*rasséjt*	*messéjt*
	PFV 2.SG	*rasséjt*	*messéjt*
	PFV 1.PL	*rasséj.na*	*messéj.na*
	PFV 2.PL	*rasséj.tu*	*messéj.tu*
RAD1	PFV 3.M.S	*ráss*	*méss*
RAD3	PFV 3.F.S	*rás.set*	*més.set*
RAD4	PFV 3.PL	*ras.séːw*	*mes.séːw*

perfective sub-paradigms

		RASS 'press'	MESS 'touch'
RAD5	IPFV 1.SG	*nróss*	*nmíss*
	IPFV 2.SG	*tróss*	*tmíss*
	IPFV 3.M.S	*jróss*	*jmíss*
	IPFV 3.F.S	*tróss*	*tmíss*
RAD6	IPFV 1.PL	*nrós.su*	*nmís.su*
	IPFV 2.PL	*trós.su*	*tmís.su*
	IPFV 3.PL	*jrós.su*	*jmís.su*

imperfective sub-paradigms

```
<table name="CVCC" rads="[:C:][:V:][:C:][:C:]">
  <item name="S1"/>
  <item name="S2" source="S1" append="ej"/>
  <item name="S3" source="S1" operation="" />
  <item name="S4" source="S1" append="e"/>
  <item name="S5" source="S1" operation="changeV1(o)" rads="[:C:]a[:C
    :][:C:]"/>
  <item name="S5" source="S1" operation="changeV1(i)" rads="[:C:]e[:C
    :][:C:]"/>
  <item name="S5" source="S1" operation="changeV1(i)" rads="[:C:]i[:C
    :][:C:]"/>
  <item name="S6" source="S5" operation="" />
</table>
```

Fig. 8. Regular stem allomorphy (MaltLex data, after Camilleri and Walther [10])

allomorphy involves up to six distinct stems (RAD1 to RAD6). The examples in Table 3 involve four stems, indicated by four distinct cell background colors (two of the stems are syncretic with others: RAD1 and RAD2 on the one hand, and RAD5 and RAD6 on the other hand).

The other way to account for multiple stems in Alexina$_{PXRSLI}$ is to provide them explicitly in the lexical entry. It is the natural way to deal with irregular stem allomorphy, i.e., cases where stem creation is not dealt with by the grammar but constitutes a lexical irregularity of the lexical entry at hand. If one considers that French verbs have twelve stems (often syncretic), following Bonami and Boyé [6] and retaining the same stem identifiers from stem 1 to stem 12, each of these stems corresponds to a slot after the / symbol in the lexical entry, sorted and separated by a comma. For example, in the case of ALLER, as shown in Figure 9, suppletive stems specified in the lexicon are stem 2 *va-*, stem 7 *aill-* and stem 10 *i-*. Other stems are deduced from these stems or from the citation form's stem *all-* by regular stem allomorphy rules. For instance, stem 3 is deduced by syncretism with stem 2, and so on.

```
aller     v:23r/,va,,,,,aill,,,i
dire      v:3re/dis,,di,,,,,,,,,,dit/2.pl.prs.ind=dites
```

Fig. 9. Irregular stem allomorphy and form allomorphy (data from a modified L*eff*)

The original Alexina formalism had no way to encode **form suppletion**. Again, this non-canonical phenomena had to be modeled in a non-satisfying way.[13] In Alexina𝖯𝖠𝖱𝖲𝖫𝖨, it is possible to list suppletive forms in a lexical entry. They override any form the morphological grammar might want to generate. Figure 9 illustrates this on the example of the verb *dire* 'say', which has the irregular 2.PL.PRS.IND *dites* instead of the regular *disez*.

In the case of overabundant suppletive forms, the mechanism already available in Alexina is preserved: they can simply be listed explicitly as such. For example, MAR-RON 'brown' is listed in the L*eff* as inflecting for number (*marrons*). In addition, the L*eff* lists an additional plural form (*marron*).

4.3 Inflectional Layers, Zones and Patterns

Another new feature of Alexina𝖯𝖠𝖱𝖲𝖫𝖨 is that it implements inflectional layers. The original Alexina formalism could deal with one exponence layer only. The implementation of the preliminary version of 𝖯𝖠𝖱𝖲𝖫𝖨 used in [24] was dealt with one stem layer and one exponence layer only. In Alexina𝖯𝖠𝖱𝖲𝖫𝖨, a description can involve an unbounded amount of layers (`level`): Zero or one stem layer (`type="stem"`), zero to many theme layers (`type="theme"`) and zero to many exponence layers (`type="exponent"`).

𝖯𝖠𝖱𝖲𝖫𝖨 defines partition spaces as subsets of feature structure sets. They constitute one of the ways to refer to realisation zones as defined in 𝖯𝖠𝖱𝖲𝖫𝖨. In Alexina𝖯𝖠𝖱𝖲𝖫𝖨, these partition spaces can be defined on a per-layer basis. We illustrate this mechanism in Figure 10 on Maltese for the stem layer and on Latin for the exponence layer.

One of the main innovation in 𝖯𝖠𝖱𝖲𝖫𝖨, and therefore in Alexina𝖯𝖠𝖱𝖲𝖫𝖨, is the introduction of **realisation zones**. In Alexina𝖯𝖠𝖱𝖲𝖫𝖨, they can be defined in two different ways. Either directly using XML tags within a given level, or by invoking them as the intersection of a realisation class and a partition space. For space reasons we do not illustrate this here, but the morphological grammars in MaltLex and L*eff*la, which are freely available, contain many examples thereof.

In Alexina, intensional entries are associated with inflection classes. Alexina𝖯𝖠𝖱𝖲𝖫𝖨 implements 𝖯𝖠𝖱𝖲𝖫𝖨's view, according to which a lexical entry is associated with realisation zones through a **pattern**. Inflection classes are only a secondary notion: they emerge as observable generalisations that capture sets of zones often used together by lexical entries. Inflection classes are indicated by `table` tags in Alexina𝖯𝖠𝖱𝖲𝖫𝖨, zones by `zone`. As a result, lexical entries in the intensional lexicon are associated with patterns, which are defined in the grammar. A pattern contains at least one *subpattern*, which is

---

[13] Either by assigning to the entry an inflection class that would not generate forms for all cells, if any, and specifying the missing forms explicitly; or by considering (almost) the whole form as an exponent (suffix) over an (almost) empty stem.

```
<!-- Maltese (MaltLex) -->
<level type="stem" level="1">
    <partitionspace name="S1" features="3.m.sg.pfv"/>
    <partitionspace name="S2" features="1.pfv|2.pfv"/>
    <partitionspace name="S3" features="3.f.sg.pfv"/>
    <partitionspace name="S4" features="3.pl.pfv"/>
    <partitionspace name="S5" features="sg.ipfv"/>
    <partitionspace name="S6" features="pl.ipfv"/>

<!-- Latin (Leffla) -->
<level type="exponent" level="3">
    <partitionspace name="I1" features="ipfv.ind|ipfv.sbjv|prs.inf"/>
    <partitionspace name="I2" features="pfv.ind|pfv.sbjv|pst.inf"/>
    <partitionspace name="I3"
            features="prs.ptcp|fut.ptcp|fut.inf|sup|pst.ptcp|grv|grd"/>
```

Fig. 10. Definition of partition spaces (data from MaltLex and Leffla)

defined in turn as a set of realisation zones (`realzone`),[14] one per realisational layer (see Figure 11).[15] Each subpattern can only produce either zero or one form for a given feature set (i.e., for a given cell). Regular overabundance therefore requires patterns that contain several subpatterns. In addition, each pattern is provided with a *morphological category*. This allows for computing the inventory of cells that has to be filled by the pattern. How and from which information this inventory is computed is explained in the next section. Figure 11 illustrates how patterns are defined in the grammar based on Latin verbal data from Leffla.

4.4 Morphosyntactic Features and Definition of Paradigms' Cells

In the original Alexina formalism, morphosyntactic features appeared only as tags associated with (exponence) realisation rules. In ℙ𝔞ℝ𝔰𝕃𝕚, a realisational model, each form is considered as the realisation of a morphological feature structure. Alexina_ℙ𝔞ℝ𝔰𝕃𝕚 therefore explicitly models feature structures. The inventory of cells specific to a given morphological category is computed based on a unification mechanism. For a given morphological category (`category`), the cells to be realised are obtained as the combination of all attribute-value pairs that are mutually compatible. Therefore, an Alexina_ℙ𝔞ℝ𝔰𝕃𝕚

---

[14] As mentioned above, a realisation zone is either invoked as such, or by proving a realisation table and a partition space. In the latter case, if the partition space is omitted, the whole table is considered as a zone. In addition, a transfer function, in the sense sketched above, can be specified.

[15] In fact, constraints can be associated with a `realzone`, such as a partition space for which the rule is valid, one or more *variants* that must be assigned for the lexical entry in order for the rule to apply, or constraints on the input of the rule (`rads=` and `rads_except=`). Therefore, several `realzones` can be used in the same subpattern for the same level. This is one of the factorisation devices mentioned above.

```
<pattern name="v-aA" cat="v" >
  <subpattern>
    <realzone level="1" table="s-reg"/>
    <realzone level="2" table="a"/>
    <realzone level="3" table="v-A"/>
  </subpattern>
</pattern>
<pattern name="v-aAB" cat="v" >
  <subpattern>
    <realzone level="1" table="s-reg"/>
    <realzone level="2" table="a"/>
    <realzone level="3" table="v-B"/>
    <realzone level="3" partitionspace="I3" table="v-A"/>
  </subpattern>
</pattern>
```

Fig. 11. Examples of pattern definitions (data from Le*ff*la)

morphological grammar specifies for each category the inventory of attributes, each possible value for each of these attribute, as well as exclusion rules (e.g., this value for this attribute is incompatible with that value for that attribute, or with the attribute itself; or this particular feature structure is invalid).

Finally, morphological feature structure sets can be defined, and then associated with lexical entries for encoding deficiency. For example, in French, impersonal verbs are associated with the set `impers`, which only contains cells from the verbal paradigm whose morphological feature structure unify with 3.SG.

4.5   Realisation Rules

Above, we have described how morphological operations are defined, and can be invoked (including by realisation rules). Contrarily to the orignal Alexina, Alexina$_{PARSLI}$ associates realisation rules with morphological feature structures. At a given layer, a realisation rule will be applied if its feature set successfully unifies with the feature set of the form being generated.

In Alexina$_{PARSLI}$, it is possible, as in PFM, to defined rule blocks within a zone or a table. In each block, one and only one rule applies given an input feature set. In the Maltese example in Figure 12, that illustrates the unique exponence table in MaltLex, we make use of two rule blocks `block="1"` and `block="2"`. The first one realises aspect and person, the second one realises number (suffix *-u* for plural forms). As in PFM, Alexina$_{PARSLI}$ allows for writing *portemanteau* rules that span over more than one adjacent blocks, and have precedence over standard rules. In our example, `block="1-2"` allows for one rule to short-cut both blocks. Last, if more than one rule can apply for generating the same form, the first one is used (contrarily to PFM, which would use the most specific one).

```
<level type="exponent" level="3">
  <table name="exponence" rads="">
    <item block="1-2" suffix="na" features="1.pl.pfv"/>
    <item block="1-2" suffix="et" features="3.f.sg.pfv"/>
    <item block="1" suffix="t" features="1.sg.pfv|2.pfv"/>
    <item block="1" prefix="n" features="1.ipfv"/>
    <item block="1" prefix="t" features="2.ipfv"/>
    <item block="1" prefix="t" features="3.f.sg.ipfv"/>
    <item block="1" prefix="j" features="3.ipfv"/>
    <item block="2" suffix="u" features="pl"/>
  </table>
</level>
```

Fig. 12. Realisation rules (MaltLex data)

5   Use Cases

5.1   Alexina$_{\mathcal{PARSLI}}$ for Language Description

Throughout the previous section, we have used examples from MaltLex, a lexicon that covers the semitic-based part of the Maltese verbal system. The first version of this description was based on Camilleri's analysis [9], which had been formalised and implemented in Alexina$_{\mathcal{PARSLI}}$. The lexicon associated with this implementation was a quasi-exhaustive inventory of 600 semitic-based verbal entries, extracted from the list of 850 first-binyan verbs from Spagnol's *Maltese Language Resource Server* [25] by manually filtering out incorrect entries. This implementation, including the lexicon, has shown that Camilleri's analysis correctly accounts for most data on first-binyan stems. However, it has also unveiled that several phenomena were not handled, including instances of overabundance. Moreover, as it is only a model of stem alternation, it does not account for the behavior of the extension vowel, which appears in the imperfective forms of some verbs. The extension of the model for taking into account this extension vowel was greatly eased by its implementation, which allowed for generating all inflected forms and validate them. In other words, the $\mathcal{PARSLI}$ formalisation and the Alexina$_{\mathcal{PARSLI}}$ implementation, together with a large-scale lexicon (for the class of verbs at hand) were of a crucial help for correcting and extending an analysis previously assumed as complete, thus contributing to improve the understanding of Maltese verbal morphology [10].

5.2   Alexina$_{\mathcal{PARSLI}}$ for Developing Lexical Resources

The development of lexical resources for NLP can also benefit from a morphologically sound model of inflection. An example thereof is the recent development of DeLex, a new Alexina morphological lexicon for German. Apart DeLex, and to our best knowledge, there is surprisingly no freely available morphological lexicon for German, as pointed out by Adolphs [1].

German morphology is not stricly concatenative, in particular because nominal and verbal inflection involves vowel alternations (*ablaut* and *umlaut*) at the stem level, leading to stem allomorphy. In addition, overabundance is massive, in particular within nominal and adjectival paradigms, both at the stem and at the exponence levels.[16] As a result, the manual development of a morphological grammar for German was simplified and speeded up thanks to notions defined in PᴙRꟗLI and implemented in Alexina_PᴙRꟗLI. For example, our morphological grammar involves two realisational levels for adjectives and nouns, namely one stem level and one exponence level. This allows for defining only one adjectival exponence table, as all variation within adjectival inflection lies at the stem level, i.e., in the way the comparative and superlative stems are built[17] or resort to morphonology. Verbs involve an additional exponence level, which uses the unique adjectival exponence zone for inflecting the past participle.

The efficient development of this morphological grammar has been realised together with the extraction of lexical data and continuous validation of both the grammar and the lexicon via the paradigms they generate. Indeed, we extracted large-scale lexical information from the German Wiktionary[18], which provided us with unstructured, noisy and incomplete raw data. The morphological grammar proved very useful for detecting and correcting the this raw data.

The current version of DeLex now contains as many as 63,000 intensional (citation form + inflection pattern) entries generating over 2 million extensional forms (inflected form + citation form + morphological feature structure), which cover 405,000 distinct inflected forms.

5.3   Alexina_PᴙRꟗLI for Quantitative Formal Morphology

Beyond language description and analysis, a large-scale implementation (large-coverage grammar and medium- or large-scale lexicon) is a prerequisite for carrying out quantitative linguistic studies. A preliminary version of PᴙRꟗLI had already proven sufficient to implement four different description of French verbal inflection [24]. The associated implementation allowed for objectively comparing these descriptions on the basis of a dedicated information-theoretic measure [24].

New complexity assessment tools have been developed, which are now compatible with Alexina_PᴙRꟗLI as presented in this paper. They have been used for quantitatively assessing various descriptions of Latin and Maltese verbal inflections, including the descriptions of Le*ffl*a and MaltLex [31] used as examples troughout this paper. These comparisions have shed new light on formal morphological issues such as the balance between heteroclisis and deponency in Latin, or the boundary between morphonology and (autonomous) morphology in Maltese.

---

[16] For example, at the exponence level, many masculine and neuter nouns can bear the suffix -*s* or -*es* for the GEN.SG, and/or the null suffix or the suffix -*e* for the DAT.SG. The stem level also shows overabundance for these nouns, specifically for the plural stem.

[17] For example, stem suppletion (*gut* 'good', *besser* 'better' *best-* 'best'), stem-related deficiency (*alkoholfrei* 'alcool-free' has no comparative or superlative) or stem overabundance (*frei* 'free', *freier* 'freer', *freist-* or *freiest-* 'freest').

[18] http://de.wiktionary.org

6   Conclusion

In this paper we have introduced the latest version of Alexina₽ᴀᴙꙅʟɪ, an implementation of the ₽ᴀᴙꙅʟɪ model for inflectional morphology that extends the Alexina lexical framework. We have shown on examples from various languages the relevance of the model and its implementation. Our aim is now, thanks to Alexina₽ᴀᴙꙅʟɪ, to strengthen our efforts towards joint work between various specialists of morphology, be they descriptive linguists, typologists, formal linguists or computational linguists.

References

1. Adolphs, P.: Acquiring a poor man's inflectional lexicon for German. In: Proceedings of LREC 2008, Marrakech, Maroc (2008)
2. Baerman, M.: Morphological reversals. Journal of Linguistics 43, 33–61 (2007)
3. Baerman, M.: Deponency in Serbo-Croatian, Typological Database on Deponency, Surrey Morphology Group, CMC, University of Surrey,
   `http://www.smg.surrey.ac.uk/deponency/Examples/Serbo-Croatian.htm`
4. Baerman, M., Corbett, G.G., Brown, D. (eds.): Defective Paradigms: Missing Forms and What They Tell Us. Oxford University Press (2010)
5. Beesley, K.R., Karttunen, L.: Finite State Morphology. Studies in Computational Linguistics, CSLI Publications (2003)
6. Bonami, O., Boyé, G.: Suppletion et classes flexionnelles dans la conjugaison du français. Langages 152, 102–126 (2003)
7. Boyé, G.: Suppletion. In: Brown, K. (ed.) Encyclopedia of Language and Linguistics, 2nd edn., vol. 12, pp. 297–299. Elsevier, Oxford (2006)
8. Brown, D., Hippisley, A.: Network Morphology: A Defaults-based Theory of Word Structure. Cambridge University Press (2012)
9. Camilleri, M.: Island morphology: Morphology's interactions in the study of stem patterns. Linguistica 51, 65–84 (2011)
10. Camilleri, M., Walther, G.: What small vowels and a large lexicon tell us about Maltese verbal inflection. Presentation at the 8th Décembrettes, Bordeaux, France (2012)
11. Copestake, A.: Implementing Typed Feature Structure Grammars. CSLI Publications, Stanford (2002)
12. Corbett, G.G.: Agreement: the range of the phenomenon and the principles of the Surrey database of agreement. Trans. of the Philological Society 101, 155–202 (2003)
13. Evans, R.P., Gazdar, G.: Inference in DATR. In: Proceedings of EACL 1989, pp. 66–71 (1989)
14. Finkel, R., Stump, G.T.: Generating Hebrew verb morphology by default inheritance hierarchies. In: Proceedings of the ACL 2002 Workshop on Computational Approaches to Semitic Languages, Philadelphia, PA, United States (July 2002)
15. Hulden, M.: Foma: a finite-state compiler and library. In: Proceedings of EACL 2009 (demos), pp. 29–32 (2009)
16. Karttunen, L.: Computing with realizational morphology. In: Gelbukh, A. (ed.) CICLing 2003. LNCS, vol. 2588, pp. 205–216. Springer, Heidelberg (2003)
17. Matthews, P.H.: Morphology. Cambridge University Press, United Kingdom (1974)
18. Pirrelli, V., Battista, M.: The Paradigmatic Dimension of Stem Allomorphy in Italian Verb Inflection. Italian Journal of Linguistics, 307–380 (2000)
19. Pollard, C., Sag, I.A.: Head-Driven Phrase Structure Grammar. CSLI Publications, Stanford (1994)

20. Sagot, B.: Automatic acquisition of a slovak lexicon from a raw corpus. In: Matoušek, V., Mautner, P., Pavelka, T. (eds.) TSD 2005. LNCS (LNAI), vol. 3658, pp. 156–163. Springer, Heidelberg (2005)

21. Sagot, B.: Building a morphosyntactic lexicon and a pre-syntactic processing chain for Polish. In: Proceedings of LTC 2005, Poznań, Poland, pp. 423–427 (2007)

22. Sagot, B.: The Le*fff*, a freely available, accurate and large-coverage lexicon for French. In: Proceedings of LREC 2010, Valletta, Malta (2010)

23. Sagot, B., Clément, L., Villemonte de la Clergerie, E., Boullier, P.: The Le*fff* 2 syntactic lexicon for French: architecture, acquisition, use. In: Proceedings of LREC 2006, Lisbons, Portugal (2006)

24. Sagot, B., Walther, G.: Non-canonical inflection: Data, formalisation and complexity measures. In: Mahlow, C., Piotrowski, M. (eds.) SFCM 2011. CCIS, vol. 100, pp. 23–45. Springer, Heidelberg (2011)

25. Spagnol, M.: A Tale of Two Morphologies. Verb structure and argument alternations in Maltese. Ph.D. thesis, University of Konstanz, Constance, Germany (2011)

26. Stump, G.T.: Paradigm function morphology. In: Brown, K. (ed.) Encyclopedia of Language and Linguistics, pp. 171–173. Elsevier, Oxford

27. Stump, G.T.: Inflectional Morphology. Theory of Paradigm Structure. Cambridge University Press, United Kingdom (2001)

28. Stump, G.T.: Heteroclisis and paradigm linkage. Language 82, 279–322 (2006)

29. Thornton, A.: Overabundance (multiple forms realizing the same cell): A non-canonical phenomenon in Italian verb morphology. In: Maiden, M., John Charles Smith, M.G., Hinzelin, M.O. (eds.) Morphological Autonomy: Perspectives From Romance Inflectional Morphology. Oxford University Press (2011)

30. Walther, G.: Measuring morphological canonicity. In: Perko, G. (ed.) Les frontières Internes et Externes de la Morphologie, Linguistica. Faculty of Arts, vol. 51, pp. 157–180. University of Ljubljana, Ljubljana (2011)

31. Walther, G.: Sur la canonicité en morphologie – Perspective empirique, formelle et computationnelle. Ph.D. thesis, Université Paris-Diderot (2013)

Verbal Morphosyntactic Disambiguation through Topological Field Recognition in German-Language Law Texts

Kyoko Sugisaki and Stefan Höfler*

University of Zurich, Institute of Computational Linguistics,
Binzmühlestrasse 14, 8050 Zürich, Switzerland
{sugisaki,hoefler}@cl.uzh.ch
http://www.cl.uzh.ch

Abstract. The morphosyntactic disambiguation of verbs is a crucial pre-processing step for the syntactic analysis of morphologically rich languages like German and domains with complex clause structures like law texts. This paper explores how much linguistically motivated rules can contribute to the task. It introduces an incremental system of verbal morphosyntactic disambiguation that exploits the concept of topological fields. The system presented is capable of reducing the rate of POS-tagging mistakes from 10.2% to 1.6%. The evaluation shows that this reduction is mostly gained through checking the compatibility of morphosyntactic features within the long-distance syntactic relationships of discontinuous verbal elements. Furthermore, the present study shows that in law texts, the average distance between the left and right bracket of clauses is relatively large (9.5 tokens), and that in this domain, a wide context window is therefore necessary for the morphosyntactic disambiguation of verbs.

Keywords: Morphosyntactic disambiguation, topological field model, Constraint Grammar, law texts, German verbs, POS-tagging.

1 Introduction

This paper reports on the development of a rule-based system for the morphosyntactic disambiguation of verbs as a preprocessing component of a supertagger for law texts. The morphosyntactic disambiguation of verbs is a crucial step for recognising clause structures in a morphologically rich language like German. German verbal complexes are often realised as discontinuous constituents. Moreover, German verbal morphology exhibits some degree of syncretism: verbal inflectional forms and morphosyntactic features are not always in one-to-one relationships. Especially for the legislative domain, the morphosyntactic disambiguation of verbs is a challenging task since clausal structures in law texts are particularly complex. Due to the frequency of verb phrase coordinations and embedded clauses (cf. [8,17]), the distances between the heads of clauses (e.g., finite verbs and complementisers) and their verbal complements are often relatively long and intricate.

---

* This project was funded under Swiss National Science Foundation grant 134701.

C. Mahlow and M. Piotrowski (Eds.): SFCM 2013, CCIS 380, pp. 135–146, 2013.
© Springer-Verlag Berlin Heidelberg 2013

In this paper, we present a rule-based system for morphosyntactic disambiguation of verbs that exploits the concept of topological fields, and we explore to what degree our linguistically motivated rule-based system can resolve verbal morphosyntactic ambiguities in law texts.

The paper is organised as follows. In the next section, we describe the general architecture of our supertagger. In section 3, we present the two major components of verbal morphosyntactic disambiguation. In section 4, we evaluate the performance of our system and discuss the rate of the reduction in part-of-speech tagging errors.

2   Overview: Supertagger

We have been developing a supertagger for the syntactic analysis of Swiss law texts written in German. Suppertagging is an "almost parsing" approach in the sense that the supertags represent rich syntactic information such as valence, voice and grammatical functions [5,9,15] and a parser needs then "only combine the individual supertaggs" [1]. Our supertagger is part of a project aimed at detecting style guide violations in legislative drafts [12]. To detect stylistically undesirable syntactic constructions, our supertagger aims at tagging core syntactic structures such as topological fields and grammatical functions. It consists of a pipeline with the following components:

1. Sentence segmentation and tokenisation
2. Morphological analysis
3. Morphosyntactic disambiguation of verbs
4. Morphosyntactic disambiguation of nouns
5. Grammatical function recognition

Sentence segmentation and tokenisation (component 1) are carried out as described in [12].

For the morphological analysis (component 2), our system employs Gertwol [7]. Gertwol is a classical two-level rule-based morphological analyser and provides fine-grained morphosyntactic features. However, Gertwol does not provide any analysis if it cannot not find the root of a word in its lexicon. In these cases, the system uses the analysis of the statistical decision-tree-based POS-tagger TreeTagger [19] to complete the output of Gertwol: the system identifies the set of possible morphosyntactic features on the basis of the inflectional endings of the tokens unknown to Gertwol and the POS-tags that TreeTagger returns for them. If a token has, for example, the ending -en and is analysed as an infinite verb by TreeTagger, two possible morphosyntactic feature sets, that for verbs in 3rd person plural indicative and that for infinitives, are generated. TreeTagger has proven to be robust and its performance with regard to unknown words is relatively high [21].

The three main components of the system, dedicated to the morphosyntactic disambiguation of verbs (component 3), the morphosyntactic disambiguation of nouns (component 4) and the recognition of grammatical functions (component 5), respectively, have been implemented in the framework of Constraint Grammar. Constraint Grammar [13] is a grammar formalism that has been successfully employed for tasks such

Table 1. Exemplification of the topological field model: occupation of the left and right brackets in the templates of the three clause types as found in sentence (1)

Vorfeld	Left Bracket (LB)	Mittelfeld	Right Bracket (RB)	Nachfeld
Verb-first clause (V1):		LB = finite verb, RB = verb complements		
	Stellt	*die Zollverwaltung Unregelmässigkeiten*	*fest,*	
Verb-second clause (V2):		LB = finite verb, RB = verb complements		
so	*verweigert*	*sie den Abschluss des Transitverfahrens*		
[und]	*hält*	*die Sicherheit*	*zurück*	
Verb-final clause (VL):		LB = subord. conj. / compl., RB = verb complex		
	bis	*die mit bedingter Zahlungspflicht veranlagten Einfuhrzollabgaben*	*bezahlt sind.*	

as English POS-tagging [22] or NP chunking [23]. We employ VISLCG2[1] to compile hand-crafted Constraint Grammar rules.

In the remainder of this paper, we will focus on component 3 and its strategies for the morphosyntactic disambiguation of verbs.

3 Verbal Morphosyntactic Disambiguation through Topological Field Recognition

The morphosyntactic disambiguation of German verbal elements is a challenging task: German verb forms are morphosyntactically highly ambiguous as syncretism is very common in German verb paradigms. The inflectional ending *-en*, for example, is used to mark 1st person plural (e.g., *wir trink-en* 'we drink'), 3rd person plural (e.g., *sie trink-en* 'they drink') and infinitive (e.g., *trink-en* 'to drink'). On top of that, in tenses other than present and preterite, verbal morphosyntactic properties such as mood and diathesis are realised via periphrasis (i.e., multiword expressions). Depending on the clause type in which they occur, these periphrases appear as continuous or discontinuous constituents.

3.1 The Topological Field Model

Traditionally, German clause structure has been described in terms of topological fields [4,14]. The topological fields of a clause are the different positions in which non-verbal constituents can appear: the vorfeld, the mittelfeld and the nachfeld. They are defined relative to the positions in which the heads of the clause (e.g., finite verbs and complementisers) and their verbal complements (e.g., infinitives, participles and separable verb prefixes) can be placed: the left and right bracket of the clause, respectively (cf. Table 1).

---

[1] http://beta.visl.sdu.dk/ (last visited on 15/05/2013)

Depending on the position of the verbal elements in a clause, the topological field model distinguishes three types (or templates) of German clauses with a different template each: verb-first clauses (V1), verb-second clauses (V2) and verb-final clauses (VF) [3, pp. 864ff]. Table 1 illustrates how the following example sentence is analysed according to this distinction:

(1)   Stellt die Zollverwaltung Unregelmässigkeiten fest, so verweigert sie den Abschluss des Transitverfahrens und hält die Sicherheit zurück, bis die mit bedingter Zahlungspflicht veranlagten Einfuhrzollabgaben bezahlt sind.[2]

'If the customs administration recognises irregularities, it refuses the completion of the transit procedure and retains the security until the import customs fees rated with conditioned duty of payment have been paid.'

Depending on the clause type, different elements can occupy the left and right bracket of a German clause. The left bracket of verb-first clauses (imperative sentences, interrogative sentences, certain conditional clauses) and verb-second clauses is occupied by the finite verb. The right bracket is filled by verbal complements such as separable verb prefixes and, where the finite verb is an auxiliary or a modal, infinitives and participles. In contrast, the left bracket of verb-final clauses (most types of subordinate clauses) is occupied by a subordinating conjunction or a complementiser, whereas the whole verbal complex of these clauses appears in the right bracket.[3] The verbal complex is thus a continuous element in verb-final clauses but can be realised as a discontinuous periphrasis in verb-first and verb-second clauses.

3.2 Approach

Taking into account the language-specific morphosyntactic configurations mentioned above, we propose a verbal disambiguation system for German that is based on the topological field model. The topological field model was first employed for the identification of clause boundaries by Neumann et al. [16]; since, it has also been applied in the pre-processing routines of deep syntactic parsers [2,6,10]. In our system, it is used for defining rules for verbal morphosyntactic disambiguation. Table 2 shows a selection of the heuristics used by our system and the syntactic rules on which they are based.

Our system proceeds in two steps: in a first step, it disambiguates verbal elements in left-bracket position and determines the clause type, and in a second step, it disambiguates verbal elements in right-bracket position. The second step depends on the completion of the first step as heuristics for right-bracket elements frequently build on knowledge about left-bracket elements (cf. Table 2, rules R1ff.): the morphosyntactic features of verbal elements in right-bracket position are disambiguated by checking the compatibility of their features with those of the corresponding left-bracket elements.

---

[2] Art. 155 para. 2 Customs Ordinance (SR *631.01*).

[3] In the present study, relative pronouns have also been considered to occupy the left bracket, although, from a theoretical perspective, they actually appear in vorfeld position. For practical reasons, this simplification seemed justifiable as, in standard German, the left bracket of relative clauses always remains empty.

Table 2. A selection of the heuristics used by the system and the hard topological-field rules on which they are based. (For exhibitory purposes, some of the heuristics are rendered in a slightly simplified form.)

Nr.	**Rule:** Heuristic
General	
G1	**A past participle requires an auxiliary verb:** If a potential past particle is not preceded or immediately followed by an auxiliary verb within the same sentence, then discard the features PART PERF.
...	...
Left Bracket	
L1	**The left bracket of V1 clauses is a single finite verb:** If a verb appears in sentence-initial position, select the feature FINITE from its set of possible features, mark it as left bracket and identify the clause type as V1.
L2	**The left bracket of V2 clauses is a single finite verb:** If a verb in sentence-internal position is not preceded by an auxiliary or modal in the left bracket of a V1-clause, select the feature FINITE from its set of possible features, mark it as left bracket and identify the clause type as V2.
L3	**The left bracket of V1 and V2 clauses is a single finite verb:** If a modal verb is not adjacent to other verbal elements, select the feature FINITE from its set of possible features, mark it as left bracket.
L4	**The left bracket of VF clauses is a conjunction or a complementiser:** If a potential conjunction is indirectly followed by a finite verb and a punctuation mark or a coordinating conjunction, then mark it as left bracket and identify the clause of VF.
...	...
Right Bracket	
R1	**A modal verb requires an infinitive:** If a potential infinitive is preceded by a modal verb at the left-bracket position of a V1 or V2 clause, then select its feature INFINITIVE and mark it as right bracket.
R2	**The auxiliary *werden* requires an infinitive for future tense:** If a potential infinitive is preceded by *werden* at the left-bracket position of a V1 or V2 clause, then select its feature INFINITIVE and mark it as right bracket.
R3	**The auxiliary *haben* requires an infinitive for perfect tense:** If a potential infinitive is preceded by *haben* at the left-bracket position of a V1 or V2 clause, then select its feature INFINITIVE and mark it as right bracket.
R4	**The auxiliaries *werden/sein* require a past particple for passive voice:** If a potential past participle is preceded by *werden* or *sein* at the left-bracket position of a V1 or V2 clause, then select its feature PAST PARTICIPLE and mark it as right bracket.
R5	**The right bracket of VF clauses contains a finite verb:** If a verb is directly followed by a punctuation mark or a coordinating conjunction and preceded by the left bracket of a VF-clause, then select its feature FINITE and mark it as right bracket.
R6	**Lexical verbs can have a separable verb prefix:** If a potential verb prefix is directly followed by a punctuation mark or a coordinating conjunction and preceded by a lexical verb at left-bracket position, then select its feature VERB PREFIX and mark it as right bracket.
...	...

Table 3. Incremental morphosyntactic disambiguation of elements at brackets in sentence (1)

	Stellt	*fest*	*verweigert*	*hält*	*zurück*	*bis*	*bezahlt*	*sind*
Input: Gertwol	PL2 PL2 SG3 PP	ADJ PREF	SG3 PP PL2 PL2 PL2	SG3	PREF ADV	CONJ PREP ADV	SG3 PL2 PL2 PP	PL1 PL3
Step 1a: Morphosynt. disambiguation	SG3		SG3	SG3		CONJ		
Step 1b: Topological field recogn.	LB-V1		LB-V2	LB-V2		LB-VF		
Step 2a: Right brackets disambiguation		PREF			PREF		PP	PL3
Step 2b: Right brackets labeling		RB-V1			RB-V2		RB-VF	RB-VF

The details of what is being checked fall from the morphosyntactic properties of the predicate as a whole (e.g., mode, tense, diatheses) and the type of the clause.

In each step, the heuristics exemplified in Table 2 are applied in a specific order. The order is relevant as some heuristics build on the output of other heuristics. An example is Rule L2, which is concerned with detecting left brackets of verb-second clauses and disambiguating the morphosyntactic features of the corresponding verb form: it exploits information that has previously been added by Rule L1, namely information on the presence of the left bracket of a verb-first clause in the respective context. Morphosyntactic disambiguation thus happens incrementally not just between the two steps but also within.

3.3 Step-by-Step Example

In what follows, we illustrate the two-step procedure of our system by tracking how it processes the aforementioned sentence (1), which we repeat in (2):

(2)   Stellt die Zollverwaltung Unregelmässigkeiten fest, so verweigert sie den Abschluss des Transitverfahrens und hält die Sicherheit zurück, bis die mit bedingter Zahlungspflicht veranlagten Einfuhrzollabgaben bezahlt sind.[4]

'If the customs administration recognises irregularities, it refuses the completion of the transit procedure and retains the security until the import customs fees rated with conditioned duty of payment have been paid.'

---

[4] Art. 155 para. 2 Customs Ordinance (SR *631.01*).

Table 3 gives an overview of the morphosyntactic analyses Gertwol returns for each bracket candidate contained in the sentence, i.e., for each token that is a potential left or right bracket (Input), and it illustrates how these analyses are gradualy disambiguated in the processing steps performed by our system (Steps 1a–2b).

Step 1: Left bracket detection and disambiguation

Step 1 is concerned with detecting word forms that serve as left brackets and with determining the clause type. At the same time, the morphosyntactic analyses of word forms identified as left-bracket elements are disambiguated.

The first left-bracket candidate encountered by the system is the verb form *stellt*. Gertwol yields the following possible morphosyntactic analyses for this token:[5]

(3)   "stellt"
        stell~en   V IND PRÄS PL2
        stell~en   V IMP PRÄS PL2
        stell~en   V IND PRÄS SG3
        stell~en   V PART PERF

The system applies a domain-specific heuristic and discards these two analysis because, in general, there are no second-person statements in legislative texts.

The third analysis identifies the word form as a third-person singular verb (V SG3); the fourth analysis interprets it as a past participle (PART PERF). The fourth analysis is discarded because past participles in sentence-initial position are always followed by an auxiliary verb (e.g., *Gekauft habe ich aber dann doch das billigere Auto*), which is not the case in the present sentence. The only remaining analysis is thus the one that interprets the word form in question as a third-person singular verb in present tense indicative.

Given the constraints described by the topological field model (cf. Table 1), the fact that a finite verb occurs in sentence-initial position means that the respective token is the left-bracket of a verb-first clause (cf. Rule L1 in Table 2). The system thus labels the token *stellen* accordingly (LB-V1).

The next left-bracket candidate to be considered by the system is *verweigert*. Gertwol returns the following five morphosyntactic analyses for this token:[6]

(4)   "verweigert"
        ver|weig~er~n   V IND PRÄS SG3
        ver|weig~er~n   V PART PERF
        ver|weig~er~n   V IND PRÄS PL2
        ver|weig~er~n   V KONJ PRÄS PL2
        ver|weig~er~n   V IMP PRÄS PL2

---

[5] To keep the morphosyntactic features of verbs unique per token, redundant features generated by Gertwol are deleted. Tags: V = verb, IND = indicative, PRÄS = present, PL2 = 2nd person plural, IMP = imperative, SG3 = 3rd person singular, PART = participle, PERF = perfect.

[6] KONJ = conjunctive

Once more, the system discards all analyses that identify the token as a second-person verb (i.e., the last three analyses listed) as legislative texts generally do not contain second-person statements.

The second analysis listed, containing the feature combination PART PERF, is also discarded by the system: if *verweigert* was a past participle, it would have to be either preceded or immediately followed by an auxiliary verb (Rule G1).

The token *verweigert* has thus been morphosyntactically disambiguated as a third-person singular verb in present indicative. The fact that it is a finite verb and that it is preceded (a) by a verb-first clause and (b) by a comma followed by the adverb *so*, furthermore indicates that *verweigert* is the left bracket of a verb-second clause; The system labels it accordingly.

In a similar fashion, the following two left-bracket candidates, *hält* and *bis*, are identified as the left bracket of a verb-second clause and a verb-final clause, respectively, while the final two candidates, *bezahlt* and *sind*, are identified as not being left brackets (cf. Table 3).

Step 2: Right bracket disambiguation and labeling

Step 2 is concerned with detecting right brackets; at the same time, the morphosyntactic analyses of the respective word forms are disambiguated. Specifically, the system detects and disambiguates tokens that serve as right brackets by checking the compatibility of their morphosyntactic features with those of the left brackets preceding them.

The first right-bracket candidate encountered by the system is the token *fest*. Morphosyntactically, *fest* can either be a predicative adjective or a separable verb prefix. However, only the latter analysis is compatible with the lexical verb in preceding left bracket (*stellt*); The system thus discards the former analysis and tags the token as the right bracket of the respective verb-first clause (Rule R6 in Table 2). By applying the same rule, the next candidate, *zurück*, is disambiguated and identified as the right bracket belonging to the verb-second clause with the finite verb *hält*. The remaining two candidates, *bezahlt* and *sind*, are disambiguated and identified as right brackets by applying Rules G1 and R5, respectively.

4   Evaluation

The strategies for verbal morphosyntactic disambiguation and topological field recognition presented in the previous section have been evaluated over 100 sentences (2,370 tokens) that were randomly selected from the the Swiss Legislation Corpus [11].

4.1   Verbal Morphosyntactic Disambiguation

To evaluate the performance of our verbal morphosyntactic disambiguation system against a gold standard, we manually annotated all potential left- and right-bracket elements (bracket candidates, i.e., potential verbal elements, subordinating conjunctions, complementisers, relative pronouns) in the test sentences. We then processed the same

Table 4. Performance of the system at detecting and disambiguating bracket candidates: Recall

	correct	wrong	total
TreeTagger	281 tokens (89.8%)	32 tokens (10.2%)	313 tokens (100.0%)
Our system	308 tokens (98.4%)	5 tokens (1.6%)	313 tokens (100.0%)

test sentences with our system and compared its automatic annotations with those provided by TreeTagger. To be able to compare the output of the two systems, we converted our Gertwol-based output into the Stuttgart-Tübingen Tagset (STTS) [18] used by TreeTagger.

As shown in Table 4, 308 of the 313 tokens that were tagged in the gold standard were analysed correctly by our system; Our system had a *recall* of 98.4%. In comparison, TreeTagger only achieved a recall of 89.8%. The results of our system thus constitute an improvement of 8.6% from those obtained by TreeTagger.

30 of the 32 tokens wrongly analysed by TreeTagger (i.e., 93.8%) were correctly analysed by our system. Our system mainly proved superior to TreeTagger at tagging right-bracket candidates. Right-bracket candidates are always verbal elements, and verbal elements generally exhibit a relatively high degree of morphosyntactic ambiguity: on average, Gertwol returned 3.3 analyses per token for the verbal elements in our test data. Consequently, all tokens wrongly analysed by TreeTagger were morphologically ambiguous verb forms, e.g., verb forms with the inflectional endings *-en* or *-t*.

The most frequent type that TreeTagger failed to analyse correctly were finite verbs ending in *-en* that appeared in the right bracket of a verb-final clause (9 of 32 tokens). TreeTagger wrongly interpreted these verb forms as infinitives.

To correctly disambiguate right-bracket candidates, information about the corresponding left-bracket elements is required. Our system performed better at the task precisely because it has access to such information. In contrast, the context window used by TreeTagger and other n-gram-based taggers does not seem to be wide enough for domains with relatively complex clause structures such as law texts. Indeed, we found that in the sentences we used for the evaluation, the distance between the left and right bracket amounted to a comparatively high average of 9.54 tokens.

An additional but related explanation of why our system performed better than Tree-Tagger arises from the fact that some of the tokens for which TreeTagger returned wrong analyses occurred in syntactic structures that are frequent in law texts but not in the newspaper texts TreeTagger was trained on (e.g., verb-first clauses and adverbial participle phrases with participle inversion).

There were also three tokens that were wrongly analysed by our system but correctly analysed by TreeTagger. These errors in the output of our system were caused (a) by the correct analysis not being included in the output provided by Gertwol (*aufrecht* not analysed as prefix), (b) by our system wrongly interpreting a definite article as a relative pronoun, and (c) by a specific syntactic structure not yet taken into account in the disambiguation rules (extraposition of a prepositional phrase within a relative clause in the vorfeld of a verb-second clause).

Our system achieved a *precision* of 99.7%. As shown in Table 5, 308 of the 309 tokens tagged by our system were analysed correctly. TreeTagger achieved a slightly lower precision of 98.3%.

Table 5. Performance of the system at detecting and disambiguating bracket candidates: Precision

	correct	wrong	total
TreeTagger	281 tokens (98.3%)	5 tokens (1.7%)	286 tokens (100.0%)
Our system	308 tokens (99.7%)	1 tokens (0.3%)	309 tokens (100.0%)

Table 6. Performance of the topological field labeling system

Recall	Precision	F1-score
95.3%	99.7%	97.4%
(286/300 tokens)	*(286/287 tokens)*	

The one incorrect analysis returned by our system was a relative pronoun erroneously tagged as the definite article of a participle phrase. In comparison, TreeTagger misinterpreted three relative pronouns as definite articles; another two mistakes were caused by the phrases *wie folgt* ('as follows') and *von sich aus* ('on its own').

In summary, TreeTagger achieved an F1 score of 93.8% while our system achieved an F1 score of 99.0%. These results indicate that rule-based morphosyntactic disambiguation can indeed substantially improve the performance of a part-of-seech tagger.

4.2 Topological Field Labeling

We have also used the test data described above to evaluate the performance of our system with regard to recognising topological fields by determining the left and right brackets of clauses. To this aim, we manually annotated the left and right brackets (300 tokens in total) contained in the sentences selected from the corpus. As shown in Table 6, our system correctly detected 95.3% (286 tokens) of all brackets (recall), and 99.7% (286 tokens) of the tokens that our system marked as brackets (287 tokens) had been identified correctly (precision). In sum, our system thus achieved an F1-score of 97.4% at the task of recognising left and right brackets.

Of the 15 errors (14 false negatives and 1 false positive) that occurred, 12 were the direct or indirect result of a wrong morphosyntactic disambiguation: failure to detect a left bracket (e.g., because a subordinating conjunction had been wrongly analysed as an adverb) frequently also lead to a failure to detect the corresponding right bracket (e.g., because the next finite verb would then be correctly identified as a right-bracket element).

5   Conclusion

The morphosyntactic disambiguation of verbs is a crucial pre-processing step for the syntactic analysis of morphologically rich languages like German and domains with complex clause structures like law texts. In this paper, we explored how much linguistically motivated rules can contribute to the task. We presented an incremental system of verbal morphosyntactic disambiguation that exploits the concept of topological fields. In the evaluated sentences extracted from a corpus of German-language law texts, our system achieved a F1 score of 99.0%

The system proved to be capable of reducing the rate of POS-tagging mistakes from 10.2% in a state-of-the-art statistical tagger to 1.6%. Our evaluation showed that this reduction was mostly gained through checking the compatibility of morphosyntactic features within the long-distance syntactic relationships of discontinuous verbal elements in the left and right brackets of clauses. The present study also showed that in law texts, the average distance between the left and right bracket of clauses is relatively large (9.5 tokens), and that in this domain, a wide context window is therefore necessary for the morphosyntactic disambiguation of verbs.

The present study suggests that such a rule-based system, if employed as a post-processing component, may be able to make a significant contribution to improving the quality of POS-tagging, especially in long-distance discontinuous verbal periphrases in German.

In the future, we plan to use information on the left and right brackets of clauses as additional input for determining grammatical functions.

References

1. Bangalore, S., Joshi, A.K.: Supertagging: an approach to almost parsing. Computational Linguistics 25(2) (1999)
2. Becker, M.: Frank. A.: A Stochastic Topological Parser for German. In: Proceedings of COLING 2002, pp. 71–77. Association of Computational Linguistics, New York (2002)
3. Dudenredaktion (ed.): Duden - die Grammatik: unentbehrlich für richtiges Deutsch, Duden, vol. 4. Dudenverlag, Mannheim (2009)
4. Dürscheid, C.: Syntax: Grundlagen und Theorien. Vandenhoeck & Ruprecht, Göttingen (2012)
5. Foth, K., By, T., Menzel, W.: Guiding a constraint dependency parser with supertags. In: Bangalore, S., Joshi, A.K. (eds.) Supertagging: Using Complex Lexical Descriptions in Natural Language Processing. MIT Press, Cambridge (2010)
6. Frank, A., Becker, M., Crysmann, B., Kiefer, B., Schäfer, U.: Integrated Shallow and Deep Parsing: TopP Meets HPSG. In: Proceedings of ACL 2003, pp. 104–111. Association for Computational Linguistics, New York (2003)
7. Haapalainen, M., Majorin, A.: GERTWOL: ein System zur automatischen Wortformerkennung deutscher Wörter. Technical report, Lingsoft (1994)
8. Hansen-Schirra, S., Neumann, S.: Linguistische Verständlichmachung in der juristischen Realität. In: Lerch, K.D. (ed.) Recht verstehen: Verständlichkeit, Missverständlichkeit und Unverständlichkeit von Recht, Die Sprache des Rechts, vol. 1. Walter de Gruyter, Berlin (2004)
9. Harper, M.P., Wang, W.: Constraint dependency grammars: Superarvs, language modeling, and parsing. In: Bangalore, S., Joshi, A.K. (eds.) Supertagging: Using Complex Lexical Descriptions in Natural Language Processing. MIT Press, Cambridge (2010)
10. Hinrichs, E.W., Kübler, S., Müller, F.H., Ule, T.: A hybrid architecture for robust parsing of German. In: Proceedings of the 3rd International Confererence on Language Resources and Evaluation (LREC 2002), Las Palmas, Gran Canaria (2002)
11. Höfler, S., Piotrowski, M.: Building Corpora for the Philological Study of Swiss Legal Texts. Journal for Language Technology and Computational Linguistics (JLCL) 26(2), 77–89 (2011)
12. Höfler, S., Sugisaki, K.: From Drafting to Error Detection: Automating Style Checking for Legislative Texts. In: EACL 2012 Workshop on Computational Linguistics and Writing, pp. 9–18. Association for Computational Linguistics, New York (2012)

13. Karlsson, F., Voutilainen, A., Heikkilä, J., Anttila, A. (eds.): Constraint Grammar: A Language- Independent System for Parsing Unrestricted Text. Mouton de Gruyter, Berlin/New York (1995)
14. Kathol, A.: Linear syntax. Oxford University Press, Oxford (2000)
15. Nasr, A., Rambow, O.: Supertagging and full parsing. In: Proceedings of the 7th International Workshop on Tree Adjoining Grammar and Related Formalisms (TAG+7), Vancouver, British Columbia, Canada, pp. 56–63 (2004)
16. Neumann, G., Braun, C., Piskorski, J.: A divide-and-conquer strategy for shallow parsing of German free texts. In: Proceedings of the Sixth Conference on Applied Natural Language Processing (ANLC 2000), Seatle, WA, pp. 239–246 (2000)
17. Nussbaumer, M.: Rhetorisch-stilistische Eigenschaften der Sprache des Rechtswesens. In: Fix, U., Gardt, A., Knape, J. (eds.) Rhetorik und Stilistik / Rhetoric and Stylistics, Handbooks of Linguistics and Communication Science, vol. 31(2), pp. 2132–2150. Mouton de Gruyter, Boston/New York (2009)
18. Schiller, A., Teufel, C., Stöckert, C., Thielen, C.: Guidelines für das Tagging deutscher Textcorpora mit STTS (kleines und grosses Tagset). Technical report, Universität Stuttgart/Universität Tübingen (1999)
19. Schmid, H.: Improvements in Part-of-Speech Tagging with an Application to German. In: Proceedings of the ACL SIGDAT-Workshop, Dublin (1995)
20. Schneider, G., Volk, M.: Adding Manual Constraints and Lexical Look-Up to a Brill-Tagger for German. In: Proceedings of the ESSLLI 1998 Workshop on Recent Advances in Corpus Annotation, Saarbrücken (1998)
21. Volk, M., Schneider, G.: Comparing a Statistical and a Rule-Based Tagger for German. In: Lang, P., Frankfurt, A.M. (ed.) Proceeding of the 4th Conference on Natural Language Processing (KONVENS 1998), Berlin, Bern, New York, Paris, Wien, pp. 125–137 (1998)
22. Voutilainen, A.: NPtool, A Detector of English Noun Phrases. In: Proceeding of Workshop on Very Large Corpora: Academic and Industrial Perspectives, pp. 48–57. Ohio State University, Columbus (1993)
23. Voutilainen, A.: A Syntax-Based Part-of-Speech Analyser. In: Proceedings of the Seventh Conference on European Chapter of the Association for Computational Linguistics, EACL 1995, pp. 157–164. Morgan Kaufmann, San Francisco (1995)

Author Index